CORINTHIAN

AND

CRICKETERS

✠ ✠ ✠ ✠ ✠

AND TOWARDS A NEW SPORTING ERA

By
Edward Grayson

With Forewords by
C.B.Fry, Hubert Doggart and Gary Lineker

(First Published in 1955 by The Naldrett Press: London
entitled *"Corinthians and Cricketers"*)

ISBN 1 874427 71 2

Published by:
Yore Publications
12 The Furrows, Harefield,
Middlesex. UB9 6AT

Printed and bound by: Biddles Limited

To the memory of
my parents

and
the spirit of Corinthians
worldwide

FOREWORD BY C.B.FRY
(As appeared in the original edition)

This book, full of interest and information about an important period in the history of field-games, is in the nature of a Pindaric ode in prose. Its central subject is one man - his fame and prowess in football. But that select personality is a theme song, as it were, that introduces, among kindred topics, a great Public School, a great University, a great Club, and a great formative era of what is now a great national and international entertainment. Some would say an industrial entertainment.

Pindar, by the way, is not a stiff and turgid reference to the Classics. Quite remarkable it is how easily forgotten or overlooked is the influence upon our mental attitudes and moral standards in athletics and field-games, as in the reputedly superior worlds of art and literature, of the relatively small but none the less powerful universe of ancient Hellas.

The Olympic and Isthmian Games figure as a kind of architectural monument setting something of a pattern; not only in the technique of practice and training, but in procedure and management, and even in terminology. Perhaps the Greek equivalent of professional would be *athletes,* and of amateur *idiotes,* which latter name might also indicate the spectator and the reporter as distinguished from the player. As a Bishop once said in an after-dinner speech: 'Of course, all laymen were called idiots by a Greek writer.' This I do not myself accept as true, but regard rather as heretical and nowadays unorthodox. The Bishop had stroked his College boat!

All this, however, by the way. Nevertheless may one suggest, in spite of such arbiters of taste as Mr Wyndham Lewis and Mr Gilbert Harding, both of whom have a poor opinion of cricket and football, that these field-games, being quite a major interest, indeed perhaps the major interest, of a people who have won two world wars, cannot be of negligible inherent value humanly considered. There may be something in them, and the reader of this book may discover that something. I by no means equate Mr H. with Mr L.

In our present category there is no doubt that neither football nor cricket would have developed as they have but for the Public Schools, and if either game has any good standards, this is due largely to that influence. The Public Schools are considered at Trades Union Conferences to be feudal in origin and development, and to be anti-equalitarian, or, as the silly term is, anti-democratic. In fact they are quite the reverse, no matter how many Old Etonians may have climbed into the Cabinet on merit. You can tell an audience at Marble Arch, if you like, that the games we now enjoy were developed from the back-alleys of London, Birmingham, Leeds or Wigan (all fine cities), but the appeal, although emotional, would not be true to fact. You will find out how and why if you read this book.

The elegant and blameless football now seen on occasions, e.g., at Wembley, did not come from the Midland and Northern industrial towns, though of the skill a good deal did, but from the now supposedly obsolete Old Boys teams. Indeed, but for the Old Boys Clubs - Carthusians, Etonians, Westminsters, Salopians, Reptonians and the like - the world of soccer would never have seen the Corinthians, in their day the greatest of all amateur football clubs yet known or likely to be known.

This epoch-making club came into existence through the selective and organising ability of N.L. Jackson. He saw that if he avoided cup-tie competition he could skim off the cream of the Old

Boys clubs into a quasi-international amateur team. This he did, and in 1886, he being on the Selection Committee, ten Corinthians and one professional appeared at Hampden Park to represent England v. Scotland. There has never been a stronger England team.

But let us now consider G.0. Smith, our hero, and his compeers, if any, and his times. A genius in football he was. Like all geniuses he rose on stepping-stones of his real self by taking infinite pains in terms of his natural gifts.

He came up to Oxford from Charterhouse with as big a name as any Freshman ever in Association football. He was not alone as a Carthusian eminent - E.C. Bliss, E. Farquhar Buzzard, R.J. Salt and C.D. Hewitt were all Blues with him. In the 1893-94 Varsity match when I was captain we had the strongest team that ever played for either University, but we lost, as you will see from these pages. The ground was frozen at Queen's Club and was more suited to skating than football. We had five internationals, but not for skating. G.0. played extremely well all the same, and he was as good a centre forward then as ever afterwards. A gem.

His rating as the finest man in his place who ever played for England is generally accepted. But such rating cannot be proved correct. *De gustibus* comes in. So do changes of conditions of play. Anyhow he was the cleverest centre-forward I saw between 1888 and 1903 - my years of first-class football. Clever is not the word. He was inspired.

He was of medium height, slight and almost frail in build. He was a quick mover but not a sprinter. He was uncannily prehensile of foot and almost delicately neat. What made him was his skill in elusive movement, his quickness in seeing how best to bestow his passes, his accuracy and his remarkable penetrative dribbling. He swung a marvellously heavy foot in shooting - always along the turf and terrifically swift.

The yarn that he was a weak shot in his early first-class seasons is just a yarn. I played often with and against him, and he was as straight and hard a shot as I ever met except perhaps only Steven Bloomer of Derby County, on one of Steve's special days. G.O.'s was every day. The Corinthian players of the eighties used to say that Tinsley Lindley of their great forward-line was at least as good a centre. Theirs was a great line - Bambridge, Cobbold, Lindley, Brann and either Aubrey Smith or Spilsbury. Lindley, like G.0., was slim and elusive, with a knack of slipping in unexpected shots, but he did not shoot as hard as G.0.

G.0. was, you might say, an epitomy of Charterhouse football. He was an emanation from a hot-bed of skill in the game produced by a long tradition and a fast sandy field where delay meant loss of the ball and inaccuracy a troublesome bounce.

Charterhouse, originally buried in London near Smithfield Market, was transferred to Godalming by Dr Haig-Brown its factor Headmaster. He selected a convenient table-land, built fine buildings and laid out fine grounds. He could say with Dido - *Urbem quam statui, vidi; mea moenia vidi* - The City I founded I have seen; my city walls I have seen. No wonder Dr Haig-Brown was naturally annoyed when some idiot in a complimentary speech said that the Doctor's only defect was that he was not a Carthusian! The Doctor had a beard, and it positively stood out every hair at right-angles.

There were many fine footballers bred on the hill at Godalming. The brothers Walters, P.M. and A.M., were the best pair of backs who played for England in my time; C. Wreford Brown and Blenkiron were two excellent centrehalves; and among the earlier Carthusian footballers were two fine cricketers: Major E.G. Wynyard, D.S.O., and Sir C. Aubrey Smith, the actor and film hero. Yet the strange thing was that Charterhouse cricket, though of course good, was not at that time up to the standard of the football. They had no cricket master at all. I was a classical master there for two years and only just escaped being taught by the head boy, Lord Beveridge. But I did not teach cricket - I was not allowed.

G.0. in his schooldays was a great run-getter, but he had a peculiar short-handle lean-down style. He was a formally correct off-driver and cutter with an excellent defence, but although he

scored a famous match-winning century for Oxford v. Cambridge he was not a good model for the average young batsman. Not upstanding enough and not free enough in his driving. No left arm swing. In fact he batted like a very good putter at golf. Nevertheless, a useful man on any side, he would have collected stacks of runs in Australia.

By the way, he had curiously fine grey eyes and eye-lashes such as any girl would envy. He read History at Oxford and the Keble Dons thought well of him. I guess he taught well as a schoolmaster; he was kind, quiet and peculiarly patient.

He is worth reading about, as also are many of his contemporaries, and much of his conspicuous context.

October 1955

1996 FOREWORD BY HUBERT DOGGART

To have accepted Edward Grayson's invitation to write a second Foreword to 'Corinthians and Cricketers' - alongside that of Charles Burgess Fry, the greatest of all Scholar-Sportsmen, may appear to savour of Hubris - and Hubris is, perhaps, fitting for one who bears my Christian name, inherited from a Corinthian and Cricketer of the early twenties whose well-known surname was Ashton. Fry, who won first-class honours in Classical Moderations at Wadham, knew well that Hubris is always visited by Nemesis - and I would rather that Nemesis could be kept at bay a little longer.

Perhaps my acceptance of Edward's invitation could rather be called a combination of, on the one hand, pleasure at being asked to add a chip or two to Fry, and, on the other, a sympathy with the vehemence of the author's belief in the importance of the Corinthian ideal. This vehemence was given youthful shape by his visit to G.O.Smith, the finest of all Corinthian centre-forwards, and his daring to ask him for his autograph. It was sustained by the ideas and ideals of the Corinthian Football Club in two distinct eras; given new hope by the appearance at Wembley of the Pegasus Football Club in 1951 and 1953, and of the Corinthian-Casuals in 1956; and received a further stimulus by to-day's decline from Corinthian standards and the consequent need for their restatement.

Why in the world was it I who was asked, not to match Fry - that would be hubristic indeed- but to complement Fry and reflect the 1990s rather than the 1950s? First, I went to Cambridge rather than to Oxford - and I suspect that Edward thought that a Light Blue would neatly supplement a Dark. Secondly, my father was a great Corinthian of the twenties, scoring 167 goals in 170 matches and in 1924 being selected for the full England side against Belgium - and Edward perhaps thought that Graham's Corinthian spirit might well have been handed down to me especially as my mother spent hours in the British Museum researching F.N.S.Creek's 'A History of the Corinthian Football Club'.

And thirdly, my own experience might be able to add to Fry's in Corinthian terms: for I had been a boy at Abberley Hall under Gilbert Ashton, Captain of Cricket at Cambridge in 1921; I had been imbued with some at least of the approach of Colin Hunter, Captain of Soccer at Cambridge in 1920, who was my housemaster at Winchester, and of Harry Altham, the author of the 'History of Cricket', who taught me my first-ever period there in 1938. It was, if I recall correctly, a Greek period about Thucydides. To have been a player as well as a coach of both soccer and cricket, and to have been involved with M.C.C., which continues to guard both the Laws and the spirit of Cricket, perhaps counted in my favour - as did my continuing Presidency of the English Schools Cricket Association, to whom Corinthian standards are important.

To re-read C.B.Fry's Foreword from 1955, not long before he died, is to catch the flavour of a Golden Age of sport and of those he met and played with. His memory is remarkable and his powers of observation acute. The Foreword ranges allusively and naturally from Pindar to Pa Jackson, the founder of the Corinthians, but his recollections of G.O.Smith are especially vivid and the most pertinent to the book. How wise of the author to retain his Foreword in this new edition!

It is easy to exaggerate, but it is clear to historians, of whatever persuasion, that the prevailing ethos in much of today's sport is markedly different both from that of the late Victorian era in which C.B.Fry applied his intelligence to the games he played, and from the mid-fifties when he wrote his Foreword.

From the start of the sixties, the historians tell us, there was a gradual sea-change in values and moral climate, and that sport was inescapably bound up in this decline. Before the sixties, Soccer was unfettered by commercialism, the telescopic lens and a win-at-all-costs mentality, which all too often latterly would lead to negative play, the stretching of the rule of law, and aspects of violence totally alien to the way the Corinthians played.

Cricket too has suffered - from the loss, after 1962, of the amateur, who was not playing the game for a living and was thus not beholden to his county committee in the same way as his professional colleagues; from a growing commercialism, with its inherent risk of the game being market-led rather than cricket-led; from a greater intrusion by those whose priority is human rather than cricket interest; and from an atmosphere which, for one reason or another, reduces the level of sheer enjoyment of those who play.

It has been said that each sport has in itself the seeds of its own decay. One of the qualities that will prevent that deterioration is the Corinthian ideal, which colours what goes on off the field as well as on it. Self-evidently, the Corinthian ideal has to be applied to each new age to match the changing circumstances, but by definition its core and its characteristics are unchanging.

The Corinthian ideal should be both a touchstone and a talisman for all involved. Its relevance and importance are why Edward Grayson's story is as fresh now as it was in 1955, when the original book was published (and in 1983, the year of its reprint), and why I commend it warmly to a new generation of readers.

Hubert Doggart

June 1996

FOREWORD BY GARY LINEKER

We live in dramatic times for sport. As I write, it is far from certain that England will field a rugby union team in the Five Nations Championship which, for decades, has been the mainstay of the winter calendar. The power-play off the pitch looks set to be as dramatic as any rolling maul on the field of play. In the last year, rugby league has been transformed into a summer sport. Track and field athletics has been buffeted by some well documented litigation in the lead-in to the Atlanta Olympics. With the TV rights and income now riding on success in any sport, there are influences and pressures which could not have been contemplated twenty or thirty years ago. The English national games of football and cricket have been central to all of this. Indeed these sports have generated some of the most important legal actions of all.

The days when a top level cricket and football career could be combined are long gone, but in *'Corinthians & Cricketers and Towards A New Sporting Era'*, Edward Grayson takes us back to an era when they did things rather differently. G.O.Smith was the forerunner of all the footballing cricketers, with a brief but illustrious career in the early 1900's. His letters will provide interesting reading for anyone with even a passing interest in the evolution of British sport.

I noted that G.O. as long ago as 1942 believed that, football strikers undertook an *"incessant amount of heading"* - a man after my own heart! I hope you enjoy *'Corinthians & Cricketers and Towards A New Sporting Era'*.

G.W.Lineker
August 1996

AUTHOR'S NOTE & ACKNOWLEDGEMENTS:

The triple purpose explained in the Introduction for re-issuing this homage to the Corinthian ideal of fair play in sport has become more urgent with every passing day. This occurs because the need to explain for a sceptical public opinion why and how Parliamentary and Court actions are required to protect against abuses of sporting traditions on and off the fields of play is as crucial as the need to protect victims of road traffic, and every other land, sea and air transport outrage against the public interest and its safety, in a secular orientated society.

In particular there is an ever widening culture gap between the publicly commercially sponsored and subsidised sport as a segment of the global entertainment televised leisure industry, and the traditional grass roots at school and village green levels, which demand a need to preserve the Corinthian ideal against onslaughts from unthinking academics, anarchists, and financial predators who would destroy it.

My sustained belief in the ideal within what Hubert Doggart in his Foreword rightly describes *"a gradual sea change in values and moral climate"*, since the book first appeared, has been heartened by so much encouragement that space alone permits acknowledgement here to only those for whom omission would amount to gross ingratitude.

Dave Twydell, my publisher at Yore Publications, has balanced his own football enthusiasms with reasoned judgements and restraints on mine, continually supported by his wife, Fay. Each contributor of the three Forewords has responded with a common thread of Corinthian magic from his own unique football-cricketing experiences. C.B. Fry as the *beau ideal* of all sport with a vision which has stood the test of time, Hubert Doggart with his great Corinthian family traditions, and Gary Lineker, whose biographer, Colin Malam, has explained him to be *"something of a throw back to turn of the century public school heroism; a resonant echo of lofty Corinthian ideals"*.

The complex road to unite them involved Colin Malam's description of Jonathan Holmes, Special Agent; his golfing partner and Senior Partner, Peter L.T . Jacks of Fraser Brown solicitors, Nottingham; Professor John Davies, medical adviser to the Welsh Rugby Union in the Corinthian mould; and Jeff Butterfield, of the Rugby Club of London, a Corinthian Harlequin. Jean-Claude Bragard and Alan Brown, Producers of BBC2 T.V.'s "Kicking and Screaming " series, and not least of all my solicitor son, Harry, born in World Cup year 1966, for his insight to me of his generation.

E.Maurice Watkins, Chairman of the British Association for Sport and Law, a Senior partner in James Chapman & Co, Solicitors, Manchester, and a Manchester United director, steered me away from a practical pitfall with the landmark Jean-Marc Bosman Belgian court case while sustaining an Old Trafford tradition of legal expertise handed down from his solicitor predecessor of whom you can read in these pages, Harold Hardman, an Olympic Games soccer gold medalist, whose vision as Chairman of Manchester United, took Britain into European football against parochial establishment opposition. Additionally, Lord (Denis) Howell of Aston, Britain's longest-serving Sports Minister; E.W. ('Jim') Swanton, Olympian among cricket chroniclers; David Miller, modern soccer Olympian, Corinthian-Casual and Pegasus flying winger; David Harrison, Corinthian-Casuals Chairman; and Brian Glanville, doyen of soccer chroniclers and creator of Chelsea-Casuals, have all flown the flag of Corinthian idealism during that *"sea change in values and moral climate"*.

In the beginning, however, this book would not exist at all without the inspiration of those who have joined the Great Umpire in the Sky. Sir Harold ('Tommy') Thompson and his learned lieutenant and M'learned Friend, Jerry L. Weinstein guided the Pegasus chapter and Walter Lancashire and Harry ('Dick') Spooner, schoolmasters supreme, opened the door to all which has flowed from my schoolboy correspondence with a very special retired headmaster, who was not only a gentle Player, but also a Gentle man, Gilbert Oswald Smith.

9-12 Bell Yard, London, WC2A 2LF : Edward Grayson.
3rd September 1996.

CONTENTS

INTRODUCTION

 A triple purpose exists for this up-dated version of the background to a Second World War schoolboy's correspondence with a retired headmaster, G.O. Smith, who also had been Association football's greatest centre-forward during the last decade of Queen Victoria's England, and a more than useful cricketer, too. First, to fill the 40 years time span which now exists since its earliest publication in 1955; a period during which the nature of sport and games at the public as distinct from the overwhelmingly greater numerical private level has shifted from a form of physical recreation and healthy competition to a global satellite village. It was crystallised in the 40th anniversary issue, 1954-1994, of America's *SPORTS ILLUSTRATED* with the realisation

"Sometime in the second half of the century, sports became an axis on which the world turns. ...There have been comparable times in history when sports have been at the centre of a culture and seemed to dominate the landscape. Whether in Greek society or in what used to be called the Golden Ages of Sports. But everything is magnified by television."

Second, to preserve for posterity, through the original text of this book, the traditional Corinthian values of fair play, self-discipline and sheer fun of sport, within an unfolding enveloping commercial environment in the 1990's where no **effective** sanctions for misconduct appear to exist from many sporting governing bodies and their discipline committees: and thus the only protection for oppressed or physically injured victims is in the courts of law. Third, to explain how it led directly to to-day's involvement of the law with sport, and to the creation, concurrently with the modern development of Sports Medicine, of Sport and the Law as an expanding professional discipline dedicated to the world of sport.

This ranges from The Football Association's creation in 1863 to harmonise the then different school and club playing rules to such ever diverse increasing areas such as Matthew Simmons igniting Monsieur Cantona's touchline reaction at Selhurst Park during early 1995; fighting for freedom of contract in football with Ralph Banks and George Eastham and for cricket via the Packer Revolution and its London High Court landmark ruling in *Greig v. Insole* in 1978; or Jean-Marc Bosman's Belgian litigation at the European Court of Justice ending in 1995, and the consequent abolition of transfer fees within the European Union, where a player moves at the end of contract, from one member state to another; tax-free charitable status for sporting educational trusts, and above all else, the general failure of domestic and international sporting governing bodies to create realistic and fair and just penal policies on and off the field of play, to meet the Gilbert and Sullivan criteria: of "let the punishment fit the crime". Here a greater use of "sin-bins" comes readily to mind.

G.O. Smith has always been regarded as one of the greatest centre-forwards in the game's history. During a time when only three international matches were played each season between England, Scotland, Wales and Northern Ireland before football circled the globe, he played 21 times for England, often as the Corinthian Football Club's amateur captain alongside, and in competition with, the leading professional players of his era. He bridged the 19th and 20th centuries with his last appearance for England against Germany at Tottenham Hotspur's ground in 1901. He also merited an accolade from one of cricket's most eminent chroniclers, Sir Pelham Warner, who wrote of a memorable fourth-innings century during 1896 in the Oxford-Cambridge Varsity match, in his *Lord's 1787 - 1945*, explained in detail at Chapter IV, Varsity Cricket in the Nineties.

"As long as there is a history of Oxford and Cambridge cricket the name of G.O. Smith will be emblazoned on its roll".

That century was scored three months to the day after he had led the full England pro-am as centre-forward against Scotland at Ibrox Park, Glasgow, alongside such talented professionals as John Goodall, then of Derby County, and William Isiah (Billy) Bassett of the club for which he became a distinguished chairman before the Second World War, West Bromwich Albion. Fourteen years earlier in 1882, the Mark McCormack of his day, N. Lane "Pa" Jackson, had created the Corinthian Football Club out of the leading public school and university amateur players of the period before professionalism was authorised in 1885, and the Football League formed in 1888, in order to challenge the more scientifically structured Scottish international victories over England.

I had enjoyed a Second World War schoolboy correspondence with him after responding to a schoolmaster's challenge by cycling 20 miles to obtain his autograph when he was living in retirement on the South Coast from the joint headmastership of Arthur Dunn's foundation, Ludgrove School, then and to-day, one of the main Preparatory Schools to Eton College. There he had succeeded that earlier England international and Old Etonian F.A. Cup winning finalist centre-forward, Arthur Dunn, in whose memory the long-standing Public Schools Old Boys Cup competition was inaugurated. After having suffered a badly treated broken leg following my own ill-judged tackle during the Oxford University soccer trials, which prevented further playing activity, I was able, with G.O. Smith's earlier encouragement, and in such moments as I could spare from commencing practice at the Bar in Lincoln's Inn before moving to the Temple, to frame the letters I had preserved against a background to his life and times.

This decision was stimulated and sustained by a post-Second World War phenomenon: the creation in 1948 of a joint Oxbridge soccer team, Pegasus, coached by their professional Tottenham Hotspur tutors under the magnetic management of Arthur Rowe, with Alf Ramsey, Billy Nicholson and Vic Buckingham, all inspiring in the Pegasus play their memorable message, "Make it simple, make it quick" for the "push and run" technique. It also sustained the G.O. Smith footballing-cricket tradition of predominantly talented schoolmasters alongside other worthy citizens.

That pattern of duality, unintentionally, imperceptibly and almost unknowingly stirred original interest in a legal googly thrown up by various Court decisions which subjected footballers' benefits to income tax, whereas cricketers were tax-free. It began a never ending legal innings which is now identified as the combination of Sport and the Law.

Pegasus, with Test Match cricket captains Donald Carr (England) and Gerry Alexander (West Indies) (on the second occasion) drew two 100,000 crowds to Wembley Stadium for F.A. **AMATEUR** Cup Final victories, against Bishop Auckland, 2-1, in 1951, and Harwich and Parkestone, 6-0, in 1953. Three years later in 1956 some of the Pegasus finalists appeared again at Wembley Stadium in an F.A. Amateur Cup Final against Bishop Auckland, on this occasion before an 80,000 crowd for the amalgamated Corinthian-Casuals. The merger of the two clubs, Corinthians, and Casuals, in 1939, had been too close to the outbreak of the Second World War to make any high profile public impact before Pegasus followed a path prepared by the Corinthians of the 1880's and 1920's for flying the genuine amateur flag in a professionally dominated game at the public level. Shortly after the second of those two Pegasus triumphs in 1953, yet another 100,000 crowd at Wembley Stadium witnessed the last minute dramatic F.A. Cup Final defeat of Bolton Wanderers by Blackpool, for whom the (Sir Stanley) Matthews' magic at outside-right mesmerised the Bolton Wanderers left-back, Ralph Banks. This in turn set in motion a sequence of events two years later in 1955 which became the first step on the road which has led ultimately to Jean-Marc Bosman's arrival at the European Court of Justice in 1995, and its resultant need to consider how to replace the transfer system with its associated funding now outlawed by the Court's judgment: an issue considered in the final Chapter X: Towards a New Sporting Era.

During that second half of this 20th century football moved into public perception as the world's most popular team game, and away from its incorrect but usually mythologised image as the opiate of the cloth-capped artisan classes. Cricket expanded its horizons - from its earliest expatriate old colonial British Empire and Dominion base to an International Cricket Council which now absorbs forty-one cricket playing nations, comprising nine full members, twenty-one associate members and eleven affiliate members. Each game is now part of the worldwide entertainment and leisure industry. Yet each game still retains its natural roots in the schools, clubs and village greens of the United Kingdom, from where the pioneers carried this great slice of British culture, with its concepts of fair play and law and order, to their multi-racial converts in the four corners of the globe; and during the euphoria experienced in England for the Euro '96 competition, soccer became a cult concept transcending areas of interest which earlier had dismissed it as an artisan indulgence.

Before television's global village in the 1970's and 1980's dissolved nature's traditional sports divisions into winters for football and summer for cricket, they had allowed the two dimensional talents of footballing-cricketers over an eighty years period to straddle both games, many of whom played for the amateur Corinthian Football Club, and in the years after the Second World War following the 1939 amalgamation with Casuals, for Corinthian-Casuals, too. A round dozen Double Internationals who represented England at both national games emerged as the apex of a widely based pyramid which covered F.A. Cup finalists, Test Match cricket captains, professional players of both games, as well as scores of double Oxbridge Blues.

C.B. Fry is best known for having illuminated this trend. He followed on an F.A. Cup Final appearance, on leave from his schoolmaster duties and the Corinthians, for Southampton at the old Crystal Palace against Sheffield United on Saturday, by scoring runs for Dr. W.G. Grace's London Counties XI at Kennington Oval two days later on Monday in 1902. Additionally he was capped for England at both games. A more modern example was the umpire Chris Balderstone during 1975 in his playing days motoring up the M1 after helping Leicestershire clinch the county cricket championship to aid Doncaster Rovers to a 1-1 draw against Brentford in the Football League; and the same post-war period recalls Denis Compton's Football League and F.A. Cup Final honours at outside-left with Arsenal during 1948 and 1950 after war-time soccer international appearances alongside his Middlesex and Test Match centuries. One of his successors on Arsenal's other wing at outside-right, Arthur Milton, became the last of a rare breed when selected to open England's batting from Gloucestershire against New Zealand, in 1958, alongside his soccer cap against Austria in 1952.

From a decade before G.O. Smith's the first two of this rare breed, however, symbolise, conveniently, the then social structure of both games and the now obsolete divisions into Gentlemen and Players, and also contrast the role of lawyers and doctors in sport, then and now. During the 1880's William Gunn not only opened the batting for Nottinghamshire and England (with Dr. W.G. Grace); he also played for Notts County, Nottingham Forest - once - and became a director of the County, and founder of the sports goods firm of Gunn and Moore. The uncle of Jazz trumpeter Humphrey Lyttelton, the Honourable Alfred Lyttelton, played for England and Old Etonians in the winning and losing F.A. Cup Finals, of the 1870's; with Middlesex and for England with Dr. W.G. Grace, all before he was called to Bar, took silk and died prematurely as a Cabinet Minister in Asquith's Liberal Government before 1914. Yet his services were never required for sport, comparable to the way in which Dr. W.G. Grace never became associated with any Sports Medicine development - something which is now epitomised by the National Sports Medicine Institute at St. Bartholomew's Hospital in London, and its developing satellite services throughout the country.

Nevertheless, a year after Lyttelton's England -v- Scotland soccer appearance in 1877, the first-ever recorded prosecution for a soccer injury, a fatality, took place at Leicester Assizes in 1878; and a second occurred, coincidentally at the same location, in 1898. Even earlier, the first-ever traceable and reported case for personal injuries associated with a sporting activity had taken place in 1870 after a grandstand collapse at Cheltenham

Races in 1866; and when one of Lyttelton's successors in an Old Etonian F.A. Cup winning team during 1882, J.P.F. Rawlinson, the goalkeeper, was briefed thirty years later as a Q.C. in 1912 to plead the case for professional football and freedom of contract from restrictive practices, he took his eye off the ball, and was ruled offside by the trial judge, for having chosen the wrong legal remedies to tackle what was then an easily identifiable restrictive retain system on players' contracts. It did not surface again for another forty years, when I proposed in two articles a solution to a legal googly, whereby footballers' benefits or testimonials were subject to tax, but cricketers were not. This brought to my Lincoln's Inn Chambers the then Chairman of the Professional Footballers' and Trainers' Union now the Professional Footballers' Association: the PFA, James Guthrie, who had captained Portsmouth's 1939 F.A. Cup winning team against Major Frank Buckley's "monkey glands" Wolverhampton Wanderers side captained by Stanley Cullis.

Supported by Guthrie and his Union, the opportunity to redeem that restrictive contract position came when after that 1953 F.A. Cup defeat by Blackpool and Stanley Matthews, Ralph Banks was released by Bolton Wanderers. He joined Aldershot in 1954 for a transfer fee which Aldershot wished to recoup when Banks was invited to move on a year later in 1955 to another club Weymouth. Under the then contractual conditions existing for professional Football League players Aldershot had a retention control over Banks' services, even if he did not re-sign. When he refused so to do because of a proposed reduction in his wages, Aldershot sued for possession of his house owned by the Club.

Banks counterclaimed that the Aldershot plea was tainted with illegality, inherent in the restraint of trade legal penalty area. In due course, after a County Court Judge's suspended possession order but before a threatened appeal could be mounted, he was released to join Weymouth. It was the beginning of a road for freedom of contract for players which wound its way to the High Court - through George Eastham for football eight years later in 1963, in cricket with the Packer revolution in 1978, and ultimately at the European Court of Justice with Jean-Marc Bosman, in 1995.

Concurrently with these issues, that taxation googly bounced into action while preparing this book. A House of Lords ruling in 1927 had pronounced the publicly subscribed cricketers benefits to be tax-free. A clutch of High Court cases during 1928 and 1941 excluded professional footballers from comparable relief, because of contractual conditions. The action proposed in the two articles was adopted by the then Professional Footballers' and Trainers' Union, activated with success against the revenue in 1957 at Peterborough United, which was then outside the Football League, and has lasted until this day to create tax-free arrangements for professional footballers as well as cricketers, by deleting the contractural conditions within the regulations.

At the same time, Pegasus' exclusive Oxbridge F.A. Amateur Cup triumphs with its schoolmaster, academic and general educational backgrounds, attracted profits which also appeared to qualify for tax-relief as an educational sporting charity. The revenue would not agree, and over quarter of a century had to pass before a House of Lord ruling endorsed this opinion, based upon an earlier High Court decision concerning a gift for a fives Court at Aldenham School.

Throughout all the time, while preparing the book over a seven year period, and after, and even within the G.O. Smith letters which inspired it, the current diseases of violence and drugs, V.D., in sport, did not enter any assessment. During 1966, however, the World Cup in England witnessed the brutal ejection of Brazil's Pele by violent foul play bordering on criminality by Bulgarian and Portuguese players identified in his book *'MY LIFE AND THE BEAUTIFUL GAME'*; without any effective retribution or compensation by either F.I.F.A. or the courts. Three or four years later, however, Lewes Assizes in 1969 and London's High Court in 1970 recorded a £4,000 damages award for a broken leg from a foul play soccer tackle in a minor Sussex County League game. In 1971 the crowd disaster at Glasgow's Ibrox gave rise to the safety of Sports Grounds Act 1975, and by 1977 an invitation arrived to contribute a series of *Sunday Telegraph* articles on *Sport and the Law* which was followed up a year later with a 76-paged booklet under the same title. In due course, Butterworths law publishers expanded the title to 376 pages in 1988, and 536 in 1994.

Concurrent with these individual productions were responses to invitations for co-authorship and co-editing of *Medicine, Sport and the Law, Medico-Legal Hazards of Rugby Union,* and *Sponsorship of Sport, Arts and Leisure,* to reflect respectively the developing involvement of sporting injuries and commercial sponsorship within the sporting arena. The world had thus moved on since that Second World War schoolboy's correspondence with the retired headmaster concerned only with the personalities and play of the Victorian era, when none of the modern horrors of hooliganism, violence and drugs had entered the chronicles or consciousness of sporting lore. Nevertheless, it formed the genesis and inspiration for all of those legally based publications, which led ultimately to the formation of the British Association for Sport and Law, in 1993, forty years after the British Association for Sport and Medicine.

Furthermore, the traditional sporting values of "fair play, self-discipline or sheer fun of sport", shared by the professional and amateur players alongside G.O. Smith at public levels have always remained as ideals and practised at school and club levels down to our own day.

After the Easter holidays, 1996, on the eve of Euro '96, the Headmaster of C.B. Fry's old school, Repton, G.E. Jones, preached a sermon on the Corinthians spirit. For the competition itself the organising body, UEFA, produced a Code of Ethics dealing with football. Lord [Denis] Howell, Britain's longest serving Minister with responsibility for sport, explained in a House of Lords debate on "Society's Moral and Spiritual Well-being", [5 July 1966] how nobody knew about it because it was not mentioned by the Press.

Accordingly, for the 2nd Butterworth's 1994 edition of *Sport and the Law,* the first two of 15 Appendices dealt designedly with concepts of the Corinthian Spirit in Sport and Sportsmanship from two modern Corinthians and Cricketers, Hubert Doggart, now another retired headmaster in the G.O. Smith and general Corinthian tradition, and Douglas Insole (the nominal Defendant in the *Greig v. Insole* Packer cricket litigation). Each had played for Pegasus and in due course for the amalgamated Corinthian-Casuals in the F.A. Amateur Cup Competition.

One reviewer, however, while generously commending the legal qualities of the text, expressed a reservation about

> "the values of fair play, self-discipline and the sheer fun of sport. These are laudable values but, in an era when much of professional sport is money-dominated and played in a 'win at all costs' spirit, they are arguably naïve and inappropriate in a modern treatise devoted to the legal environment of sport".

How far that impression is shared can never be gauged with certainty. If it means that

> "when much of professional sport is money-dominated and played in a 'win at all costs' spirit"

the

> "the values of fair play, self-discipline and the sheer fun of sport"

are really "inappropriate", the question must arise, where is sport, what are its true values?

This book **may** help to find some answers, as well how and why "sports became an axis on which the world turns". It **will** certainly explain why *THE TIMES* leading article commented on the Football Association's abdication of responsibility when it failed to penalise adequately the collective hooligan mis-conduct of its England representative players on the eve of the Euro '96 competition, before their opening game,

"Nobody expects the gladiators who play it at the highest level to be statesmen or saints, or even mythical Corinthians of the legendary old school, for whom playing up and playing the game was more important than winning. That is not what they are paid millions for. But the latest bad behaviour by the supposedly grown men of the England squad confirms a depressing image of English football after its age of innocence."

That "age of innocence" emerges from the pages which follow. Furthermore, while these pages were being prepared during the EURO '96 competition, it was more than appropriate that Colin Malam, the *Sunday Telegraph* Football Correspondent, whose late father, Albert Malam, had graced Huddersfield Town in the days of Roy Goodall, Ken Willingham and Alf Young, among others, in the years between the Two World Wars, should draw my attention to a crucial contribution by his colleague, Patrick Barclay, in the columns which allowed me the privilege to argue that the RULE OF LAW on the playing fields for SPORT is as crucial for the RULE OF LAW in SOCIETY, to preserve civilised behaviour and avoid anarchy. Barclay wrote after the Croatia v. Turkey game:

"No matter how many treats Euro '96 has in store, the Croatian substitute Goran Vlaovic's late winner against Turkey will go down among the goals of the tournament. It ought also to be hailed as a vindication of strict refereeing. The liberal use of yellow and red cards may be hurting, but this was a spectacular piece of evidence that it's working.

When Vlaovic burst over the halfway line, hurdling a rash challenge to earn a clear run at the Turkish goalkeeper, the only way he could have been stopped was for the pursuing Alpay Ozalan to stick out a leg, pull his shirt, or otherwise foul him. The thought must have crossed Alpay's mind like every other in a Nottingham stadium dominated by Turks. But the defender desisted, knowing he would be sure - not just likely - to incur dismissal and suspension from the next match.

Cynics argued afterwards that Alpay should have sacrificed himself nonetheless, that Turkey would probably have survived the consequent free-kick and cling on for a point with 10 men. How tiresome. How old-fashioned. The game's rulers should be congratulated on their campaign against such debilitating negativity, even if it seems to be taking an age for some observers to recognise the link between the hard line established in the 1994 World Cup and a perceptible tilting of the balance towards entertainment.

The complaining classes tend to forget how morally brutalised top-level football had become before FIFA, alarmed by the dull, fear-filled World Cup of 1990 and the distressing submission of a great player, Marco Van Basten, to the violent tackle from behind, at last resolved to act. So the odd case of excessively zealous refereeing is a price worth paying for what we have now. The tactical foul is almost an anachronism; when Victor Onopko committed one on Italy's Roberto Mussi at Anfield, the Scottish referee Les Mottram raised his yellow card less in anger than sorrow at the accomplished libero's carelessness. The offence stood out like a sore thigh amid the ebb and flow of a match whose constant creative endeavour would have been a pleasant surprise in the early stages of any tournament. Again, I'd say, cause and effect.

Not that enlightened refereeing will ever produce good football. It simply gives encouragement to players and their coaches who respond in different ways, the more adventurous providing heroes for the neutral to adopt."

Space alone, no doubt, prevented Patrick Barclay from referring to the classic abdication of refereeing and governing body control from the 1966 World Cup when the great Brazilian, Pele, as explained previously, was brutally and criminally assaulted out of the competition. The law of the land does not stop at the touchline or boundary. It did on that occasion, and demolishes those who claim the Corinthian ideal to be.....

"arguably naïve and inappropriate in a modern treatise denoted to the legal environment of sport".

18

CHAPTER 1

MODERN SOCCER AND CRICKET

Into the full glory of the Victorian era, Gilbert Oswald Smith was born at Croydon, in Surrey, on the 25th November, 1872. Exactly thirty years afterwards, at the beginning of that sunny period known as Edwardian days, he relinquished his position in England's international football sides. During that decade cricket and football, the games he graced, grew up from their infancy as recreations of the village green, school fields and playgrounds to their adult stage as the commercial entertainment which sweeps the country today.

In fact, 1872 was a year of sporting destiny and a year in which to be born to sporting greatness. The F.A. Cup Final, before 2,000 spectators at Kennington Oval, and the England v. Scotland match were each played for the first time. W.G. Grace embarked on his first Australian tour, and G.O. Smith's great contemporaries, C.B. Fry, Ranjitsinhji and J.T. Tyldesley, were also born.

No 100,000 crowds then existed or were dreamed of. No five-day Test Matches were required to subsidise the finances of a bankrupt County Cricket Championship. W.G. Grace, by his development of forward and defensive play in batsmanship had just begun to revolutionise cricket technique and to suggest the game's box-office possibilities. The footballers, too, had just begun the evolution of their theme on which Meredith and Matthews and other modern maestros have built the rhythms of their play. Yet, by then., the way had already been prepared by the Industrial Revolution for the public acclamation of both games.

Cricket is, of course, at least a century older than modern football. That cricket took the lead was due as much to the Hambledon Club and the beginning of the M.C.C. in 1787 as to its rural growth amidst the agrarian revolution of the eighteenth century. Football, although sufficiently prominent in Tudor times, was, in the words of Stubbes' *Anatomie of Abuses in the Realme of England,* published in 1583, rather 'a friendlie kinde of fyghte than a play or recreation - a bloody and murthering practice than a felowly sport or pastime.' Even so, this ancient form of football is still celebrated in certain parts of the country as far afield as Derbyshire and Dorsetshire. Thus on Shrove Tuesday and Ash Wednesday whole townships, following the tradition of centuries, close down for an afternoon and strive in friendly combat to steer the magic ball between goals sometimes miles apart. Nevertheless, like the cricket we know and play today, football is barely a hundred years old.

Not until the great provincial centres of industry, after their rapid growth and development in the mid-nineteenth century, joined forces with the public schools and Oxford and Cambridge Universities did our national games in summer and winter begin to speak in their modern idiom. For their technical developments could take place only after the expansion of industry had started the mass migration from the agricultural acres to those northern centres in which are concentrated our famous industrial and sporting areas today. Those hives of sporting activity which now exist around Headingley, Bradford, Halifax and Huddersfield; or around Old Trafford, Bury, Oldham and Tranmere were not uncovered by chance. Working hours created leisure hours. New sources of active and passive enjoyment were needed which could never be satisfied by the miniature battlefields of cock-fighting or the boxing ring. Hence, while William Clarke was taking his All-England Cricket XI up and down the land, spreading the gospel of cricket in the counties, the railways were spreading their network and the populace for the creation of new towns and sporting centres. The growth of church and working clubs and the development of playing-fields gave rise to the modern town organisations. Bolton Wanderers descended from the local Christ Church Sunday School; Derby County from a football section of the Derbyshire County Cricket Club; and Wolverhampton Wanderers from the enthusiasm of a band of scholars and choristers.

The result of these fresh sources of energy is discernible in the rapid growth of football. In 1855 the oldest Association football club in the world was founded at Sheffield. Seven years later, in 1862, the oldest of the modern League clubs, Notts County, was formed. The Football Association was born in the next year, 1863, a year which also saw the foundation of the Yorkshire County Cricket Club. In 1871, when W.G. Grace was at his zenith, the Football Association Challenge Cup competition was inaugurated; and in 1888 came the foundation of the Football League, perhaps the perfection of all regular organised competitions.

Could the early pioneers of the games have visualised the magnitude of their creations in the years to come? The F.A. Cup and the Football League competitions have attracted an interest and an enthusiasm reserved for no other single institution. Cricket and international football politics have at times merited the attention of the League of Nations or U.N.O.; and it is by a neat twist of history that in the same year, 1888, in which Gladstone by his Local Government Act created the London County Council and other County boroughs, William McGregor, a Presbyterian member of Aston Villa, founded the Football League. One might be forgiven for thinking that it is the second of these happenings which has given the inhabitants of a locality the greatest reasons for civic pride. Preston became 'proud' because eleven men in white shirts and blue shorts won the F.A. Cup and the first Football League Championship in the same year. Everton became more famous for its team than for its toffee; and before the Second World War the potters of Arnold Bennett's *Five Towns* were to hold public meetings to keep within the City of Stoke the man whose exploits had made that district more well known than had Wedgwood of industrial fame. To mention Stanley Matthews here is almost superfluous.

Yet these developments were merely the form and shape of things to come. The substance and the laws of football grew in a much quieter way, far from the smoke and city, among the cloisters of the seats of learning, the schools and universities. Each school had its own rules depending upon the size of its playground and. its facilities for playing-fields. Indeed, at Charterhouse and Westminster, two traditional homes of Association football, only the cloisters or a walled-in space of hard ground were available for play in the days before Vincent Square was created for Westminster and Dr Haig-Brown moved Charterhouse from the London square which still bears its name to the hills of Godalming. Thus physical restrictions confined football in these schools to dribbling and no more. In other schools, too, the rules of football as played there showed the future pattern of development. So the Cheltenham College regulations allowed a player to throw the ball in from touch; at Harrow a rule provided that the umpire should 'put out of the game any player wilfully breaking any of the football rules'; whilst Eton contributed the off-side principle by a rule that 'a player is considered to be "sneaking" when only three, or less than three, of the opposite side are before him and the ball behind him, and in such case he may not kick the ball.'

Montague Shearman, later Sir Montague (Mr Justice) Shearrnan, himself an Old Merchant Taylor who had obtained a Rugby Blue at Oxford alongside the famous Harry Vassall, summed up the position in the schools with judicial clarity. In his volume on the game, in the *Badminton Library* (under the title Athletics and Football, 1st ed. 1887), he wrote:

'The different schools, in adopting as a pastime the national game of football in which any and every method of getting the ball through the goal was allowed, included only such parts of the game as were suitable to their ground, or, to put the case in another way, eliminated from the game every characteristic which was necessarily unsuitable to the circumstances under which the game could be played. As far as we can discover, however, no school but Rugby played the old style of game where every player was allowed to pick up the ball and run with it, and every adversary could stop him by collaring, hacking over and charging or any other means he pleased. No doubt the majority of schoolmasters thought, with Sir Thomas Elliot, that the original football was unworthy of a gentleman's son, and dangerous to limb as well as to clothing, and in the days when butcher's meat was cheap, and the cloth was good but dear, the clothing question was a matter of some consideration. What causes led the Rugby authorities to differ from the managers of other schools it is difficult to see, but it is tolerably plain that the "Rugby game" was originally played at Rugby School alone, while other schools adopted more or less modified forms of the kicking game... The Association of "kicking" game came before the world from Eton, Harrow, Westminster, Charterhouse, and other schools where something of the same style of game was played. All these schools had rules differing in many essential characteristics from one another, but all agreeing in forbidding any seizing of the ball and running with it.'

Far more important than its leaning towards modern Rugby football, however, Rugby School also had about this time as headmaster, Dr Thomas Arnold, the father of Matthew Arnold, the poet and author. Dr Arnold reformed entirely the public school system of the country, and perhaps the most important factor in his aim to shape an administrative class for an expanding empire was the development of the team and sporting spirit on the playing-fields. It was only natural that the old boys of schools with their own particular brand of football should desire to carry forward their enjoyment to university; and it is therefore not surprising that the universities should see the first attempt to originate a code of rules which would overcome the difficulty brought about by the variations in school rules. In 1846 at Cambridge University some old boys from Shrewsbury and Eton, two of the most famous Association football schools, joined forces to form a club. Although it did not last long, clearly the thoughts of unity were active. Two years later, in 1848, another and more successful attempt resulted in the 'Cambridge Rules' which were pasted up on Parker's Piece. By the time they were refined in 1862 to those issued by J.C. Thring, a master at Uppingham, and one of the pioneers of 1846, the scene was set for almost complete concord; and in early October, 1863, a more developed set of regulations emerged from Cambridge entitled 'Cambridge University Football Rules.'

There is now no doubt, as early historians have shown, that legislation had so oppressed football by the early part of the last century, that the game would most probably have been forgotten altogether had not most of our leading public schools included it among those they adopted when the great athletic revival commenced. Slowly the popularity of the game was taking root. Between 1850 and 1860 football became a regular feature of the winter time-table in the schools. As has been seen, clubs began to be formed rapidly up and down the country, and in 1863 the modern Stoke City Club was created by a group of Old Carthusians.

But the interchange of fixtures was not assisted in the sixties by the fact that while many of the clubs such as Sheffield, Forest (not of Nottingham but of Epping, which later altered its name to the Wanderers, the most famous of the early F.A. Cup winners) and Barnes, as well as the schools, were adhering to the general principles of the Association game, Richmond and Blackheath among others played the Rugby version. On 26th October 1863, fifteen clubs therefore resolved at the Freemason's Tavern, Great Queen Street, Lincoln's Inn Fields, 'that the clubs represented at this meeting now form themselves into an association to be called the Football Association.' Thus was born the world-famous F.A.

The first problem was to produce a set of rules to please both schools and clubs. Ultimately it was decided to base them upon those drawn up at Cambridge University in October of the same year, and they were adopted by the Association on 8th December, 1863. Immediately a great dispute arose as to whether or not hacking should be included. This appendage to the game which consisted of cheerfully kicking the shins of the opponent instead of the ball, was practised by a number of clubs and schools without being generally approved or followed.

The majority view, however, which was opposed to this practice, prevailed, and hacking was omitted completely from the new code. Thus the laws turned against the view of the game current at the time: 'Yer kicks the ball if you can, and if you can't you kicks the other man's shins.' 'But we haven't got a ball,' was the rejoinder. 'Oh, - the ball!' was the reply; 'let's start the game.'

Up to this point it had been hoped that all the existing clubs would support the revised laws, but the decision upon hacking caused the Blackheath Football Club formally to withdraw. The president of the new Association made an appeal to Blackheath not to insist on 'a dangerous and painful practice, very brutal when deliberate and unlikely to prevent a man who had due regard for his wife and family following the game.' The Blackheath and other clubs remained obdurate, however, and eight years later, in 1871, they assisted substantially in the foundation of the Rugby Union. Thus it was 'hacking' and not 'handling of the ball' which was the real basis of the difference between the two codes, for until then the Association game had not altogether disallowed handling, and did not abolish it until a few years after this early code, namely, in 1866. Subsequently hacking was rigidly barred in the Rugby game, or from the wording of its rules at least.

Not for over a quarter of a century after the Association and Rugby games had parted ways did the famous tablet appear on the garden wall of the headmaster's house at Rugby School:

> THIS STONE
> COMMEMORATES THE EXPLOIT OF
> **WILLIAM WEBB ELLIS,**
>
> WHO WITH A FINE DISREGARD FOR THE
> RULES OF FOOTBALL, AS PLAYED IN HIS
> TIME, FIRST TOOK THE BALL IN HIS ARMS
> AND RAN WITH IT, THUS ORIGINATING
> THE DISTINCTIVE FEATURE OF
> THE RUGBY GAME.
> A.D. 1823

Mr Harold Abrahams, the famous Olympic runner and sports journalist, and Mr G.R. Paling, CBE, a Director of Brighton and Hove Albion F.C., first suggested for me that the tablet created a fiction, when, at a meeting of the International Sports Fellowship, they appeared in a mock trial of the ghost of William Webb Ellis who was charged with contravening the laws of football as played in his day. The facts which have now emerged clearly indicate that a committee of Old Rugbeians set up

the inscription as recently as 1900. They had been incensed by Montague Shearman's exposure which had entirely destroyed the myth suggested by the wording of the tablet. Moreover, H.C. Bradby, in his *Rugby* (1900), has pointed out that the only evidence for attributing the first carrying of the ball to Ellis was not first-hand; for a Mr Matthew Bloxam, who suggested it, was not an eye-witness. In 1823 the rules of football in general, as distinct from those created by particular schools, had never been contemplated, and holding the ball, so far from contravening or comprising a fine disregard for 'the rules ... as played in his time,' was then part and parcel of the game. No doubt the more generous-minded Rugby players and followers would be content to fall back upon the conclusions which the Association Football Correspondent of *The Times* has ascribed to a certain Chancellor of Cambridge University who, confessing complete ignorance of all football, was asked to sum up a debate on the Association and Rugby games. 'It is clear,' he said, 'that one is a gentleman's game played by hooligans; the other a hooligan's game played by gentlemen.' Since the formation of Pegasus and the revival of Oxford and Cambridge Association football, however, the one defect in this aphorism has become apparent.

About some time between the parting of the ways and the end of the nineteenth century, although the actual date can never be certain, the shorter and more popular term 'soccer' came to be applied to the Association game, being derived from the 'soc' in 'association.' Here again aristocratic origins are evident, for Mr Erie Partridge, the recorder of colloquial English, has traced a return to the Oxford habit, now somewhat obsolete, of slurring its names by adding the suffix of 'er.' Hence, the swot was known as a mugger, rowing men still speak of toggers and football enthusiasts quickly adopted the terms of rugger and soccer.

Despite all these happenings, however, it is hardly likely that the world would have seen the fantastic spread of the game but for the inauguration during the season of 1871-72 of that most dazzling of sporting competitions, the F.A. Challenge Cup. From the original entry of fifteen amateur clubs the trophy drew, its competitors like a magnet, and after seven years the professional invasion from the north began. With the growth of local tournaments and inter-town rivalry the competition became keener. The appearance of Scotsmen in the ranks of the northern sides could no longer be explained as a mere novelty or accident. Rumours of a trek from over the border to better jobs and wages in the cotton mills of Lancashire seeped through to the refined southern ears of the game's administrators. In 1884 the Upton Park Club, after losing a famous Cup-tie with Preston North End, protested that the ultimate 'Invincibles' had employed professionals. Major W. Sudell, football's first great *professional* manager, on behalf of Preston, promptly threw the cat among the pigeons, by admitting the truth of this allegation and in effect said 'So what.' The F.A., with a far-sightedness probably instilled by its clear-thinking secretary, C.W. Alcock, who held a similar position with the Surrey County Cricket Club, bowed to the inevitable. In 1885 professionalism was legalised. Three years later William McGregor, stimulated by the desire to avoid cancelled and irregular fixtures, sent out his suggestion of forming a Football League; and the game was launched upon what has proved to be the most triumphant and successful career in modern British sport.

Different in taste and temperament as Scotsmen are from Englishmen, their lack of interest generally in cricket is not reflected in football. Although the rugger-soccer struggle in the schools in Scotland has been, and still is, more intense among the middle classes than even in southern England, the Association game quickly took a hold over the border. The now world famous Queen's Park Club in Glasgow was founded in 1867, four years after the Football Association, and other clubs sprang up in Glasgow and Edinburgh. It would not be wrong to claim for Queen's Park the building of Scottish football almost single handed. The Club arranged the first two international matches against England in 1872 and 1873, and was instrumental in forming The Scottish Football Association in the same years. It has wielded a profound influence in fashioning the technique of the game, and its development of scientific passing and cohesion between the half-backs and the forwards as a counter to the traditional dribbling and individuality is reflected in the fact that in the dozen odd years after those first two internationals England gained only one victory, in 1878-79, and this was entirely due to the spirit of a superb rally turning a half-time deficit of 1-4 into a 5-4 victory.

During those barren years England's teams consisted of amateur players from many different clubs such as N.C. Bailey (Old Westminsters), E.C. Bambridge (Swifts), J.F.M. Prinsep (Old Carthusians) and R.H. Birkett (Clapham Rovers), who had to combine their individuality without any pre-match knowledge of each other's play. The pre-match conferences at Cabinet level, which exist today, were then a long way ahead. Not surprisingly, England failed to beat an enemy nurtured on scientific combination. This position might have continued much longer until the flood tide of professionalism had its inevitable effect; but one of the most industrious and enthusiastic of the game's earliest legislators, N. Lane ('Pa') Jackson, who was then honorary assistant secretary of The Football Association, sought a more immediate solution.

N.L. ('PA') JACKSON
Founder of the Corinthians.

'At that period,' he has recorded for us in his autobiography, *Sporting Days and Sporting Ways,* 'public school and university men provided most of the players for the English side, so I thought that by giving these plenty of practice together they would acquire a certain measure of combination.' Thus were laid the foundations of the most famous of non-professional clubs in the history of the game, the Corinthian Football Club.

G.O.Smith wrote to me in 1943 that," Pa" Jackson was one of the greatest managers the world had seen in matters of organisation. He founded the Corinthians, the Sports Club and golf clubs galore. A genius in many ways.

Certainly that genius had no greater monument than the Corinthian pillar which rose from the assembly at his barely furnished office one evening in London's Paternoster Square of a handful of zealous footballers who, with Jackson, ushered the new club into the world. The year was 1882, the same year in which a group of Sunday School boys in another part of London on another evening, around a street lamp, formed Tottenham Hotspur, one of the most famous of professional clubs in the history of the game. This link in time between the two clubs was later to be forged on the field where there were enjoyable and memorable episodes in their histories, continued in our own time through Oxford and Cambridge and Pegasus. The view of Jackson which caused the creation of the Corinthians was, in his own words, 'fully justified, for in the nine years preceding the 1884-85 season the Scots had won eight matches and lost only one, whereas the next nine years saw England win four matches and lose twice only while three were drawn. The players during those nine years of improvement included forty four Corinthians, many of whom played on several occasions.'

Indeed, the end of the barren years in 1885 saw the England team against Scotland composed of nine Corinthians and two players from Blackburn Rovers, only one of whom, James Forrest, was a professional. It is only fair to point out that Scotland's empty period here coincided with the advance of professionalism in England after its legalisation in 1885. For the combination of the Corinthians and the professionals in England's

team ended Scotland's superiority until recognition of the inevitability of the paid player crossed the border and Scotland again entered the scene.

If the immediate reason for the foundation of the Corinthian Football Club was to raise the prestige and standards of English international football against Scotland, its effect was of a far greater importance. Within twenty years the Corinthians were to become the greatest and most attractive team that football had then known. With an intelligent nonchalance and in their tailored shirts and well-cut shorts they brought a quality and culture to the game which, since their leisure and talents were dimmed by the First World War, Pegasus alone have recaptured. Corinth produced a brand of progressive attacking football still wistfully remembered by those who saw it: and its essence is amply acknowledged by the adoption of those basic principles beneath it as modified by the continental styles of to-day.

In this respect the Moscow Dynamos during their tour of Britain in 1945 come particularly to mind. For with regard to their football - leaving aside their irritating behaviour off the field of play - Ivan Sharpe has suggested in his fascinating *40 Years of Football,* 'hadn't these darling Dynamos played with the style and touch of the old Corinthians?' Further, Sir Godfrey Ince, now a vice-president of Pegasus, who, in 1914, captained London University, the first British Eleven ever to play soccer in Moscow, wrote after the Dynamos' tour:

'I count myself fortunate to have seen Moscow Dynamo twice during their brief tour in Britain. Especially fortunate in seeing their brilliant display in the opening match against Chelsea. In my view it was about the finest football exhibition I have seen in Britain since the Corinthians were a great side; classic combination and team work; superb ball control - the true Corinthian style, now called the Scottish style.'

Although the Corinthians' membership was primarily confined to old public school boys or university men, there was nothing schoolboyish about their approach. They played football as it should be played, and in the words of B.O. Corbett, himself a famous Corinthian and international of the early 1900s, 'Goal is the main objective, and theoretically all finesse which entails loss of time or ground must give way as far as possible to forging ahead.' Swiftly the Corinthians became a power in the land. The leading professional clubs were met and beaten, sometimes thrashed. As *Gibson and Pickford ('Association Football and The Men Who Made It'*, ed. by Alfred Gibson and William Pickford, 4 vols., The Caxton Pub. Co., London, 1907) put it:

'The Corinthians undoubtedly kept the game going in the South during those dull and dead seasons which followed the decline of the old teams, such as the Wanderers and Clapham Rovers, and preceded the establishment of professionalism in London and South of the Thames. Interest in football was at a minimum during those years, and nothing but the sparkling play of the Corinthian amateurs kept it from flickering out. Cockneys were proud of the men who could thrash League teams before their eyes, and they would patronise a Corinthian match where they would not glance at another.'

During the first twenty-five years of the Club's existence until the ill-fated break with The Football Association in 1907, its players had filled a third of the places in the English XI against Scotland, and nearly the same proportion against Ireland and Wales, while on two occasions against the Welshmen, in 1894 and 1895, it had provided the whole England team. It was the first English club to blend continually the separate arts of dribbling and passing, which reaped their reward with the sensational victory by 8-1 over Blackburn Rovers, the outstanding professional team of the day, at Blackburn in 1884. The Lancashire club's neighbours across the River Ribble at Preston were the disciples who learned the lesson. Their Cup and League double of 1888-89 proved this - although in the year if not the season of their triumph, November of 1889, they in turn were trounced by the men of Corinth, 5-0 at Richmond. In that match the giant Corinthian forwards, H.B. Daft, George Brann, G.H. Cotterill and .G. Veitch, brilliantly led by Tinsley Lindley in the centre, swept the 'Invincibles' off their feet and the ball into the net with an equal facility.

Many of the great Corinthians were also great cricketers, and the growth of English soccer and cricket now takes on a parallel course. For as the nineties unfolded, England entered its Golden Age of sport. The period between 1890 and 1914 has justly been called the Golden Age. As Neville Cardus wrote in *his English Cricket:* 'It was based, like most ages of gold, on an aristocracy. This was the period of the amateur cricketer ...' It was the Golden Age of the amateur footballer, too, based on an aristocracy, that of Corinth. At school, at university and afterwards, the men of Corinth had the time and the inclination to devote their leisure in summer and in winter to reap the harvest of the principles sown by the pioneers from the sixties to the eighties. Before the highly trained professional at football dimmed their star, the Corinthians scintillated and dazzled their way through the northern lights of Birmingham, Preston, Sunderland, Manchester and Scotland.

Their healthy, robust, cultured play and good old-fashioned shoulder-charging did more to balance the so-called artisan flavour engendered by professionalism than any levelling of social reform could ever hope to achieve. They brought to the game personality and distinction which, as a counter-balance to the efficiency of the professionals, were to blend with the traditions of the famous professional clubs in putting soccer on the map in such a way that it could never be rubbed off. The position was neatly summed up by *The Times* in 1909:

'The great professional clubs like Aston Villa, Preston North End and Sunderland of the past, and Everton, Sheffield Wednesday and Manchester United of more recent times, and the brilliant Scottish amateurs, Queen's Park, had all their great years, but they never won such general and lasting affection as the Corinthians. Their football ' although of a different type, may have been equally fine, but underlying it has been the thought that it was a business first and a pleasure second. It is human nature that it should be so. But the Corinthians's football has always been a pleasure and nothing else. They gained nothing by their skill but the satisfaction which the exercise such skill could give.'

The story of soccer and cricket in this period is the story of a prosperous Britain at play, with her sport untrammelled by economic or domestic or foreign upheavals. It was no mere coincidence that the professional players and teams greatest in character and colour both in football and in cricket existed side by side. All were stimulated by the amateur players in their ranks and the unique flavour and tone which the presence of the amateurs brought. When Wolverhampton Wanderers defeated Everton, the favourites, in the F.A. Cup-Final of 1893 at Fallowfield, Manchester, all but one of the twenty-two players were professionals. Yet it is interesting to note that in *The Official, History of the F.A. Cup,* Geoffrey Green has written of the Wolves' victory,

'more than anything else it was a triumph of team work, though it is said that R. Topham, one of the most popular of amateur players, was outstanding on the right-wing. The Wolverhampton prof-essionals were very fond of Topham. He was a wonderful influence on the side, and his enthus-iasm was a source of great strength to the others.' A generation later, the same could have been said of the late Rev. K.R.G. Hunt, who scored the Wolves' first goal in their victorious Cup-Final against Newcastle United in 1908, a week after playing for Oxford v. Cambridge.

There were, of course, many amateurs playing alongside professionals; for, as clearly appears, the amateur both at football and at cricket was the welcome foil to the professional. Southampton were enriched by the presence at full-back of C.B. Fry, fresh from his cricketing triumphs with Sussex; while Sussex in turn looked to George Brann's entry in the batting lists with Fry and Ranji when he was not tearing down the wing for the Corinthians. Farther north, William Gunn had played soccer for Notts County and England before professionalism was legalised, and then went on to form one of the most famous professional batting partnerships with Arthur Shrewsbury for Nottinghamshire.

This situation, nevertheless, could exist only because the training fever had then hardly infected professional football in the manner of which the monkey-gland Cup-Final of 1939 between Wolverhampton Wanderers and Portsmouth was merely symptomatic. Hence in June, 1942, when I mentioned, in a letter to G.O. Smith, the first book on the Corinthians, *Annals of the Corinthian Football Club,* edited by B.O. Corbett in 1906, he wrote back to me:

'Corbett's book I have got and I don't think he rates the Corinthians in the nineties too highly. In those days without training they met the best professional teams and won more often than not. The English team v. Wales in 1894 and 1895 was solely composed of Corinthians.'

By way of confirmation, G.O. wrote to me some three months later, in September, 1942, that:

'The Corinthians of my day never trained, and I can safely say that the need of it was never felt. We were all fit and I think could have played on for more than one and a half hours without being any the worse.'

That the Corinthians, representing England, could defeat and draw with a Welsh team, which included professional players, shows clearly that no difference existed then between the professional and the amateur player in fitness and stamina. How far the game has changed since in this respect was clearly seen when Pegasus, successors to the Corinthians, won the F.A. Amateur Cup against Bishop Auckland in 1951, with a classic exhibition of artistic, attacking, constructive football. It was suggested that Pegasus should be invited to meet the F.A. Cup winners or the Football League Champions for the F.A. Charity Shield.

Their opponents would have been either the professors of Newcastle United, who won the F.A. Cup in a far less aesthetically satisfying game on the same ground a fortnight later against Blackpool, or their own tutors from Tottenham Hotspur, the League Champions. For reasons of stamina alone, these proposals were laughed away. Yet as will be seen later, Pegasus have not performed inadequately against professional opponents; certainly in the matter of style. Perhaps it had been forgotten that in 1904, a couple of years after King Edward VII was crowned, the Corinthians, the leading amateur side, had beaten

Bury, the leading professional team and F.A. Cup holders by 10-3 to win the Sheriff of London Shield.

The magnificent Sherrif of London Shield

With the end of the Edwardian era the shadows fell over public amateur sport; and between 1910 and 1914 the Golden Age of the Corinthians and cricketers began to fade. More so did that of the Corinthians who were finding the improved training methods of the professionals increasingly difficult to counter, while the 'split' with the F.A. in 1907 crippled their fixture-lists. The First World War killed the Golden Age of Corinthians and cricketers. The years between the First and Second World Wars buried it.

Nevertheless, for a time during the 1920s the flames of life flickered on through such men as B. Howard Baker, A.G. Bower, A.G. Doggart, R.W.V. Robins and the Ashtons - Hubert, Gilbert and Claude. But they were exceptional. The age of specialisation and the increased premium placed upon success set in. These together with the Arsenal defensive system wailing mournfully like a dirge around the ears of lovers of the game became the keynote of soccer, while the pad-play of Yorkshire and Lancashire dourness became the fashion of modern cricket.

The society in which we now live is as remote from the Golden Age as that was from the glittering era of Dr Johnson and his circle a century before. It now takes us less than fifty years to bury a past which in turn took a hundred. Yet just as the classics of an earlier period in the different spheres of Shakespeare, Milton and Ben Jonson are still the masterpieces of to-day, so must the patterns of the Golden Age always contain the secret of success on the soccer and cricket fields of any day. The batsman who attacks like MacLaren or Jessop; the bowler who bowls a length with hostility of purpose, wins Test Matches for the West Indies and Pakistan. The footballer who keeps the ball on the ground and passes with accuracy into open spaces for intelligently positioned colleagues wins world football titles. These are the principles which created the Golden Age of British sport at the century's turn. They can do so again, whether at football or cricket, whether in Manchester and Lancashire, Tottenham and Middlesex, or Oxford and Cambridge. Yet while the principles of play remain essentially unaltered, the structure and framework upon and within which our national games are built have changed: and nowhere was this more clearly seen than on the last Saturday of March, 1952.

During that afternoon the F.A. Cup Semi-Final Tie between Blackburn Rovers and Newcastle United was played in Yorkshire. In Surrey, at the same hour, the Final Tie in the Arthur Dunn Cup Competition was played during its jubilee year between the Old Etonians, appearing in their first Dunn Cup Final, and the Old Salopians, jointly with the Old Carthusians, the first holders of that trophy. At Hillsborough, Sheffield, 60,000 saw the Rovers' captained by Eckersley, then England's left-back, gamely surrender to the side who were to emulate their own sixty-year-old record a few weeks later by winning the F.A. Cup in successive seasons. At Tooting a mere handful saw the Old Salopians celebrate the four hundredth anniversary of their foundation at Shrewsbury with their seventh Final victory. Yet exactly seventy years earlier, in March, 1882, these two losing clubs, Blackburn Rovers and the Old Etonians, had contested the F.A. Cup at Kennington's historic Oval in Surrey. The Old Etonians won that match through the material assistance at outside-right of the same Arthur Dunn in whose memory the competition bearing his name was established in

1902, after his death. This was the game for which the Blackburn supporters prepared the following lines, with an optimism equalled only by the Brazilians who composed a victory samba before the conquest of their country's team by Uruguay in the Final of the World Cup soccer tournament in Rio de Janeiro in 1950:

> 'The Old Etonians'
> 'All hail, ye gallant Rover lads!
> Etonians thought you were but cads:
> They've found at football game their dads
> By meeting Blackburn Rovers.'

The paths which these two cup finalists of 1882 have trod underline the changes which the years have brought. Blackburn Rovers went on to five F.A. Cup successes in the following ten years, and triumphed again in 1928 against Huddersfield Town's greatest team. In the years after the Second World War, the Rovers have shown their intention to return as soon as possible to the First Division of the Football League where tradition demands their presence. The Old Etonians, whose famed Field Game created football's earliest dribblers, dropped out of the F.A. Cup, the university elevens, the public eye, and even for a time ceased to exist as a football team. By the time that a group of Old Etonians at Oxford, inspired by Pegasus, decided in 1950 to revive the team, the gulf which by then separated the professionals from the amateurs made a replay of the 1882 Cup-Final little more than a sad dream.

In the passing of those seventy years the apathy of the public schools and the crazy commerce of professional football enabled the cultivation of a fallacy. The ill-informed and socially prejudiced middle classes came to believe that soccer, born into the purple at its public schools and ancient universities, refined and still played there while being taken the world over by their Old Boys and disciples, was little else than a vehicle for the football pools and professionalism to which no gentleman should pay attention. Nothing could have been further from the truth. The long arm of coincidence, which stretched out in 1952 to link the fashionable Cup Competition of the professionals and the unfashionable Cup-Final of the public schools with the only Cup-Final which had mattered seventy years earlier showed this.

Behind the headlines of the professional game which dominate Fleet Street and Portland Place, there is played what Bernard Darwin in his essay *British Sport and Games* has described *as 'the game of the people in Britain ... to fully the same extent as cricket, and, perhaps even more so, a school game which everybody plays. It is also a village game in that nearly every village has its team, and it is the game of innumerable clubs of young men of different occupations and different classes who, having no strictly local bond, yet join together for their games on a Saturday afternoon.'* Alongside this superb assessment of the true position of soccer in its native land the force can be seen of Professor D.W. Brogan's comment in *The English People, a* book which he wrote for the American public during the War: 'Professional football is by far the most important game from the spectator's point of view but it is only the cream of a very deep milk-jug.'

The schools which were responsible for shaping that milk-jug as well as for filling it, still continue to provide for their pupils those lessons of true sportsmanship and character which even the psychologist will admit a football field so finely allows. Such lessons can be provided on the field only by cricket and the *pure* football game. Whether the Duke of Wellington did or did not claim the Battle of Waterloo to have been won on the playing fields of Eton, the home of early Association footballers, is a matter to be left now for research degrees at American universities. What cannot now be doubted is that not the least contribution to Britain's triumph in the Second World War came from the grammar schools, the majority of which have refused to follow those, who, for reasons best known to themselves, have forsaken the more skilful and intelligent football game for the *handling* code, so aptly described by the distinguished novelist, H.E. Bates, as a 'bastard version of football.' The success of Pegasus, with its blend of old and new, the public and the grammar schools, has pointed the way in football, and, it may be, in all levels of national life, to future leadership. In Corinth's early days only the public schools and ancient universities, upon which the Corinthians drew in the main for membership, gave such a lead. At Charterhouse, one of the most famous and distinguished of those public schools' towards the end of the last century the underlying theme of this book began.

CHAPTER II

CHARTERHOUSE AND G.O. SMITH

Four years after the foundation of the Corinthians, G.O. Smith entered Charterhouse School in the wake of three elder brothers. There he was destined to follow a tradition of leadership, versatility and individuality established by such Carthusians as Wesley, Blackstone, Addison, Steele and Thackeray: a tradition to be continued firstly by his contemporaries, Sir Max Beerbohm and Sir Ralph Vaughan Williams and later by George Leigh Mallory who, while a master at Charterhouse, disappeared with Irvine on the slopes of Everest as perhaps its first conquerors in 1924, and Major General Orde Wingate. Certainly it is quite remarkable for one school to have sent out at the same time from within its walls the most outstanding of modern English caricaturists, composers and centre-forwards.

G.O.SMITH

One of the best loved of the school's housemasters and teachers, A.H. Tod, whose portrait has been so vividly painted in *46 Not Out!* the autobiography of another distinguished Old Carthusian, R.C. Robertson-Glasgow, came down as a boy when Dr Haig-Brown took the old foundation from London to Godalming in 1872. He has told us that football was probably always played at Charterhouse. In its modern form, at any rate, the game has been played there as regularly - if in recent times not quite as well - as at any other centre in the country. Moreover, it became the first of the public schools to develop Association football as a school institution.

With Westminster School, another home of famous Corinthians and cricketers, Charterhouse was a pioneer of the dribbling game. Its Old Boys, as the Old Carthusians, were among the first to play the 'combinations game, as introduced by the Scots.

By the time G.O. entered the school as a day boy attached to Hodgsonites, one of the school houses, the lists of sporting Old Carthusians were already graced by famous names: W.N. Cobbold, the authentic holder of the title, 'The Prince of Dribblers'; England's international full-backs, A.M. and P.M. Walters; C.A. Smith, whose international fame as an actor (better known as Sir Aubrey Smith) was to eclipse his reputation as a footballer and international cricketer; Charles Wreford Brown, Corinthian and international; the Army's greatest cricketer, Major E.G. Wynyard of Hampshire; and T.C. Hooman, who had played for the Wanderers' side which won that first-ever F.A. Cup-Final in 1872. A.H. Tod has also told us in his *Charterhouse* that the future defender of Mafeking and Chief Scout, Lord Baden-Powell, who kept goal for the school in 1875-76, 'took a very liberal view of a goalkeeper's functions. His voice enabled him to direct the forwards at the other end of the ground, and his agility enabled him to cheer the spectators with im-promptu dances when he had nothing pressing to do.

Shortly after this, only five years before G.O. entered the school, the Old Carthusians won the F.A. Cup-Final of 1881 with the earliest English version of combined football. During G.O.'s schooldays the way was paved for him firstly by E.S. Currey, who ended his four years in the Oxford Soccer XI with its captaincy as well as appearing for England's full side in 1890 at centre-forward against Wales and inside-forward against Scotland: and then by C.W. Wright and E.C. Streatfeild, who both hit centuries in the Varsity cricket match for Cambridge. So there was inspiration and example enough among former and present alumni to stir any boy entering Charterhouse in 1886; and around the time of G.O.'s schooldays and after we have also been told by A.H. Tod that 'many a school entertainment at Charterhouse was enlivened by the appearance on the stage of Dr Haig-Brown with a telegram. Everyone knew what this meant. Old Carthusians had won yet another tie, and the news would be cheered till the roof rang.'

While cheers of another kind were beginning to be heard during the middle of the Second World War, when sporting reminiscence was as good a means of escapism as any, H.R. MacDonald, then 'Twelfth Man' of the London *Evening News,* made the following suggestion:

'A team chosen from all the boys who have learned their soccer at Charterhouse would beat any side other schools could turn out. I am imagining, of course, that all the players are still alive and at their zenith. Here is my Carthusian side of all talents.

T.S. Rowlandson

A.M. Walters   P.M. Walters

C.H. Wild   C. Wreford Brown B.C.A. Patchitt

R.H. Allen   C.F. Ryder

G.C. Vassall   G.O. Smith   M.H.Stanbrough

It seems a pity that A.G. Bower, the best Carthusian footballer between the wars, has to be left out of the Charterhouse side, but no one would think of separating the two brothers Walters, who played together for England in nine internationals. And yet Bower, more classical, I think, in his play than the Walters, was given a place in the Chelsea side, capped in modern internationals, and played in many great games in cup-ties against professional opposition.'

I sent a copy of MacDonald's suggestions to G.O., for even if a pastime of making such selections has its faults, it conjures up a colourful panorama of the past while yet requiring acute analysis of the players concerned. He replied in the following way: 'Many thanks for the *Evening News* cutting.

Oddly enough an old Westminster boy sent me another a day or two ago with a record [this showed that from 1863, when the first records were made, until 1943, Charterhouse and Westminster had played seventy games, the most persistent series of school soccer matches] of the matches between the two Schools, which I found most interesting.

I certainly don't agree with the Old Carthusian side of all the talents, as he omits the name of Cobbold and includes two players of whom I have never heard. My side would be:

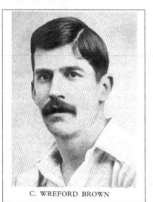

C. WREFORD BROWN

W.N.Cobbald

T.S. Rowlandson
A.M. Walters   P.M. Walters
E.C. Bliss   C. Wreford Brown   A. Amos
W.E. Gilliat   W.N. Cobbold
G.C. Vassall   G.O.S.   M.H. Stanbrough

All these players were internationals except Bliss, Rowlandson and Vassall, though the last-named could have been. Bliss had been a member of all four Oxford soccer sides in which G.O. had appeared, and in 1895 he succeeded C.B. Fry as Oxford's soccer captain. Rowlandson, the goalkeeper, who played for Sunderland, was the only player to attend Charterhouse after G.O., and in 1907 he obtained amateur international caps for England at a time when the progress of professionalism and the ill-fated split' between the amateurs and the F.A. left no room for the amateur in England's full international sides. Vassall, a brother of the famous Rugby forward, was certainly of international class.

He missed a cap by what seems now an incredible choice. For Vassall could have played for England, captained by G.O. against Ireland in 1899 alongside nine professionals, but as captain of the Oxford XI he preferred to turn out against Cambridge at Queen's Club on the same day.

Appropriately enough, G.O.'s disagreement with MacDonald's team was concerned entirely with the positions now line drawn through the wing-halves and the inside-forwards. regarded as the square-root of all modern football elevens. At inside-left, G.O. naturally selected the 'Prince of Dribblers'; at inside-right he chose a later Corinthian, Gilliat, who had played alongside G.O. when they both made international debuts against Ireland in 1893; and at wing-half, as well as Bliss, he chose Amos who was among the Old Carthusian F.A. Cup-Final winners and an international.

Of those selected by MacDonald, Patchitt will be remembered as one of the last amateurs to play alongside the professionals in England's full international side, twice against Sweden in 1923. Ryder was in and out of Corinthian sides around the turn of the century and once played for England

alongside G.O., against Germany in 1901, but comparison with Cobbold attempts the impossible. Wild made too few appearances for teams other than the Old Carthusians and the Corinthians to be properly traced, and R.H. Allen is just untraceable.

To G.O., Cobbold was indeed the Prince. I must have sent him someone else's views, for he wrote to me in April, 1943:

'Many thanks for your letter and for the article on "Nuts" Cobbold which I have read with great interest. He was a great friend of mine and I put him first of all the forwards I have known. I rather fancy he played a few times for Kent at cricket, but he was hardly a first-class cricketer, though a very useful one.'

The reference to Cobbold as 'Nuts' has been explained by C.B. Fry as the nickname which Cobbold's friends created 'possibly because he was of the very best Kentish cob quality, all kernel and extremely hard to crack.' In fact Cobbold played only once for Kent at cricket, in 1887, and scored four runs. So he could hardly be said to have made his mark at cricket,'although he had played at Charterhouse in the School XI whose wicketkeeper at the time was P.M. Walters. In a minor key Cobbold also represented Cambridge at athletics without gaining his Blue: before lawn tennis became fashionable he had played for Cambridge against Oxford. With H.W.W. Wilberforce, who later (as Sir Herbert Wilberforce) became the popular chairman of the All-England Lawn Tennis Club, Cobbold formed a doubles partnership in 1885, and together they won all their matches against Oxford without dropping a set.

To be placed 'first of all the forwards' G.O. had known, however, was praise indeed from the man who had Played alongside the immortal Steve Bloomer and nearly every other great forward before 1914. A similar tribute to Cobbold's genius comes from 'Pa' Jackson who 'unhesitatingly' described him us as 'the best Association forward' he ever saw. Why was Cobbold known as the 'Prince of Dribblers'? Well, he appears to have done all the right things swiftly, correctly and fairly. While his physique was that of the middle or light heavyweight, and his sturdy legs and hips supported massive shoulders, Cobbold anticipated the professionals, for in order to avoid getting hurt, he turned out swathed in rubber bandages and ankle-guards.

Although he had a grim determination, his Charterhouse and Cambridge training in the seventies and eighties taught him to use his weight merely as a last resort, and to defeat defences by shuffling with the ball in the way Stanley Matthews has immortalised for us. Cobbold, however, never varied his pace in the same devastating manner as Matthews. Rather did he run straight through in the style of the other Stanley, Mortensen; and he shot from all angles and at all times. If his syllabus for the Army tuition, which he undertook when his playing days were over included marksmanship, then his soccer shooting would have an appropriate example. In addition to all this, as if to confirm his skill as a dribbler pure and simple, Cobbold eliminated all heading from his play - this preference *foot*ball is, of course, a characteristic of Matthews also - for, as G.O. implied in a later letter, heading is never really *foot*ball at all.

Another of Cobbold's colleagues in the Charterhouse cricket XI was C. Aubrey Smith, later nicknamed 'Round-the-Corner' because of his peculiar approach to the wicket when bowling. C.W. Alcock, in the notes to the photograph of Smith in his *Famous Cricketers and Cricket Grounds,* refers to him as 'one of the best forwards at Association Football for some years,' and I must have mentioned this to G.O., for his letter dealing with the best Carthusian XI ended in the following way:

'I played cricket with Aubrey Smith years ago, but I never saw him play football and he was never in the School Eleven. Despite C.W. Alcock's reference to him I don't think he was first-class at the game. He was, of course, a great cricketer and played four years for Cambridge and ten years for Sussex, besides captaining an English side in Australia and South Africa. He is a wonderful man for his age and a great actor on the films.'

C. Aubrey Smith clearly had limitations as a footballer - perhaps he was too tall for the positions he chose on the wings. This did not prevent his selection at outside-left alongside Cobbold, Wreford Brown and the brothers Walters in what was virtually the last fling of the Old Carthusians or any Old Boys side in the F.A. Cup after professionalism had been legalised in 1885. Against Preston North End, in 1887, the season before the 'Invincibles' brought off the first Cup and League 'Double,' the Carthusians, after extra-time, went down 1-2 in the QuarterFinals; and A.H. Tod has recorded, 'Early in the game C.A. Smith had the professionals' goal at his mercy, when he was tripped from behind, and the play then became decidedly rough.' How that roughness was distributed can fairly be imagined. For with the brothers Walters at full-back rolling up their sleeves and each flexing his thirteen stone, one can be sure that the Old Boys gave as much as they received.

A bare half-dozen years earlier than this, in 1881, the Old Carthusians had won the Cup, and one of their two centreforwards, Major E.G. Wynyard, was a quarter of a century later to captain the M.C.C. side which toured New Zealand in 1906. Within that span Major Wynyard, with other Army cricketers, did much to establish Hampshire's reputation at the beginning of its first-class County career, and in 1896 he played at the Oval in the last England side which W.G. Grace led to victory against Australia.

Apart from his batting - in 1899 he joined another Hampshire Major, R.M. Poore, against Somerset to set up the sixth-wicket record of 411 for both country and county - he could also bowl lobs, keep wicket and field superbly anywhere. The story is told that he once turned up in a match at Sandhurst dressed as W.G. and carried off the impersonation; although the Commandant, who had been introduced to the 'Doctor', did not appreciate the joke Wynyard must have made a Picturesque figure as he fielded' for he wore his I Zingari cap, of polo shape, balanced at the) military angle with a strap under the chin. G.O. wrote me the following cameo of him:

'I stayed with Teddy Wynyard at Sandhurst when I was sixteen and knew him intimately for many years. Oddly enough he never got into the Cricket Eleven at School, but, as you know, played against Australia in 1896 and was a great batsman for Hampshire for many years. He was a sturdy, forceful footballer of the old type, but not perhaps a great one. A good soldier and a magnificent all-round athlete.'

All-round was perhaps the keynote to Carthusian and Corinthian sporting activity in those days. So one is hardly surprised that G.O.'s star shone as brightly with a cricket bat and ball in his hand as with a ball at his feet. This was as much due to natural talent as anything else. It is curious that in a school of the size and with the traditions of Charterhouse cricket, in great contrast with football, appears to have been somewhat neglected until the end of the nineteenth century. Since then, however, the balance has been redressed through such personalities as the late G.D - Kemp-Welch and J.M. Lomas, H.A. Gilbert, O.T. Norris, R.C. Robertson-Glasgow, J.T. Morgan and P.B.H. May.

The reasons for the neglect of cricket have never been hidden, and in the voluminous *Surrey Cricket: Its History and Associations,* edited by Lord Alverstone, then Lord Chief Justice of England, and the ubiquitous C.W. Alcock, the explanation can be found:

'To begin with, the ground in the early days of the school at Godalming was deplorable. Tradition does not quite go to the extent of attributing to Charterhouse the story of the partridges which were flushed at the commencement of a match by the bowler, but it might well have done so. Rabbits at any rate found the pitch their most delectable playground, and a Charterhouse historian records that the botanist and geologist made it their special study. Cricketers of those days vouch for the fact that the noble art of self-defence was practised not so much with the idea of preventing physical violence as of avoiding the relentless bowler's attempts to break his rival's head; for no groundsman was kept, and the soil being light and sandy, and therefore essentially requiring constant and careful attention, fell into a wretched state.

The headmaster, who took it under his special protection, soon discovered that it was the one thing in the new foundation which refused to yield to his treatment. Assuredly he did not reap as he sowed, for one year the only result of a dressing of the ground was a plentiful supply of cinders.'

By G.O.'s day matters had improved in regard to facilities. In March Of 1943 he wrote:

'I think the reasons why Carthusians have not been prominent in County cricket is due to two things:

(1) That the great tradition of the School in my day lay in Association football, and cricket in a sense was a minor matter; we had no master to coach us and not much interest was taken in the summer game.

(2) That very few, if any, Carthusians had the necessary £.s.d. Almost everyone after their Varsity days were over had to make their own living and unless they became paid amateurs - not a pleasant business - cricket was really out of the question for them.

I do not think the future will see any Carthusian playing for Surrey. The question of £.s.d. has become more acute in the future, and I greatly fear that amateurs in first-class cricket will be unknown, which will be a thousand pities.'

This prophecy by G.O. was disproved when Peter May became the first Old Carthusian to command a regular place in the Surrey side. Yet this was only possible through the arrangements made by the firm which May joined on going down from Cambridge. Certainly G.O. had no illusions about the position of the amateur in first-class cricket. As for his own cricketing schooldays, G.O. will always be remembered for his batting, although as he wrote to me:

'Oddly enough I got my cricket school colours for bowling, though after my school career few captains were foolish enough to put me on."

It was his batting, however, which took G.O., at the age of sixteen to the head of the School averages in

1889, his first year in the Charterhouse XI. During the following season he was captain, and he led a very raw team which, with ten newcomers, not surprisingly left a moderate record and low figures. In 1891, however, his average of 57.5 was described in the red *Litlywhite Cricketers' Annual* as 'phenomenal.' Similar figures to-day are no cause for sensational acclamations, but when placed in their true perspective, G.O.'s figures were really worthy of such a description. He played 16 innings, scoring 633 runs, and although he was five times not out, there was no doubt as to the soundness of his batting. Clearly he had taken heed of *Lillywhite's* admonition after his first season in the School XI: 'A most promising bat, hits especially well to leg but must learn not to try and hit straight balls in that direction.' For fine batsman that he became, G.O. could never afford the licence one has always associated with several more renowned cricketers.

Before leaving Charterhouse, however, G.O. had cultivated a fine defence which his timing transformed into the loveliest strokes: a magnificent off-drive and a beautiful cut, indicating that co-ordination of eye, mind and muscle which made his football immortal. He could field perfectly anywhere, and as a bowler, in 1891, he headed the School averages with 33 wickets for 219 runs in 101 overs. But above all figures there were already portents of his future displays of leadership in the Oxford, Corinthian and England sides. As the mainstay of the team he had pulled it together after two extremely poor years; imbued it with some of his own keenness and energy, and fired it with the confidence which the warmth of his personality breathed into every team he led.

G.O.'s last year at school, 1892, was one long triumph. Centuries were hit in the big matches against Westminster and Wellington and his 229 out of 260 against the former was then the largest innings ever played in a school match. It still remains the highest ever played for Charterhouse; and Roy Webber, through his *Playfair Book of Cricket Records,* has let us see that in over sixty years since, the achievement has been equalled only once and surpassed on only six occasions - by schoolboy batsmen who have not possessed either the time or the talent, or have lacked both, to fulfil their early promise. On the second morning of his remarkable innings against Westminster, the whole school was allowed out early to see G.O. complete his second hundred; and the next highest score, that of F.L. Fane, was 24!

There was no doubt that G.O. was the best bat in the team, although E.H. Bray, his successor as captain (later Sir Hugh Bray of the Viceroy of India's Council), and F.L. Fane (later of Essex and England) were both first-class batsmen too. He also proved himself the best captain Charterhouse had had for many years. Indeed, since 1850, no one else has been captain of cricket at Charterhouse for more than two years. Finally, the red *Lillywhite* accorded G.O. the distinction of being 'the best school bat of the year' despite the presence of the diminutive P.F. Warner at Rugby, H.K. Foster at Malvern, and H.D.G. Leveson-Gower and J.R. Mason at Winchester.

At football it is not possible to assess a schoolboy's qualities in cold figures as can be done for cricket. A collection of goals scored, certainly in schoolboy football, is no indication of a player's value to his team. This is true of football in general, for one need recall only the rarity with which the late Alex James scored a goal to realise the danger of statistics as an absolute, or even a relative, guide in this matter. Moreover, talent at soccer, for the reasons just mentioned, as well as through latent developments of physique and ability, may be less easily recognised than cricketing prowess.

That great full-back A.G. Bower, for example, one of the few amateurs to gain a full England cap and captain the national side after the First World War, could not rise above the third soccer eleven at Charterhouse; while P.M. Walters, who obtained his cricket colours there, failed to get them at soccer.

No such experiences as these were the lot of G.O. In 1942 he wrote to me:

'I believe I hold a record in one thing, namely that I was in both cricket and football teams at Charterhouse for four years and Captain of both for three years.'

But although he wrote to me in the autumn of that year that he did not think he had 'anything interesting to say' about his schooldays, he was to show clear signs at school of his later greatness. Moreover, his own ability must have been well above average. For, just as in his triumphant career he was surrounded, but never overshadowed, by players of the highest calibre, so at school the team was outstanding. As he wrote to me:

'I don't think we ever lost to Westminster - our chief opponents, and I fancy one of the Elevens of our day had seven future Blues in it - a rare occurrence I should say.'

Like his cricket, G.O.'s soccer contained an early fault that was later eradicated. In Alcock's *Football Annual* for 1890, the following appeared under the report on the Charterhouse XI, 1888-89: 'G.O. Smith, outside-right. Improved towards the latter part of the season, dribbles and passes well but is rather slow.' Perhaps it was this slowness which, according to a tale at Charterhouse, caused him to keep fit by walking from his home to chapel each morning at 7.30 with the last mile up-hill. Three years later, after his last season in the XI, the same *Football Annual* for 1892 recorded: 'G.O. Smith (Captain). Has made an excellent captain throughout the season. His dribbling and shooting are splendid. He will be a very great loss to the School XI next season, leaving after a captaincy of three Years, a term of office we believe to be unprecedented.'

In any event, the irregular variations of football played at Charterhouse must have assisted G.O. in eliminating any slowness. Unlike Eton, Harrow and Winchester with their indigenous and insular forms of football played alongside the general version, Charterhouse never departed from real football, which had become by 1900, in A.H. Tod's words, 'the main amusement of the whole school from September to the end of March.' In just the same way as youngsters in less fortunate circumstances, who have become star professional players, generally begin by kicking a pile of rags around a Lamppost, or a tin-can near a coal-mine, so one of the greatest of all footballers, professional or amateur, began by a kick-about, though in his case it took place at school. For at any odd time during the day, chiefly between school-periods and dinner, the most important of what may be termed 'casual' games would take place, known as run-about. The random number of players who began and left off play as and when they pleased did not have to change their clothes. Everyone played forward; handling, hard kicking and long shots at goal were forbidden. Hence the players were forced to develop what the modern theorist would call ball control and ball-play. There was clearly no organised coaching, and natural talent found its own way to the top.

In regard to this it is significant that G.O. never once made any reference to coaching whether at school or in his later days. I never troubled him on this point. Yet I am sure that if G.O. had been consciously coached at any time during his schooldays he would have mentioned the fact when dealing with his cricket and football at Charterhouse, for his modest references to himself were always as trenchant as they were complete. Somewhere I must have seen a reference to G.O.'s dribbling through the whole of the school while playing *run-about,* for he wrote to me:

'I don't think I ever dribbled through the whole school at Charterhouse, but I am sure "run-about" was a great help to learning the art of dribbling and kick-about, when you were allowed to take the ball as it came to you, taught one a lot.'

There were other irregular variations, too, in G.O.'s day, known as *punt-about and shoot-about,* which explain themselves, designed for the improvement of back play and shooting respectively. But their monotony soon adversely affected the quality of the forwards so that one finds A.H. Tod writing in N.L. ('Pa') Jackson's *Association Football:* 'Carthusians had better stop shoot-about, play less punt-about and more run-about.' Eventually the house system of regular competitive football must have stamped out such pleasing and useful *divertissements,*for no reference was made to them by Michael Whinney, Charterhouse 1st XI captain in 1948, in his valuable contribution on Public School football, published in *The F.A. Book for Boys* for 1949-50. The picture of Charterhouse football in the days of G.O. and his great contemporaries makes all the sadder reading when one considers the present decline of football at the School. The warning which A.H. Tod gave in 1900 that 'run-about is the best and most vigorous of games; it is this which has trained school forwards, and when run-about decays the school eleven always deteriorates,' seems to have been justified. For since the end of the Second World War only three Carthusians - P.B.H. May, J.D.P. Tanner and D. Miller - have gained football Blues at either university. Where, then , are your G.O. Smiths, Wynyards, Cobbolds or 'seven future Blues' of to-day?

It should not be imagined that G.O. Smith passed his school career entirely upon the playing-fields. *Mens sana in corpore sano* may be trite, but in the case of G.O. it's true enough. He did not strike the intellectual spark to reach the dozen or so elect out of 500 odd boys who formed the Sixth Form of his day. Yet he spent three years at Charterhouse in the Under Sixth where his diligence may not have brought its true scholastic reward, because of what the author of a charming memoir in *The Carthusian* described as 'his being almost too conscientious.' Perhaps some explanation may be found in his own words, expressed after a kind thought, in a letter to me in the summer of 1942:

'I hope you did well in Matric and expect you did; examinations have always been a bugbear to me.'

So they have also been to more distinguished scholars than G.O. Smith.

Above all his bare achievements, however, his school career revealed a quality of that modest grace associated with the truly great sportsman.

'On Saturday mornings', continued the author of the memoir in *The Carthusian,* 'we would rush out of school on to Green, fully expecting him to be batting. And afterwards we realised that this man whom we so much admired as small boys, had never presumed on his success and popularity to lord it over others or call attention to himself in any way; it would have been impossible to connect him with anything dishonourable. He was an example to all without thinking about it.'

When the time came, in the summer of 1892, for G.O. to leave behind the stones of Greyfriars amidst the hills above Godalming for Oxford, he had laid the foundation for as outstanding a university sporting career as any young man can dream of. How that developed in a manner partly different from and partly similar to our own day, the next two chapters will tell.

CHAPTER III

VARSITY SOCCER IN THE NINETIES

The Oxford to which G.O. went up at the commencement of the Michaelmas Term in the autumn of 1892 was vastly different from that of to-day. It was not a mixture of milk-bars, motor-cars and medieval masonry, but a city of leisure and tranquillity: a University whose college rooms in the High, where grass grew in the roadway, were as coveted for their atmosphere as to-day they are avoided for the bustle and noise which breaks the line and charm of one of Europe's oldest thoroughfares.

At Keble College, however, G.O. doubtless found, as have many others since his day, compensation for that foundation's gloomy architecture in its closeness to the Parks and University football and cricket. For not until seven seasons later, the last of the nineteenth century, was the ground of the University Association Football Club moved from its home in the Parks, where it had been since the Club's foundation in 1872, to the first of its sites in the Iffley Road.

The 1870s had seen Oxford University win the F.A. Cup, by defeating the Royal Engineers, and lose three more Finals. The 1880s had heralded a period of consistent Cambridge successes in the Varsity Match: and from 1884 to 1888 five consecutive wins were recorded when W.N. Cobbold, A.T.B. Dunn and A.M. Walters graced the Cambridge teams. Then came the 1890s with Oxford losing 1-3 to Cambridge, who fielded an all English international forward line, and gaining their revenge the following season, by 2-1. In 1892 Oxford lost again, however, 1-5, with the first Varsity match appearance of a Wadham freshman from Repton at left-back, C.B. Fry. The arrival of G.O. Smith, therefore, had more than formal significance.

At Charterhouse he had played outside-right for the first two years and centre-forward in the last two. Then, as he wrote to me early in 1943, 'On going up to Oxford in the autumn of 1892 I was put

outside-right till Wreford Brown, a very old friend of mine, suggested to the Oxford Captain that I should be tried at centre and I played there in my first Varsity match in 1893.'

Perhaps Wreford Brown's suggestion was based upon his own experiences. He had been keeping goal regularly for the Old Carthusians in the 1880s, in which position, among others, he had played at school. Before a game with Oxford University the Old Carthusians were short of a half-back, and, finding another goalkeeper on the spot, they tried Wreford Brown successfully at centre-half. In the next Varsity fixture, against West Bromwich Albion, he played there again, and, in the words of a pre-1914 publication, *50 Years of Sport*, *'shadowing the pro. centre forward excellently,* he stayed there until the end of his time.' When that was no one has ever been able to discover. C.B. Fry has told us, however, 'He was playing for England against Scotland at centre-half before I began first-class football, and he was still going strong in good-class football years after I stopped. I saw him playing against a strong side when he was well over fifty.' Wreford Brown, like so many of his generation, was a genuine all-rounder. At Charterhouse he had captained both the cricket and the soccer elevens, and after he had been awarded his Blue for cricket as well as for soccer in 1887, only a badly split finger kept him out of the Varsity match at Lord's. This let in Lord George Scott, who, as a last-minute choice, scored an historic century in an Oxford victory just as G.O. was to do nine years later: and for the following season Scott retained his place while Wreford Brown was Oxford's twelfth man. That Wreford Brown was to be reckoned with as a batsman, however, can be judged from his achievements in 1891 when, with Lord Hawke's team, he toured America after occasional appearances with the Graces for Gloucestershire, with whom he had a birth qualification. He headed the batting averages above Lord Hawke, C.W.. Wright and H.T. Hewitt, Somerset's 'Colonel.' After going down from

OXFORD SOCCER XI – 1893
(*Back, l. to r.*): E.F. Buzzard, G.O. Smith, G.B. Raikes, W.J. Oakley, T.C. Robinson.
(*Middle*): J.A. Walker, C.B. Fry, F. Street (Capt.), E.C. Bliss, C.D. Hewitt. (*Front*): R.J. Salt.

Oxford he followed Tinsley Lindley, a future County Court Judge, the Walters brothers and W.R.Moon into the legal profession, and I shall always recall meeting him on one occasion at the Oxford University ground in the Iffley Road shortly after the Second World War. At the age of eighty he appeared as delighted at having been selected to play for Oxford's Past and Present against Cambridge at chess as if he were being capped at soccer.

During Wreford Brown's England days in the 1890s at centre half his tireless tackling and scientific feeding of his forwards made him outstanding among such masters of that position as John Holt of Everton, Tom Crawshaw of Sheffield Wednesday and James Crabtree of Aston Villa, in a period when one had to be a *footballer* to play there. Before the end of the Second World War he was chairman of the International Selection Committee of The Football Association, of which body he was a life vice-president until his death: and his committee was responsible for, the choice of so many great England sides in the late 1930s. When he died in 1951, a link was broken which had bound the International Selection Committee to the Golden Age and international experience on the field of play. Not until the humiliating performances against the Hungarians and in the World Cup Competition in 1954 had exposed the decayed standards of English professional football, was the first attempt made to re-forge that link, with the appointment to that Committee of the former captain of the Corinthians and England's professionals in the 1920s, A.G. Doggart, a Vice-President of The Football Association, too. Nevertheless, Association football, alone of all the national sporting spheres, continues to be denied in *quantity* the experience and guidance of former players. It may therefore well be that only when The Football Association follows the M.C.C., and once more welcomes to its selection committee the background and knowledge of former international players, can England at the national level expect to compete successfully with foreign nations in the football world.

The suggestion by Wreford Brown - that G.O. should play at centre-forward - has had many illustrious applications. For example, after the Second World War, Jackie Milburn inspired Newcastle United from the outside-right position both before and after he had won the 1951 Cup-Final and international caps in the centre-forward position: and appropriately enough, J.D.P. Tanner followed G.O.'s pattern with the Old Carthusians, Oxford University and England before moving to centre-forward. This switch from the wing to the centre positions was but one example of the versatility of G.O.'s day. In the second-half of the Varsity match of 1893 he scored the first of Oxford's three goals by which they rubbed off a two-goal half-time deficit to win 3-2. Then as G.O. wrote to me,

'After the Varsity match I was chosen v. Ireland and put inside-right as G.H. Cotterill was the Corinthian centre of that day. The forwards were Sandilands, Walter Gilliat, George Cotterill, self, R. Topham. After that I have never played anywhere else but centre, and Cotterill was put inside right for Corinthians matches. In other first-class matches I have played in every position at one time or another including goalkeeping.'

By modern specialist standards, the selection of G.O. at inside-forward may appear unusual. Yet it is not so surprising when the numbers who have interchanged the three inside-forward positions are recalled. For the tradition has been perpetuated from V.J. Woodward, G.O.'s great amateur successor alongside the professionals in England's elevens, down to Billy Walker and Dai Astley of Aston Villa, not to mention Hidegkuti of the Hungarians. The fallacy that a centre-forward cannot play elsewhere, which is prevalent especially among schoolboys, for example, is here clearly exploded. Specialisation is certainly desirable if a football eleven is to be soundly created: but the natural footballer, as G.O. indicated in his letter, and as historical examples support, is often to be found playing 'in every position at one time or another including goalkeeping.'

Perhaps most significant of all G.O.'s remarks here, however, is the casual reference to his playing at inside-right for England because Cotterill was the Corinthian centre of the day! For even if G.O. was then ready for the England team, he had to step down for the Corinthians in favour of the player who had the prior tenancy to this position in the club side. Tall, moustached and slightly balding, G.H. Cotterill may be regarded as a typical Corinthian forward of those days, of heavyweight build when the Club's attack often averaged nearly thirteen stone in weight. He had captained the legendary Sammy Woods at Brighton College - the school which around this time also produced L.H. Gay, one of the select dozen or so who have represented England in full peace-time cricket and soccer internationals.

In later times this same school produced one of the few genuine 'characters,' in the true sense of that much abused word, namely, W.H.V. Levett, wicket-keeper of Kent's colourful elevens of the 1930s. Cotterill, so C.B. Fry has told us, had a great gift for pushing the ball through at the end of his long stride; and one can well imagine the charging which took place when professional defenders such as Holmes of Preston North End and Underwood and Clare of Stoke-on-Trent, as well as the Oxonians against whom he captained the Cambridge XI of 1890, hunched their shoulders to tackle him.

By way of contrast, the inside-left in that England side v. Ireland mentioned by G.O., WE Williat, another of G.O.'s Old Carthusian contemporaries, was described by 'Pa' Jackson as becoming 'unfortunately, too much damaged to play in many first-class matches." He was a dribbler in the Cobbold mould, with some of that master's shooting qualities. For although this game produced his only cap, he left his mark by settling the issue with a brilliantly taken hat-trick in the first half. One wonders how many other international footballers have done this and then never played in their national side again. Like a number of his contemporaries, Gilliatt took Holy Orders and was little seen in the first-class game thereafter.

All the forwards who comprised the England attack mentioned by G.O. against Ireland were Corinthians. His partner at outside-right was the same dashing Topham who won his F.A. Cup medal with Wolverhampton Wanderers a month after the international. Equally speedy on the other wing was R.R. Sandilands, probably the finest footballer ever produced by Westminster School with the exception of Stanley Harris who arrived a decade later. It is really difficult to understand why that old foundation, loyal to and steeped in the traditions of the game, has failed to produce a soccer Blue or international amateur or professional, since the Second World War.

As for the Ireland match, G.O. himself scored a fourth goal before the interval after Gilliatt's trio to give England a 4-1 lead. When the teams crossed over, another Old Westminster, the England centre-half, W.N. Winckworth, 'with an exceptionally brilliant shot' (from *centre-half!)* scored the fifth; and since Sandilands cleverly shot the sixth, one may well say that Charterhouse and Westminster won the day for England.

It is worth noting, too, that nearly 8,000 turned up at Perry Bar, Birmingham, the old Aston Villa ground, to see the match. Eight thousand for the first international of the season! From their hotels, the Irishmen at the 'Colonnade,' and the English-men at the 'Queen's,' the two teams drove to the ground in style with bugles and fours-in-hand. Of greater significance than all that, however, was the selection of the England side immediately after the Varsity match, just as the Gentlemen of England cricket sides against the Players are selected during or following the Varsity cricket match at Lord's. The Cambridge captain, N.C. Cooper, another, Old Brightonian - why have they, too, forsaken their traditions? - and G.O. alone from that game were chosen alongside nine other amateurs, three of whom were playing with professional clubs. One of these clubs, Small Heath, had just then become the first leaders of the newly formed Second Division of the Football League. Later it changed its name to Birmingham, and after the Second World War added the suffix City. Yet despite the club's lack of fashionable success, down the years from this game in 1893 it has continued to supply England's national soccer elevens with their last line of defence through such men as Tremelling, Hibbs and, in 1953, Merrick. The England team lined up as follows:

C. CHARSLEY
(*Small Heath*)

F.R. PELLY		A.H. HARRISON
(*Old Foresters*)		(Old Westminsters)

ALBERT SMITH	W.N. WINCKWORTH	N.C. COOPER
(*Nottingham F.)*	(*Old Westminsters*)	(*Cambridge Un.)*

G.O. SMITH		WE GILLIAT
(*Oxford University*)		(*Old Carthusians*)

R. TOPHAM	G.H. COTTERILL	R.R.SANDILANDS
(*Wolverhampton W.*)	(*Old Brightonians*)	(*Old Westminsters*)

Twelve months later, in 1894, the Oxford side arrived at West Kensington under C.B. Fry's captaincy as strong favourites for the game. The defence contained the current or future English internationals, G.B. Raikes, W.J. Oakley and Fry, a strong Old Carthusian half-back line, and G.O. was at centre-forward. They had a record of 14 wins, 2 draws, 1 defeat, with 74 goals scored against 8 conceded. Cambridge, with only one future international, L.V. Lodge, at left-back, had won 12 games, lost 9 and scored only 56 goals as against 38. Oxford, therefore, had the pull all round on paper; and when they scored first, the expected result was awaited.

Direct from the restart, however, Cambridge equalised, and on a bone-hard, uneven surface, as so often has happened before and since, fast, open tactics rather than repute carried the day. C.B. Fry has told us in *Life Worth Living* that the day before the game had brought a thaw in the winter weather to Oxford. All his men arrived at the frozen pitch with long knobs on their boots, but as it was still freezing at Cambridge, their team turned up with shallow bars of felt. Fry could have agreed to a postponement, but rejected it. He and Oakley fed their forwards well enough in what is imagined to be exclusively a modern style; but when the opportunities came, they were lost by the forwards in elaboration and the short pass, and so was the match. 'Probably the best side that ever represented Oxford at Association football got beaten.' wrote Fry, 'and, what is more, on the play of the day, on its merits.' Cambridge scored twice more without reply after they had equalised; and their vigour and energy, aided by considerable skill, triumphed over a great Oxford team, which apart from defence, failed to do itself justice.

But what a defence! G.O.'s era draws our eyes to its accent on attack, yet the University defenders of his day could stand comparison with any among the professionals that have come after. Raikes, Oakley and Fry were shortly to capture over twenty international caps between them in those days of only three international games a season; and Lodge, from Cambridge, gained five caps. Here, then, were easily the equivalent of Moss, Male and Hapgood, to go back no further than Arsenal and England of the 1930s for a modern yardstick.

G.B. Raikes was merely one in a long line of Corinthian goalkeepers and cricketers. As G.O. wrote:

'Apart from W.R. Moon, the great Corinthian goalkeeper in my day was L.H. Gay, who played cricket for England, too, and G.B. Raikes who played behind C.B. Fry and W.J. Oakley in the Oxford Elevens of my time. Both Gay and Raikes played against Scotland. There have been others very good, but Howard Baker would rank higher than any others except these I have mentioned.'

B.Howard Baker is considered in the text in company with his fellow-Corinthians of the 1920s, the last flickers of the Glory that was Corinth. L.H. Gay is, of course, unique. For he is the only goalkeeper among the select group of double internationals. He carried on the Brighton College traditions of G.H. Cotterill and S.M.J. Woods of obtaining double Blues against Oxford. Gay kept goal in 1892 and wicket in 1893. Had he not been contemporary with Gregor MacGregor, one of the greatest wicket-keepers of all time, he would have received recognition for his talents in that position even earlier than he did. Nevertheless, his performances for Cambridge were of such excellence that A.C. McLaren, the famous England captain, has related in the *Country Life* volume of *Cricket* that A. E. Stoddart invited Gay to tour Australia during the winter of 1894-95 without ever having had the opportunity of seeing him perform behind the stumps.

In the sensational first Test Match at Sydney, which England won by 10 runs, Gay kept wicket effectively to the bowling of Bobby Peel of Yorkshire and Johnny Briggs of Lancashire, but immediately afterwards he lost his form and also his place. Not unnaturally he was described by 'Pa' Jackson as being 'wonderfully clever with his hands, taking the football almost as readily as if it were a cricket ball.' He kept goal for England against Scotland in 1893 and 1894, and against Wales in 1894 behind ten other Corinthians, and was never on the losing side for his country.

W.R. Moon missed this distinction on only one of the seven occasions upon which he played for England between 1888 and 1891, in 1889 against Scotland, because of a weakness in that most vulnerable of positions, centre-half. In the previous season, Moon's exhibition during the first fifteen minutes of the same fixture, in Glasgow, was described by 'Pa' Jackson as 'little short of marvellous,' and the victory of his side by 5-0 was undoubtedly as much due to his defensive work as to the splendid attacking powers of the English forwards. Just over sixty years later, in 1949, James Cowan of Morton repeated this performance at Wembley when Scotland ran out winners by 3-1 in a game that will live in the minds of those who saw it or heard it broadcast. Like Gay, Moon had been a wicket keeper, and when he died in 1943 I wrote of him to G.O. In his reply G.O. mentioned Moon's uncanny anticipation. Anticipation has been fundamental to the goalkeeper's art at all phases in the history of the game, the continued success of Harry Hibbs in the 1930s as one outstanding illustration coming readily to mind. For, unlike all other positions on the field, the principles governing the strategy of goalkeeping, with its limited range, have never changed. G.O. wrote:

'Many thanks for your letter. I was very sorry to see the death of Billy Moon: he was a great friend of mine and I played football with him and against him on numberless occasions. His name will always be associated with the brothers Walters and together they were a great trio in defence: a goal against the Corinthians in those days was none too easy to get. He was a sturdy goalkeeper, who gave as good as he got in the matter of charging, and was also very quick at foreseeing where a shot would come from. He kept wicket for Middlesex occasionally but his cricket was mostly confined to the Hampstead Club. He was a solicitor by profession and a member of my club in London, so I saw a certain amount of him in after life. There was an obituary notice of him in *The Times*.

In a match between Old Carthusians and Old Westminsters at Vincent Square he and I collided head to head - I was knocked unconscious, but my head broke his cheekbone and smashed the retina of his eye. Mercifully, this was cured - at that time, I believe, an unknown occurrence. His younger brother played a lot for Middlesex and was a good inside-left besides.'

The younger brother mentioned by G.O., L.J. Moon, gained cricket Blues at Cambridge alongside G.L. Jessop, E.R. Wilson, John Daniell and S.H. Day in 1899 and also with E.M. ('Toddles') Dowson and R.N.R. Blaker in 1900. In both these years Moon also gained soccer Blues, as did Day and Blaker.

S.H.Day

L.J.Moon

He scored only 23 and 31 in the Varsity match in 1899, but was probably compensated for this by a glorious 138 against the Australians and the bowling of Ernest Jones, M.A. Noble and W.P. Howell. In the 1900 Varsity match Moon succeeded with scores of 58 and 60, and afterwards frequently opened the Middlesex batting with Sir Pelham (then P.F.) Warner.

In 1905-06 he went with Sir Pelham's M.C.C. team to South Africa and played in four Test Matches. Although not up to his brother's standard at soccer Moon emulated Arthur Dunn in changing from the inside-forward position, where he was strong and speedy with a good shot, to full-back. There he may well have gained the highest honours but for a knee injury, for in 1905 he played at full-back for the Amateurs of the South against the Professionals of the South in the international trial match.

The third of the great Corinthian goalkeepers was G.B. Raikes, and he certainly maintained the tradition. At that great home of public school soccer, Shrewsbury, Raikes was captain of cricket as well as football when W.J. Oakley as an inside forward was preparing for his internationals at full-back. The same *Football Annual* which had criticised G.O. at Charterhouse also recorded in its report on Shrewsbury School: 'G.B. Raikes. Goal. Knows how to use his hands better than his feet, as his kicking is erratic. With improvements in this latter respect is likely to become good.' He did, too, for with his flawless style he kept goal for the all-Corinthian England eleven against Wales in 1895, and a year later played in all three home internationals while J.W. Sutcliffe, the Rugby international back who became the Bolton Wanderers' goalkeeper was still in form, and Foulke and Robinson were advancing with Sheffield United and Derby County respectively. After playing against Scotland in his last year at Oxford in 1896 he entered the Church and could devote no more time to first-class soccer. Yet having obtained a cricket Blue in 1895, he went on to play cricket for Norfolk for many years (except for an interlude with Hampshire from 1900-02), and in 1905 and 1910 he led Norfolk to win the Minor Counties Championship, two notable landmarks in the history of perhaps the strongest and most famous cricketing county outside the major County Championship.

A final glimpse of Raikes in the fashion of our modern goalkeepers such as Swift, Williams and Ditchburn, as they dovetail with their colleagues, may be seen from the commencement of his last Varsity soccer match under G.O.'s captaincy in 1896. *The Times* report tells us that the first thing of note in the game was a long run by the Cambridge University cricketer and international outside-left, C.J. Burnup, 'who finished with a long side shot, which Raikes took well and then he threw the ball over to Oakley.'

Oakley and Butler from America's famous musical success, *Annie Get Tour Gun,* are doubtless more familiar to-day than Oakley and Fry or Oakley and Lodge from the internationals of the 1890s. But Thickett and Boyle of Sheffield United at the turn of the century, Wadsworth and Barkas of Huddersfield Town from the 1920s, Male and Hapgood of Arsenal in the 1930s, or Carey and Aston of Manchester United and Ramsey and Willis (or Withers) of Tottenham Hotspur of our own day, to mention but a few since 1900, had nothing on those undergraduate pairs when they turned out for their university or country in the 1890s.

This is not surprising, for around this time 'Pa' Jackson wrote that 'amateurs usually supply better backs than professionals. They learn to kick cleanly and well at school and generally show better judgment in placing the ball to their forwards than the professors, who do a lot of vigorous charging and hard wild kicking, but are not really finished players.'

Of the distinguished backs of this period the best are W.J. Oakley (Oxford), L.V. Lodge (Cambridge), A.H. Harrison (Cambridge) and C.B. Fry (Oxford); these being closely followed by Crabtree (Aston Villa) and Holmes (Preston North End). F.M. Ingram (Oxford) and F.R. Pelly (Old Foresters), although differing greatly in physique, both deserve their places in the first class.' Other cultured professional backs before and after this period we know existed, and Nicholas Ross of the great Preston 'Invincibles' and somewhat later, Crompton of Blackburn Rovers with his England partner, Pennington from West Bromwich Albion, all enriched the game; but on the whole the amateur had the edge on the professional in G.O.'s day.

Apart from that, the most significant feature of defensive play around this time was the versatility of players. Specialisation in one position with the accompanying use of only one foot was unheard of. Oakley, Fry and Lodge switched their full-back positions with the ease of a politician changing, his parties; while Crabtree played for England in every defensive position except that of goalkeeper. Over fifty years passed before Jack Froggatt, then of Portsmouth, in 1951, proved versatility still to be attractive and admired. For, two years after his first cap against Italy at outside-left, the selectors put him where true football is no longer expected - at centre-half. Later, when injured against Wales at Wembley in 1952 and forced on to the wing again, he returned the compliment with as fine a headed goal and a display of courage as one can ever wish to see.

No less courageous a display was W.J. Oakley's against Scotland in 1900 at Celtic Park, Glasgow. Within five minutes of the start he collided with his goalkeeper, J.W.Robinson, then of Southampton, and Bobby Walker of Heart of Midlothian who was advancing goalwards. Oakley was knocked out - blood flowing from his nose and mouth. Suffering from concussion, he played on instinctively throughout the match, and his first remark on returning to the dressing-room was, 'Who's won?' His partner, Crabtree, declared afterwards that he could not understand how a man could play so well when in such a state. When allowed to play in a normal state, however, Oakley had come to the front at Oxford with the characteristic required of most modern full-backs - his great pace in overtaking and dispossessing opposing forwards: then he would turn to supplying his own. He must have benefited here from his feats on the athletic track where he twice won the hurdles in the Varsity sports.

In one remarkable match between Oxford and Yale he finished second in the long jump with third place going to the ultimate holder of the world record for half a century, C.B. Fry; and that authority has also told us that Oakley was a good oar in the Christ Church boat and not far off a rowing Blue.

After playing in the 1895 Corinthian international v. Wales, Oakley appeared in every international match for England during five of the next six seasons (the exception being 1899-1900), gaining sixteen caps in all. He was built for the forward line, where he had commenced at school; and *Gibson and Pickford* re-called that 'his tall, well-knit figure, crowned with a broad forehead, large earnest eyes and rather sharp-cut face was ever a pleasant picture to thousands who knew him at his best, say in 1900.' On going down from Oxford he joined G.O. at Ludgrove, one of the leading preparatory schools for Eton. They jointly wrote the Association section for the revised edition of *Football* in the *Badminton Library,* and for a few years after their retirement in 1902 they were joint honorary secretaries of the Corinthians. Not unnaturally, therefore, G.O. stated,

'I could write reams about W.J. Oakley who was my closest friend from 1892 to his untimely death. I put him first as a back and he was a wonderful player with no weak spot: he always made the game easy for his forwards the supreme test of any footballer in any position. Not so spectacular as some but, like P.M. Waiters, absolutely Sound and reliable. I always like what C.B. Fry wrote of him many years ago: "give me 'Oakers' in a rough and tumble and you may have any other man in England except Sam Woods". In a sense his qualities as a football player illustrate what he was in life - absolutely reliable and never ruffled. He was, indeed, an English gentleman in the best sense of the word.'

Oakley's famous partner for the Corinthians and England was L. V. Lodge of Cambridge University who, with his pluck and courage, was almost as good a tackler as either of the brothers Walters. Indeed, when I had enquired from G.O. what he might have considered to have been the best Corinthian eleven chosen from all periods, I can now see that it was hardly surprising that he should reply in September 1942 that this,

'Is an almost impossible task. I could, I think, put down two sides and there would be little to choose between them; for instance A.M. and P.M. Waiters were magnificent as a pair, but I doubt if they were better than L.V. Lodge and W.J. Oakley.'

C.B. Fry has told us that Lodge 'could head the ball as far as many men can kick it.' Yet the pluck of this red-haired hero, who had all the dash and fire that his colour signifies, 'must have given out, for he was missed one day, and after a long trial his body was found in a pond near Buxton; a sad mystery,' wrote J.A.H. Catton ('Tityrus') in *Wickets and Goals*. The same chronicler also pointed out the contrasts of life whereby Lodge's only fellow amateur in the England side against Scotland in 1895, R.C. Gosling, of the Old Etonians and the captain, died in his bed twenty-seven years later as an Essex squire and left a six-figure fortune.

Robert Cunliffe Gosling was described by Sir Frederick Wall as the richest man who ever played soccer for England by the side of a professional. He had appeared against Oxford in 1890 at outside-right for Cambridge: then he moved inside with the Corinthians to appear there for England, firstly in 1892. But Gosling did not appear enough again for his many supporters before receiving his last of five caps in 1895 when he captained England's professionals who included for the first time Derby County's Steve Bloomer. Jimmy Catton wrote that Gosling was 'the most aristocratic-looking man I ever saw,' and a glance at Gosling's photograph shows why C.B. Fry rated him as the best looking man of my acquaintance' as well as a person who aided 'the Corinthians in their reputation up North as a team of toffs.'

Charles Burgess Fry is renowned for so many achievements other than on the football field that one tends to overlook his appearances for England against Canada in 1891, against Ireland in 1901 and for Southampton against Sheffield United in the Cup-Final of 1902, in addition to being a member of the Southampton Championship teams in the old Southern League around this time. All this is usually forgotten in recalling the Blues he obtained at cricket and athletics as well as soccer: the one he missed for Rugby through injury: his Presidency of the O.U.D.S.: and not least on going up to Wadham from Repton, his seniority in scholarship to two future Lords Chancellor,

Birkenhead and Simon, and a future Lord of Appeal, Roche. Perhaps the neglect of his soccer is not surprising since G.O. wrote in the same letter which refers to Fry's cricket mentioned in the next chapter:

'As a footballer he was a most useful back though not up to the standard of A.M. and P.M. Walters, L.V. Lodge and W.J. Oakley and many professionals.'

The yardstick which G.O. took for measuring his full-backs, however, contained such superlative quality that it was an achievement to be brought within the borders of comparison, even without attaining the standard G.O. suggested. 'It is doubtful if the game has ever produced a better pair of defenders than the two old Charterhouse boys with the 'meridian' initials. Individually each was a great back; collectively they were superior to any club pair that ever took the field.

'Those words of *Gibson and Pickford* written before the First World War have not lost their effect since the Second. Indeed, the same chroniclers could well have been referring to Manchester United's Carey or Tottenham Hotspur's Ramsey when they recalled that if A.M. was hampered in keeping close behind his half-backs with safety 'he would, with the greatest nonchalance, pass the ball back to his brother, and they rarely or never made a serious mistake. They could pass to each other with the accuracy of well-trained forwards.'

If ever there were pioneers at soccer, the brothers Walters deserve the title. Previous to their time, during G.O.'s schooldays, combination had been thought of only for attack. It was left for them and W.R. Moon to prove its virtue in defence whereby the final three defenders worked together. So marked was their success that 1888 was the only season between 1885 and 1890 when the brothers did not play together against Scotland, because of A.M.'s absence through injury; and C.B. Fry wrote as recently as 1939 that 'with Moon in goal they formed the best defence England has ever had against Scotland.'

Tall, exceptionally fine-looking fellows of the Nordic type, as Fry put it, the Walters brothers each tipped the scales at about 13 stone. They kicked as well as to-day's masters, tackled fearlessly within the bounds of the old-fashioned shoulder-charge rule, and, attacking all the time in the true Corinthian spirit, they were always close to their half-backs, while relying on their pace and combination in the event of a breakaway. They would doubtless have added many more to the dozen or so caps each collected in home internationals had not their younger brother Hugh died from the effects of an accidental blow in the stomach by an opponent's knee during a game; and in deference to their parents' wishes they reluctantly gave up the game. Like so many of their contemporaries they were passionately devoted to football; and also like so many of their contemporaries they subsequently became prominent in the legal profession, A.M. as a London solicitor and P.M. as a Chancery barrister and a Bencher of Lincoln's Inn. They had played against each other in the Varsity match of 1884, P.M. for Oxford and A.M. for Cambridge; and in their short but glorious sporting careers they spanned the time between the old individual dribbling of Cobbold's day, when the defensive tactics employed then were obviously less involved than those required against the combined forward movements of the nineties and G.O.'s era.

It is not widely appreciated that down the years the *general principles* of defensive play have changed but little. One reads frequently of Fry and Oakley kicking a fine length for Oxford; and, in that 1894 game, of a long shot from the left for Oxford, 'which would have been effective had not Lodge been opportunely at hand and headed the ball away.' Lucky Lodge? Lucky Arsenal?

In spite of Oxford forward-line's failure in that Varsity match of 1894, a few weeks later G.O. first appeared at centre forward for England. Four to five thousand had watched the Varsity match on Wednesday, 21st February, in polar conditions. On Monday, 12th March, nearly 1,500 less turned up on the Racecourse Ground at Wrexham for the sixteenth match between England and Wales. A

far cry, indeed, from the 60,000 who now pack Ninian Park, Cardiff, for the same fixture, or the 95,000 who bought out Wembley Stadium in the first game there between the two countries in November, 1952.

This game of sixty years ago was one of the two for which the selectors paid the Corinthians the supreme compliment of choosing eleven members of the club *en bloc* to represent England. It was well repaid by five goals after Wales scored first. G.O. was not among the marksmen, and a month later only the goalkeeper, L.H. Gay, and F.R. Pelly, at left-back, remained in the England side chosen to play against the far more formidable opposition from Scotland. The Blackburn Rover's centre-forward, John Southworth, had been selected for that position, but he was forced to cry off because of injury. So G.O. was brought in. *The Sportsman* suggested that it had been thought that he might not combine well with the others, i.e. the professionals Bassett of West Bromwich Albion and John Goodall of Derby County on the right wing, and Everton 's Edgar Chadwick and little Fred Spiksley of Sheffield Wednesday on the left ; but clearly G.O. 'rendered a very creditable account of himself.' Already the growing popularity of soccer among the Northern Celts could be observed, for 40,000 turned out at Celtic Park to see this match. They also saw England's right-half, John ('Baldy') Reynolds from Aston Villa equal the score five minutes from the end and England force a 2-2 draw.

In the south on this day, at Richmond, the Old Carthusians won the first F.A. Amateur Cup -Final, just beating the Casuals by 2-1 in the presence of the Duke and Duchess of Teck and their daughter, Princess May, later so beloved as Queen Mary. The Casuals had been founded only a year after the Corinthians to suit those who were on the fringe of the Corinthian Elevens, and it gradually became a kind of junior partner to or recruiting ground for the senior club until the amalgamation created the present Corinthian-Casuals F.C. in 1939. G.O. was even more sorely missed by the Old Carthusians than was to be expected in the attack during this game, for his deputy, E.F. Buzzard, had been at wing-half in both of G.O.'s first two Oxford sides. Nevertheless, he did equalise an early goal against his side scored by the ubiquitous R.Topham less than five minutes from the start. It was just as well that the Casuals had this initial advantage. Their left back, L.V. Lodge, missed his train at Cambridge, was consequently late and took his place ten minutes after the start.

It was difficult in 1954 to imagine a similar happening in the same competition before its 100,000 audience at Wembley Stadium. Some years after that first Amateur Cup-Final, Buzzard returned to his University as its Regius Professor of Medicine and became Physician to the late King George VI as Sir E. Farquhar Buzzard. In his *Life Worth Living,* C, B. Fry commented 'Buzzard was a strong player at left-half-back. I hope he is as good a Regius Professor as he was a footballer.' Certainly he was a good enough footballer to appear with G.O. and such other distinguished Old Carthusians as the Walters brothers, Wreford Brown, Streatfeild, Bliss, Hewitt and M.H. Stanbrough in the other two F.A. Amateur Cup-Final appearances of the Old Carthusians. A year later, in the first of these, when the Cup was surrendered to Middlesbrough by 1-2, Buzzard was at left-half. When the Cup was recaptured two seasons later, in 1896-97, from the North East against Stockton by 4-1 (after a 1-1 draw), he scored two goals from inside-left alongside G.O.

If the Old Carthusians' most famous footballing member, on the occasion of his first appearance against Scotland, had not yet arrived for certain as a new star in the soccer firmament, he was certainly travelling fast in that direction. After only two seasons with the University and the Corinthians, for whom he was playing during vacations, he was just about to enter the galaxy of great centre-forwards already containing his great predecessor Tinsley Lindley, and to which our own times have so brilliantly added Lawton and Lofthouse. One defect in his play yet remained, which the predecessor of James Catton and Ivan Sharpe, as Editor, noted in *The Athletic News Football Annual:*

ENGLISH INTERNATIONAL PLAYERS
1894
Versus Scotland

G.O.Smith (Old Carthusians and Corinthians), a capital young forward, who was brought into the team owing to Southworth being unable to play. Is a pretty dribbler, but lacks shooting power.

This drawback did not take him long to overcome. If he did not come off in his only international appearance of 1895, against Wales, in which the Corinthians, as England, had to be content with a 1-1 draw, he flashed home Oxford's first goal against Cambridge after a dribble the length of the field; and the Dark Blues, after their shock of the previous season, coasted home to a 3-0 win. The experience of John Goodall was preferred by England for the centre-forward position in the Scotland and Ireland games Of 1895, but G.O.'s final and crowning year at Oxford in 1896 found him among the honours as well as the goals. By that time his shooting must have improved, for as captain he won the Varsity soccer match with the game's wonderful only goal; scored the first and fifth of England's nine goals against Wales at Cardiff, and rocked the posts against Scotland up in Glasgow. The late F.B. Wilson, father of Peter Wilson, the present sports columnist, recollected in his *Sporting Pie* that he once kept goal against G.O. in a friendly match. After connecting with one of G.O.'s friendly shots he had a strained right wrist for three weeks. While Jack Robinson, the great international goalkeeper from Derby County and Southampton, has related that he would rather keep goal against his Satanic Majesty than G.O., and he doubtless had practical reasons for such a preference.

Among other victims of G.O.'s improved shooting around this time was Tottenham Hotspur. By some divine intuition I asked G.O. about the famous Spurs in 1942 and he replied:

'I only played on the Spurs ground twice - once for England v. Germany, and once for the Corinthians v. the Spurs, so I do not know much about the Spurs side except that later on they became a great team, but that was after my day.'

47

When these words were written perhaps the Spurs' greatest days were yet to arrive, But from G.O.'s own day two remarkable games must have slipped his memory. For on the Saturday and Thursday which sandwiched that 1-1 draw with Wales on Monday, 15th March, 1895, the Old Carthusians with G.O., the Walters brothers, Buzzard and other familiar figures, twice played the North London Club. The first meeting in the Second Round of the F.A. 'Amateur' Cup took them as holders to the Spurs' old ground at Northumberland Park. 'Fully 3,000 ardent admirers of the game' saw G.O. score the final Carthusian goal in a 5-0 win. Five days later at Leyton, G.O. scored twice more for the Old Carthusians in a 3-0 victory over the Spurs in the Semi-Final of the London Charity Cup.

On both occasions Tottenham Hotspur's outside-left was Ernest Payne. Two seasons earlier, when this player left Fulham to join the Spurs, the whole of his kit was missing. His new club found him all the gear except for a pair of boots; they gave him ten shillings to buy a pair, and consequently were suspended by the London F.A. for breaking their amateur rules. Smarting under this fanatical reflection of southern disapproval of the paid player and their crushings by the Old Carthusians, the Spurs took the plunge and turned professional. Six years later, in 1901, with Sheffield United they drew 110,000 to the Crystal Palace Cup-Final and also the match, 2-2. In the deep north at Bolton they won the replay 3-1, and the Cup too, for the first southern success in twenty years. Such was the romance and rise of professionalism in London. During that year, 1901, the Spurs also gained their first international match - England v. Germany - for the new and present ground opened at White Hart Lane in 1899. This match was G.O.'s last for England, and perhaps it was fitting that it should be played at the ground of Tottenham Hotspur.

G.O.'s last year at Oxford, 1896, has been called by H.S. Altham and E.W. Swanton, in their *A History of Cricket,* Oxford's *annus mirabilis.* It was also that for G.O. His goal against Cambridge at Queen's Club on 22nd February, in a game whose brilliancy, reported *The Times,* 'exceeded anything that has been seen in the university match for many years,' was typical of many. He took the ball in mid-field, diddled the defence in dribbling down towards the goal, then slipped it over to his outside-left, Compton, of all names (unconnected with the Arsenal and Middlesex family). Compton pulled out a terrific side-shot, the goalkeeper saved at full stretch and the ball rolled away towards the dead-ball line. Then, as G.C. Vassall, Oxford's outside-right, has written:

'G.O. was twenty yards away from goal towards the corner flag, and practically on the touch-line; apparently the only thing to do was to centre, but he, noticing that the Cambridge goalkeeper had stepped forward to intercept the centre that was obviously coming, deliberately placed the ball with a left-foot slice just over the goalkeeper's head, and under the bar. No goalie could have saved it, even if he had stopped in goal, and we won the match by 1-0.'

Seven or eight thousand saw this game. On the same day a mere 12,000 turned up at Perry Bar, Birmingham, to see Aston Villa, who were to become League Champions, play Stoke; and the runners-up at the time, Derby County, could draw only 10,000 for their home fixture with Blackburn Rovers.

A fortnight later against Ireland on 7th March, G.O. was alongside the immortal Steve Bloomer in England's XI for the first time. Seven days after that he was playing against Wales. On Saturday, 4th April, he was one of the half dozen Corinthians who played alongside five professionals for England v. Scotland; and exactly three months later, on Saturday, 4th July, his century against Cambridge in the last innings at Lord's took Oxford to an unexpected and unprecedented victory.

That game against Scotland was to be the most significant of all that were played during G.O.'s Oxford days. For it marks the turning-point in the challenges that had been steadily growing to the amateurs since professionalism had been legalised in 1885 and the Football League had been founded in 1888. The southern amateur clubs had not won the F.A. Cup since the Old Etonians' victory against Blackburn Rovers in 1882, and the Old Boys clubs had now dropped out entirely from that competition. Yet professionalism in the South was only just loosening the stranglehold in which the prejudice of the amateurs had held it from birth. Royal Arsenal, founded at Woolwich in 1886, waited until 1891, the year of Blackburn Rovers' fourth F.A. Cup victory, before taking the plunge; Southampton followed two years later, and Portsmouth in 1898. The great professional clubs of the industrial midlands and the north alone could chase and win the trophies from which the Corinthians held aloof; and Aston Villa were to carry off both the major ones in the following season, 1896-97.

Nevertheless, the amateurs of the mid-nineties were far from being a spent force or a faded attraction. Ten thousand were present on a Wednesday afternoon in March of 1896, just ten days before the Scotland game, to see the annual Gentlemen v. Players fixture on the llford Club's old ground at Lyttleton Road, Leyton, in Essex. The amateurs, of course, were all Corinthians, and the players comprised the cream of the professionals. G.O. played himself into the England side with a display in which he 'showed all his best skill and with either foot seemed to have a remarkable control over the ball.' The other ten places were divided equally between the paid and the unpaid so that the team as originally selected was as follows:

G.B. RAIKES
(*Oxford University*)

CRABTREE   J. OAKLEY
(*Aston Villa*)   (*Oxford University*)

A.G. HENFREY   CRAWSHAW   NEEDHAM
(*Corinthians*) (*Sheffield Wednesday*) (*Sheffield United*)

BLOOMER   GOODALL
(*Derby County*)   (*Derby County*)

BASSETT   G.O. SMITH   C.J. BURNUP
(*West Bromwich Alb.*) (*Oxford Un.*) (*Cambridge Un.*)

Burnup had been the star of the 1896 Varsity match and kept in the ascendant during the trial to outshine Sheffield Wednesday's Spiksley, who had scored a brilliant hat-trick against Scotland in 1893. Ten years later Burnup was to overtop Surrey's Tom Hayward in the batting averages

during the halcyon Edwardian days of Kent's great side. Henfrey had been England's centre-forward against Wales in 1892 when Southworth, Devey and Goodall were all available. Now he was selected on the strength of an outstanding trial display, and as so often happens, he could not repeat his form on the big occasion.

The selectors then, however, like those of to-day, could not sit back and relax, their team chosen, their work complete. Bloomer had missed the trial because of an injury he had received for his club in the F.A. Cup Semi-Final tie against West Bromwich Albion. Now he had to miss the international. Goodall was switched to let in Harry Wood at inside-left, who had played for Wolverhampton Wanderers' Cup-winning team of 1893. He was to play for its losing side in the Final only a fortnight after this international, against Sheffield Wednesday, captained by England's selected centre-half, Crawshaw, and ended a distinguished soccer career as captain of Southampton in the old Southern League in the early 1900s. Unfortunately for England, Wood was no Bloomer, just as no one else has ever been. The withdrawal through illness before the game of Ernest 'Nudger' Needham, the 'Prince of Half-Backs,' caused Crawshaw to move over from centre to the left-half position. Aston Villa's Crabtree, who could play in any position came up to centre-half from right-back, to where Oakley was switched from left-back; and Lodge was brought in to play there, The revised team, therefore, included three undergraduate Oxonians, one Cantab and two former Light Blues, all, of course, Corinthians. It lined up, therefore:

G.B. RAIKES
(*Oxford University*)

W.J.OAKLEY   L.V.LODGE
(*Oxford University*)   (*Corinthians*)

A.G.HENFREY   CRABTREE   CRAWSHAW
(*Corinthians*)   (*Aston Villa*)   (*Sheffield Wed.*)
          GOODALL   WOOD
        (*Derby County*)   (*Wolverhampton W.*)

BASSETT   G.O.SMITH   C.J.BURNUP
(*West Bromwich A.*) (*Oxford Un*) (*Cambridge Un.*)

The Scottish selectors, whose Association had resisted professionalism until 1893, now included, for the first time, Anglo Scots engaged with English clubs; and the famous Queen's Park, residents at Hampden Park, whose matches with the Corinthians at Christmas and the New Year are among the greatest and most memorable in both clubs' histories, provided the only amateur in the home side, William Lambie, at outside left. This attempt to combine Scotland's full available strength was rewarded with a crowd of 51,346 who paid £3,264 and 'exceeded anything that has before been reached either in the company or the gate money at an international match.' The Scotsmen who turned up were certainly well repaid, for they saw their kinsmen win by 2-1.

England's amateurs did all that was expected of them, except perhaps for Henfrey. He failed to find his true form; and the playing of Crawshaw out of position at left-half meant that the English forwards waited in vain for a ball that never came through from the wing-halves, while Scotland's line advanced unchecked. Upon this point the game's fate turned, although G.O. hit a post with one of his flashing shots, and in the words of Alcock's *Football Annual,* 'for what it is worth, it deserves to be stated that serious exception was taken to the referee's decision disallowing a goal, which would have brought England on even terms.'

The reaction was summarised a month later by *The Times in* its 'Review of the Past Football Season.' 'While there was so much good amateur talent last season, the English executive were not very happy in making up the eleven that lost to Scotland. Too much reliance was placed on the form of a fine trial at Leyton. These trials are not very trustworthy, for a man is seen much more himself in a really good club game and hence it came about that a couple of players were absent from England's team who should have had precedence of the amateurs.' In view of the wing-half weakness, however, Burnup could hardly have been bettered by Spiksley, while G.O. and the old defensive firm of Raikes, Oakley and Lodge gave not the slightest cause for complaint. From the absence of Bloomer and Needham grew the defeat, and, indeed, the selectors would hardly have been remiss had they looked for Bloomer's deputy to their captain of the previous year, R.C. Gosling, who had never been on the losing side in an international.

Defeats, however, bring recriminations and in the following two seasons G.O. and Oakley alone played as amateurs in all three of England's international games. Only two others joined them, Middleditch, against Ireland in 1897, and Wreford Brown, against Wales in 1898 as captain. Oakley dropped out for 1899 when G.O. carried the amateur flag alone as captain - and all three games were won.

Nineteen hundred and the turn of the century saw a slight revival with G.P. Wilson and the great Oxford batsman, R.E. Foster, as G.O.'s inside forwards, while in the following years S.S. Harris, S.H. Day, E.G.D. Wright and non-Corinthian forwards such as Vivian Woodward and Harold Hardman appeared with the professionals in the international sides. M. Morgan-Owen, another Old Salopian and Corinthian, became to Wales at centre half in that period what Fred Keenor of Cardiff City became in the 1920s and Tommy Griffiths and Tommy Jones of Everton and other clubs became in the 1930s. But it was a rearguard action; the professionals were advancing in the F.A. Council Chamber and also on the playing-field, unless a genius like G.O. or Woodward barred their way in a particular sector - and, it will be observed for England, usually among the forwards, no longer among the defenders.

When one realises that the selection of G.O. for England was not by his fellow Old Carthusians or Corinthians, but more and more each year by administrative representatives of the professional clubs, his distinction is all the more unique. Yet Alverstone and Alcock in their *Surrey Cricket* recorded shortly after this time, in 1902, 'It is sufficient only to state that if he ' had not become the most famous association footballer of his day, his abilities as a cricketer would have been even more appreciated.' For three months to the day after that Scotland game he was entrancing an entirely different crowd from that in Glasgow at not such an entirely different game. But that is another story and also another chapter.

VARSITY CRICKET IN THE NINETIES

Coincidence alone has not brought the footwork of many great footballers to the batting-creases of cricket fields. For both our national games share the common traits of fair play and graceful charm to reflect the environment of their different seasons of the year. Cricket is the contemplative mood of a summer's day; soccer, when kept to its proper period, thrills to warm a winter's afternoon or an appetite for toast and tea. Since soccer is the game of the people, like Tauber's song, it goes round the world. Summer in England being what it is, cricket has naturally remained in the country of its birth or within those peoples who have gained their inspiration from the game's ancient home. Nevertheless, only the English with their unique climate and character could have allowed the growth of two contrasting pastimes with such a community of skill and spirit as cricket and soccer. It is hardly surprising, therefore, that one of the greatest footballers should have had his moments of summer glory too.

As has been seen, G.O. had no small reputation as a cricketer when he went up to Oxford in 1892. His school record, to say nothing of his general

G.O. Smith - The Cricketer

sporting prowess, earned him a trial. This was forthcoming. Yet as he wrote to me half a century later, in the summer of 1942:

'At cricket in 1893 I made 113 in the Freshman's match, but did little in the other trial matches so failed to get my Blue. If you don't come off in the first few games at University there is little hope of getting into the side. In 1894 I again failed in the few games I played in the Parks, so there would be no account of my play in that year, which was confined to College cricket and Old Carthusian matches.'

Similar observations on the hazards of Varsity cricket have been made by Sir Henry Leveson-Gower, G.O.'s captain at Oxford in the 1896 season. In his autobiography, *On and Off the Field,* Sir Henry has pointed out that many people do not realise how important a part luck plays in getting a Blue. The summer term at the universities is so short, only eight weeks, that unless a player strikes form at once he may be passed over for that year.

Such was G.O.'s fate, as well as that of Sir Pelham (then P.F.) Warner, for the two years he mentions. In the first of these, in 1893, Cambridge, captained by the Hon. F. S. (later Sir Stanley) Jackson, won by 266 runs. For Cambridge Kumar Shri Ranjitsinhji made nine and a duck. For Oxford, Charles Burgess Fry scored seven and, in the second innings, thirty-one out of the side's total of 64! So met, on opposite sides, at Lords, Ranji and Fry, who were to form together one of the most famous associations in the history of cricket.

'Ranji - was a contemporary of mine, [G.O. wrote to me in 1942] and I was lucky enough to come across him a certain amount. In the early nineties there was rather a prejudice against an Indian playing for the, English Varsity and I think that was the real reason why he didn't get his Blue at Cambridge till his last year (1893). That prejudice has luckily entirely gone by now and Jackson subsequently acknowledged his mistake. Ranji was wonderfully kind and generous to all he came across - perhaps to generous, as he hadn't much money in those days. However, when he was acknowledged as Jam Saheb of Nawanagar in later years he became very rich and could indulge in his generous acts to the full with no fear of debts etc. Besides being a cricketing genius he was a most likeable man and proved himself a most efficient ruler in later years. I doubt if the world will ever see his like again.'

It nearly did, though, when Ranji's nephew, Duleepsinjhi, emulated his uncle by scoring a maiden century on his first appearance for England v. Australia, and later entered loftier circles as the High Commissioner for India in Australia. For Ranji, as Jam Saheb, the statesman, nursed his little northern province of Nawanagar, between Bombay and Kashmir, to a status entirely disproportionate to its physical size; and one was reminded of this when the present Jam Saheb took his seat in the Imperial War Cabinet in London during 1941. Ranji the cricketer brought his Oriental genius to the Victorian pastime fashioned by W.G.'s breed, and cast mystical spells with the charm and grace for which his country is famed. His presence on English fields with wrists of steel gliding the ball to leg kindled more interest in his homeland than all Disraeli's additions to his sovereign's titles could ever hope to do. Ranji's presence at the League of Nations with his high sense of duty, likewise,

achieved more for the recognition of India at that assembly than any professional politician could have done; and there, in Geneva, Ranji, with Fry as his secretary, revived the memorable partnership, which had turned the small Sussex ground at Hove into a haven for the pilgrims of the Golden Age.

For that was the period at the turn of the century which Altham and Swanton in their *A History of Cricket* have called 'The Golden Age of Batting: Ranji, Fry, Jessop.' Under that title one finds the authors recording: 'It is an open secret, which he himself would be the first to admit, that it was his association with the Indian Prince that raised Charles Fry from a good into a great player.' That greatness was indicated when the Australians under M.A. Noble in the Final Test Of 1905 at the Oval prepared their field for the almost mechanical regularity of Fry's on-side play. Yet they were as surprised as his detractors to see him vary his style, at the age of thirty-two, to hit 144 run, with as crisp a rate of cutting as his driving had always displayed. The risks which this cutting involved, however, usually left no alternative to the straight hit and every kind of on-side stroke for his colossal scores controlled by concentration. That made him for years the greatest run-getting machine that modern cricket has known. So perhaps G.O. was just a shade too cryptic and conscious of the 'machine' when he wrote in the same letter in which he had described Fry as a most useful footballer:

'As a cricketer he was rather an ugly bat, but his scores speak for themselves. As an all-round athlete I should put him No.1. Apart from games he had a wonderful brain and was a brilliant classic. Had he chosen to enter Parliament, I should say there was no position he might not have attained to.'

Fry did in fact stand three times as a Liberal candidate for Parliament, but was defeated on each occasion. But as he once said to Lord Birkenhead: 'The question remains, whether it is better to be successful or ... happy.' Moreover, as G.O. put it, 'he had to earn his living and he has undoubtedly done a splendid work at Hamble.' There among his Merchant Navy cadets at the training ship *Mercury,* on the Southampton water, Fry found what he has himself described as 'A Life's Work.' It turned out to be as great, but less spectacular, a service to the nation as his college contemporaries Lords Birkenhead and Simon contributed from the Woolsack. Accordingly, if it has not gone unsung, with appropriate gratitude from officialdom, it has certainly gone unhonoured.

All the playing honours, however, came to Fry at cricket. In 1921, at the age of forty-nine, he was invited to captain England against Warwick Armstrong's Australians - and declined because of an injury and a feeling that he was no longer equal to the task. Nine years earlier, in 1912, at the age of forty, Fry had led England to success against both Australia and South Africa in the Triangular Tournament. For Oxford he had scored a captain's century in 1894 and followed a year later with a duck in the first innings, a single in the second, but with the best bowling analysis of the match. Bowling successes, however, were not exceptional to Fry. It is often forgotten that he twice accomplished the hat-trick, both occasions being for Oxford *v.* M.C.C. at Lord's. The first series was A.E. Stoddart, A.E. Gibson and W.C. Hedley; the second, T.C. O'Brien, C.W. Wright and A.H. Heath. As Fry himself put it: 'two great and four good batsmen.'

G.O., however, was no bowler. Let him take up his story:

'In 1895 I made 76 in the Senior's Match and 131 for the Next Seventeen against the First Thirteen, so I was asked to play against the Gentlemen of England plus Mold. This gave me my first chance, and oddly enough, when I was nervously going in to bat, S.M.J. Young Woods, who had come into the pavilion, on my way out said to me, "Young Fellow, I think you are nervous," to which I replied, "Yes, I am." He then said in his gruff voice, "The two first balls you will get from me will be two full tosses to leg; if you can't hit them both for four I shall bowl you out". Well, I hit them both for four and by nightfall was 57 not out. I played all that season and after making 100 not out v. Kent, was given my Blue. Oddly enough we

lost the match against Cambridge that year, though I think it was about the only match we lost that season'.

In fact they lost two other matches that season; but only the Cambridge defeat damaged their reputation as the best Oxford team for years and, indeed, one of the best of all time. Of the fixture against the Gentlemen of England (with Mold), *Wisden* recorded, 'The Dark Blues ... had the best of the match from the start, and gained a highly creditable victory by six wickets. The Gentlemen's team was powerful in batting, but except for Mold and Woods the bowling was by no means deadly.' yet Arthur Mold - especially while he maintained a Lancashire tradition for that time of 'throwing' - and Woods could be deadly enough for any batsman, be he undergraduate or professional. In the end Mold was no-balled nineteen times in one innings for 'throwing,' so he threw and bowled no more.

Before the turn of the century, S.M.J. Woods brought to the West Country, with its rugged zest and humour divorced from the rustic air of Hardy's Wessex or the gentle breezes from Kent and Sussex, the flavours of his Australian boyhood. From this fusion surged the quality of gusto throbbing throughout Victorian life, a quality now withered in the era of Strube's dehydrated 'Little Man.' While still an undergraduate Woods had played for the Australian tourists alongside Spofforth and Turner in 1888; and the force of his breakback, probably built upon beer and lobster breakfasts made him for a time the fastest bowler in the land. With a shorter ball and hard hitting, Woods was as fine an all-rounder as any when such versatility was common in the game. A week before his encounter with G.O. he had bowled the ball which enabled W.G. to complete his hundredth century. Woods himself has said how terribly nervous he was at the time, and one may perhaps be forgiven for thinking that he showed on that occasion a similar sympathy to that he showed to G.O.

G.O.'s reference to his 100 not out v. Kent that earned him his Blue in 1895 must have prompted me to draw his attention to Sir Pelham Warner's recollection of that day which I had come across in his autobiography, *My Cricketing Life.* For the elder statesman of modern cricket there recorded,

'We went to Maidstone to play Kent on the Mote Park, which had not then been levelled, and was on a most pronounced slope, which suited Walter Wright's left arm swingers to a nicety, but we batted very well and won by 215 runs. Fry made 99 in the first innings. We all stayed at Linton Park, with the Cornwallises, and had a most delightful time. There was a dance on the second night, but G.O. Smith, who was not out 8, departed to bed early. He had his reward next day scoring 100 not out, and being given his Blue.'

By way of reply, G.O. commented,

'I remember staying with the Cornwallis' at Linton very well for the 1895 match against Kent, but I fancy went to bed early not so much with the view to making runs the next day, but because I disliked dancing. I remember, too, Jack Mason's great innings in the previous Kent match that year; it was a great performance. G.B. Raikes was in the 1895 side and the first six batsmen were Charles Fry, Plum Warner, H. K. Foster, G.J. Mordaunt, Shrimp Leveson-Gower and F.A. Phillips - a pretty useful opening six. I wish in many ways one could put the clock back, but it is something to be able to recall those days by re-reading the accounts.'

One of those accounts, that of the red *Lillywhite* for 1896, tells us that G.O.'s century took two hours and twenty minutes. This was a quite exceptional rate of scoring by modern standards, on a sloping pitch against Alec Hearne, one of D.V.P. Wright's leg-break predecessors in the Kent team, and Walter Wright and Fred Martin supplying the left-hand medium-paced deliveries. The same annual also records for the previous Kent match that year mentioned by G.O., that 'The most successful run-getter for Oxford was G.O. Smith with 78 and 32,' a fact omitted entirely by G.O. with characteristic modesty. *Wisden,* for 1896, supports G.O.'s recollection: 'This match was an absolute triumph for the Old Winchester boy, J.R. Mason, thanks to

whose exertions Kent gained a brilliant and decisive victory over Oxford University by nine wickets.' Triumph it was indeed, for in the second innings Mason was undefeated for 142 out of 295 scored in just under two hours, and in the match he took seven wickets for 151 runs. This all-round performance was a fine tribute to his splendrous strokes and medium-paced deliveries. Since he was also a brilliant slip fielder, when that position was necessary, Sir Pelham Warner has understandably described him as the greatest all-rounder Kent has had with the exception of Frank Woolley.

An even more versatile all-rounder than Mason, however, G.B. Raikes, completed the Oxford cricket eleven of 1895. Ralkes had been G.O.'s goalkeeping colleague for Oxford, the Corinthians and England, and had shared in the victory of the previous summer. Now he was the last selection by the captain, G.J. Mordaunt, as an all-rounder: nor did he let the side down. The captain himself, too, could do almost everything necessary with a cricket ball, and he had good enough cause to be aware of G.O.'s batting powers. He had captained Wellington School when G.O. and E.H. Bray scored 109 and 94 respectively out of 295 off Wellington's bowling only three summers earlier. His faith was not misplaced, for G.O.'s 51 not out against Cambridge easily became the second highest score in Oxford's first innings total. During this innings the light was so poor from the pitch that Sir Pelham Warner has recalled one could see the gas-jets burning in the bar under the grandstand.

In the second innings G.O. did no better than anyone else in support of H. K. Foster, who gracefully stroked 121 brilliant runs out of the total of 196. Thanks to the fast bowling of Horace Gray, C.E.M. Wilson and W.W. Lowe, the Cambridge centre-forward of that and the following year, the stumps were hit of all the Oxford batsmen except Foster and Raikes, who carried his bat for 23. But *The Times* observed: 'If they had gone forward and hit the bowlers off their length instead of playing back as most of them did, they might have made a bold bid for victory.

OXFORD CRICKET XI – 1896
(*Back, l. to r.*): F.H.E. Cunliffe, J.C. Hartley, P.S. Waddy, G.O. Smith. (*Middle*): H.K. Foster, G.R. Bardswell, H.D.G. Leveson-Gower (Capt.), G.J. Mordaunt, R.P. Lewis. (*Front*): P.F. Warner, C.C. Pilkington.

Such back play, often to short bowling on a fast pitch, has ruined the chances of many a side.' It ruined the chances of Oxford in this game, and Cambridge won by 134 runs.

During the next twelve months we have already seen how G.O.'s fame spread at Belfast, Cardiff, Glasgow and the Queen's Club, Kensington. As a footballer he had a truly international reputation, based upon truly international standards. At cricket he had justified his schoolboy promise for his University. Yet even after the previous summer's success, his place in the Oxford side was far from being assured. As he wrote in the summer of 1942,

'In 1896 I gave up cricket as I had to face Schools, and three-day matches gave one little time for reading. I only played against the Australians in Term time so there was a question whether I should play for Cambridge. However, I luckily made 41 and 85 against the M.C.C. in the match that preceded the 'Varsity match, so was chosen at the last moment.'

That last-minute selection, as had that of Lord George Scott for Oxford and Eustace Crawley for Cambridge of nine years earlier, became a triumph. H.D.G. Leveson-Gower, the Oxford captain who made the choice, has related that he had practically resolved to play G.B. Raikes when an inspection of the wicket indicated that G.O., the better bat of the two, would be a sounder investment. As he wrote in *Wisden* for 1937, 'Experience has taught me that you can never have too much batting in a 'Varsity match. I took the risk of going into the field against a powerful Cambridge batting side with only four bowlers. It meant that I should have to work these extremely hard. F.H.E. Cunliffe and J.C. Hartley, my two chief bowlers, sent down no fewer than 88 and 92 overs in the match respectively. The last choice won the match by a superb 132, when we were set 330 runs to win.'

About the time that Leveson-Gower was making up his mind, 'Pa' Jackson was waiting outside the Pavilion at Lord's until G.O. and Raikes came out in order to learn who had been selected. As they approached, he could see that Raikes was all smiles while G.O. looked somewhat dejected, so naturally enough, in Jackson's own words, 'I assumed that the latter had not been chosen. I was wrong, however, and the fact was, I believe, that Raikes was the most pleased of the two that his friend had got his Blue, while Smith was correspondingly sorrowful at Raikes having missed his. This was true friendship indeed.' Such a tale need not be cynically dismissed as a relic of Victorian sent-imentality when one recalls the decision of B.H. Travers on the eve of the 1947 Varsity match to stand down from the Oxford side because he thought himself not sufficiently prepared for the game. Even in the present era of cut-throat competition pure sportsmanship has not become entirely the prerogative of earlier generations.

The Lord's Cricket Ground to which G.O. came in 1896 differed somewhat from the Lord's of to-day. Of the modern estate, only the pavilion then existed, and the low flat roof of 'A' Block, which now lies between the Press Box and the grandstand surmounted by Father Time, ran all the way round to the present uncovered stands at the Nursery end. The packed pavilion recalled the opening day of the first Test Match against the Australians under the captaincy of G.H.S. Trott, ten days earlier. The clergy thrived amongst the most interested attenders; during the luncheon intervals the picnic parties and strollers sprinkled

gaily on the grass with their top hats, frock coats and tossing waves of lace and tulle, and nodding hats and brilliant parasols. At various vantage points suitably chosen for a view of the play, the coaches, landaus and tents were decorated with the female company which was not gliding to and fro upon the promenade and filling the asphalt path around the ground to turn the occasion into a garden party and fashion parade that for many of the near 20,000 present on each day were as great attractions as the cricket itself.

G.O. summarised the 1896 match for me in the following way:

'The 1896 'Varsity match you know all about: Plum Warner's being run out twice, W.G. Grace's pair with his poor father resplendent in his top hat and frock coat looking on, and Frank Mitchell's fatal action in failing to make us follow on. How well I remember Harry Foster's disgust at his running out Plum twice. P.F. Warner never had a ghost of a chance and might have made a host of runs.'

Quite a host were made, though, in the Cambridge first innings. They had begun the week by scoring 509 v. M.C.C. at Lord's in the last fixture before the Varsity match, for which the highest score until then was 388. Winning the toss and batting first on a dull damp Thursday morning brightened by shafts of afternoon sunshine, they totalled 319. The innings had been saved from collapse by C.J. Burnup, England's outside right alongside G.O. v. Scotland in Glasgow three months earlier, with 'a carefully, almost tenderly compiled eighty in three hours and five minutes.'

C.E.M. Wilson, a century-maker in a later year, took even a further hour to construct the same score, and *The Times* struck a note more in keeping with to-day, 'although none the less reflective of a change in scoring values when it recorded on the following morning: 'In these days when good bowling is a lost art among amateurs, it is remarkable that on a perfectly true pitch at Lord's yesterday, the Cambridge eleven with all the advantage of first innings averaged ONLY 58 runs an hour.'

Not a little of that rate of scoring, however, was due to the supreme excellence of the Oxford fielding, clearly then not a lost art, at least among amateurs. Inspired by their captain at cover-point, they practised to perfection in the presence of W. G. his golden maxim, a run saved is a run made. Mordaunt's picking up on the run and quick returns from third man and in the long field were a revelation in brilliant ground fielding; and the whole eleven radiated a dash and keenness that amply compensated connoisseurs for the slowness of the scoring. *The Sporting Life* remarked that G.O.'s magnificent fielding alone on that first day justified his selection: he covered so much ground and blocked runs so effectively that another journal observed his hands and chest must have been sore from stopping Wilson's drives that were hard enough to reach the boundary. He jumped up for a nicely judged catch off one of Cunliffe's fast left-handers to send back Druce, who seemed to be settling down as dangerously as he did later in the second innings.

Warner and Foster, opening Oxford's batting for a few minutes on that Thursday evening, just had time to score five runs without scare; and as the curtain came down on the play's first day its pattern had hardly taken shape. 'If only something would happen! That was the universal complaint, especially among the feminine elements of the audience at Lord's yesterday,' observed *The Daily Telegraph* on Friday morning. 'Let us hope they may be gratified when Oxford face the music to-day.' They probably were from about four o'clock onwards, in a manner that nobody expected or really wanted.

When play commenced at noon, Oxford no longer faced the expresses of Gray or Lowe, although Wilson was still at hand: but a far less accurate and more physically dangerous attack came from one whose fame now rests upon other branches of the game, G.L. Jessop. Gilbert Jessop's batting inspired an American poet to call him

'The human catapult,
Who wrecks the roofs of distant towns
When set in his assault.'

In this Varsity match the victims of his wreckage were those assaulted by the balls catapulted from his hands. Perhaps he sought solace for the disappointment of the crowd as well as himself for having joined Grace junior in contracting duck's disease. Whatever was the reason, the man who became cricket's most famous and scientific hitter, and one of its finest coverpoints, distinguished neither friend nor foe in bowling short of a length. His own wicket-keeper, as well as the Oxford captain, painfully felt his force, and *The Times* passed judgment in a leading article. He broke Mordaunt's leg stump in two pieces: confused Warner to call for a run that was not there - and was doubtless ready to add England's centre-forward to his scalps as G.O. approached the wicket. But two wickets down for 44 runs with nearly two days left for play was even simpler than being 0-2 down at half-time in that 1893 Varsity soccer match, a deficit which had not deterred G.O. and his colleagues from winning by 3-2. So he promptly hit jessop for 'two spanking' fours, as *The Sportsman* put it, and the fight was on.

Foster was clean bowled by Wilson with a grand ball, presumably straight, unaffected by seam or swerve: Jessop yorked Pilkington, Eton's captain of the previous year; and Leveson-Gower came out to join his last-minute selection with four of the best wickets down for 64.

Taking a leaf from G.O.'s book, the captain hit Jessop at once for four. In his next over from that end he took a ball with his arm that bounced on to the wicket-keeper's forehead; the following delivery dropped short and hit the wicket-keeper on the mouth: then Leveson-Gower was hit and doubled up, dropping to the ground 'and there lay in the form of a Z for the moment.' More than one journal commented that the bowler was not removed or protested against; and *The Sportsman* *tells* us, 'the demon bowler, as perky as ever, for a time went on with stubborn determination.' So did the batsmen. The sun peeped through and in fifty minutes 48 was added to the total. Then G.O. failed to get right over one from Wilson which he had meant to drive, and was caught at the wicket for 37 by E.H. Bray, his successor to the

Charterhouse captaincy. He had played just the innings the time required: stubborn defence blended with some fine hitting; he was the first batsman to take the sting out of the Cambridge bowling, and once more justified selection.

The score was then 110 for 5. Leveson-Gower stayed to make 26. Yet of the first eight batsmen, G.O.'s total was the highest. The seventh wicket fell at 132 when Bardswell was caught in time for lunch. Directly after the interval, with only one more run added, the eighth wicket fell, and Oxford's bowling hopes now came together as Cunliffe joined Hartley. Twenty years later Colonel Hartley won the D.S.O., and Major Sir Hugh Foster Cunliffe, 6th Bart., died of wounds received at the Battle of the Somme. So did the last man, R.P. Lewis, the wicket-keeper. On this occasion Cambridge felt the essence of their qualities. From five-to-three till a quarter-to-four Cunliffe and Hartley manoeuvred the stroke for the better bat, Hartley, to reach top score with 43, while the partnership added 55. Then a brilliant catch by Marriott off Wilson at 'good old-fashioned point' sent back Hartley and left Oxford within distance of saving the follow-on, at that time based upon a margin of 120 between the innings. If the last Oxford wicket could not add 12 more runs they would accordingly follow on their meagre total directly with a second innings, cause the Cambridge bowlers and fieldsmen to continue their labours uninterrupted till the end of the day's play and then bat last on a possibly crumbling wicket during Saturday.

Unlike to-day, no discretion then vetsted in the captain of the fielding side to enforce or waive the follow-on rule at his option. If Oxford got the runs Cambridge would certainly have to bat again. The odds, however, hardly favoured this. Lewis, the last man and a capital wicket-keeper, had earned *Lillywhite's praise:* 'as a bat backs up well.' Cunliffe had spent two hours on his 10 runs, and the follow-on seemed even more certain than a Cambridge victory at that stage. But as *The Sportsman* put it: 'the Light Blues did not covet the worse than barren distinction that seemed likely to be theirs. To guard against it - or with singular

good luck - Shine, starting an over, sent a ball on the leg-side which counted for four byes, then he was no-balled for four, and for four more the next delivery. The fourth ball of this remarkable over went for two leg-byes and the fifth brought down Cunliffe's wicket. It was laughable. A few censors in the crowd cried, "Play cricket," and some hissed. That was what the Cantabs were playing. They thought a dozen runs not too high a price to pay for the privilege of going in next.' That events did not plan out as doubtless had been conceived was another matter. Yet the action caused a sensation and subsequently an alteration in the laws of the game.

Directly the tactic was realised, 'The crowd hooted,' as *The Times* records, 'and ... disrespectful noises were heard in the Pavilion.' That newspaper's columns subsequently carried a long correspondence on the subject; and in the words of E.R. Wilson, himself a Blue, the brother of the Cambridge allrounder in this game: 'Cantab was divided against Cantab and brother against brother.' Exactly the same position had arisen in the Varsity match of three years earlier, when another Yorkshire captain of Cambridge, F.S. Jackson, ordered similar tactics. Runs were given away and Cambridge won the match. The M.C.C. nibbled at the problem by increasing from 80 to 120 the number of runs requiring the follow-on. It was clear that this was no decisive answer: a repeat would occur whenever keenness to win revived it; and the Cambridge captain, Frank Mitchell, with typical Yorkshire daring, did so. The rule, of course, and not Mitchell, was at fault; and after England through being compelled to apply the compulsory follow-on failed to beat Australia three years later at Old Trafford through being compelled to apply the compulsory follow-on rule, a reform of 1900 introduced the present law. Even at cricket, therefore, the law always chases, but never overtakes public opinion.

If it all looks like a storm in a tea-cup to-day, at the time the tempests were more in keeping with the feelings of the Home Rule controversy, then regularly flaring up outside, or the bodyline nightmare nearly forty years later. *Wisden* devoted half its report to the incident, and when the Light Blues came off the field after the twelve runs were gained and the Oxford innings closed, they were undoubtedly unnerved by the hostility of their reception. Sir Pelham Warner has told us, in *Lord's, 1787-1945,* that 'when Oxford took the field they were greeted with loud prolonged cheering,' and, in *My Cricketing Life,* that 'there can be no doubt that one or two of the early Cambridge batsmen were upset by the hoots with which they were followed to the wicket in the second innings.'

With the last ball of his first over from the Pavilion end Cunliffe bowled W.G. Grace junior for a duck - and poor Grace had bagged a 'pairs in the presence of his famous father and family. *The Sporting Life* gently remarked: 'If, however, it is any consolation for him to know, we can assure him that he had the sympathy of the fair sex almost to a woman.' H.H. Marriott, the next batsman, was barely more successful. After a single he too was bowled by Cunliffe, who was now making full use of the slight hill at Lord's as the ball followed the swing of his left arm; and with Hartley pitching his right-hand slows, which broke both ways, with deadly accuracy at the other end, six wickets tumbled for 61 runs. Here was the turning-point of the game. Did they but know it, Cunliffe and Hartley in this wonderful hour of sustained accuracy, again backed up by phenomenal fielding, had destroyed all the advantage Cambridge had gained from their exceptional and, as events proved, justifiable tactics. Charterhouse once more came to the rescue, though only temporarily this time, when Bray joined his captain, Druce, who alone could score with any confidence. With the strokes expected in the Varsity match, Druce hit 72 out of 154 before playing Waddy straight to mid-off. Then the heavens opened and nature aided the work of man. For the rain and the wicket now conspired to prepare as thrilling a finish as any sporting event can stage. As G.O. wrote,

'The wicket, I allow, looked like getting worse, but there was slight rain on the Friday night and it rolled out perfectly on the Saturday. The wicket at Lord's was inclined to bump a bit, but the rain that

fell on Friday night was just sufficient to take the sting out of it, and it was an easy wicket, even Jessop being unable to make the ball kick.'

Equally unable were the Oxford bowlers. Bray spoilt their averages by hitting them all over the field. He took his own score to 41, the second highest to Druce, and set the Oxford sights for 330 - a total never previously reached in the fourth innings of a Varsity match.

Oxford must have started their quest as did Pegasus in their attempt to rekindle for the nation the spirit of the Corinthians more in hope than expectation of the ultimate triumphs. They also reflected the Pegasus pattern by conceding early advantage before striving on to victory. So Oxford lost their first two wickets just as they had in their previous innings. Warner was run out and Jessop bowled Mordaunt, though without breaking a stuump this time. Once more, however, the virtues of all-round play were to be seen, for *The Morning Post* wrote of Jessop and Wilson, 'the two fast bowlers, fresh and hopeful, did their very best, and were so well backed up in the field that run-getting was by no means an easy matter.' But now, to use the modern phrase, G.O.'s 'big-match temperament' in the international soccer arena overcame any nerves the occasion may have jangled: and all his schoolboy promise was consummated by what proved to be altogether his *piece de resistance* and his swansong in first-class cricket.

Two wickets had gone for 55. Foster was easily caught off one of Cobbold's leg-breaks at 60. With Oxford still wanting 270 to win and seven wickets to fall, a handsome victory for Cambridge seemed to be the more probable finish to the game. At this point, C.C. Pilkington joined G.O.; and the partnership of these batsmen made victory for Oxford just seem possible.

Let G.O. himself sketch in the setting for the last scene of the third day's play.

'Cambridge were not out until after 12 on the Saturday morning and we did not start our last

59

innings until 12.30. Foster, Mordaunt and Warner were all out for 60 runs and the score at lunch was 98 for 3 (Pilkington and I being the not outs). I had then made 13. The only other incident I recall was that at lunchtime an enthusiastic Old Carthusian and Oxonian offered me £1 for every run I made over 100. He little dreamt he might be let in for £32, but the offer did not materialise.'

Something else, however, did materialise for Cambridge. Refreshed from luncheon, G.O. paid the same respect for Jessop's short balls that, in the evening's play at the Lyceum after the day's play at Lord's, another Old Carthusian, Cyril Maude, as Sir Benjamin Backbite, and Mrs Patrick Campbell, as Lady Teazle, showed for their neighbours in Sheridan's comedy The School for Scandal. Jessop was punched out of his stride by lovely cover drives from G. O. as swift and timed along the ground as his passes always were to the wings; and drawing his slender body up to its full height, he sent any ball short of a good length scudding away to the on-side boundary.

When he had scored 32, G.O. gave a very sharp one-handed chance, low down in the slips , to H.H. Marriott; but this was the only mistake observed by contemporary reports in an otherwise chanceless innings. With some beautiful cricket that produced a stand of 84 runs for the fourth wicket in about an hour and a quarter the partnership checked the onslaught of the Cambridge attack. Then Pilkington was caught and bowled by Jessop for 44; 60 for 3 had now become 144 for 4. Less than 250 were now required with six wickets left.

'Through an atmosphere of hope tempered with unbelief, our captain walked to the wicket,' wrote Cunliffe in *Fifty Years of Sport*. When he walked away from it a hundred minutes later, caught by Bray for 41 after the keenest cricket of the day, he and G.O. had added 97 runs. With only five wickets left, 89 were still required. 'Any little accident might have turned the scale in Cambridge's favour,' wrote *Wisden of* this stage. But Bardswell, next man in, had an Uppingham reputation to regain after scoring only 9 runs in the first innings, G.O. was in full cry, and the Light

Blues were on the retreat. Oxford could actually win, and Cambridge knew it.

Mitchell marshalled all his talent, and ground every ounce of bowling from it to stem the advancing total. Burnup, Druce, himself, all batsmen rather than bowlers, were tried as well as Jessop, Wilson, Shine and Cobbold. But fast balls, slow balls, high balls, low balls - all came alike to England's centre forward. With Bardswell at the other end, the counter-attack swept all before it. Now the cuts were flicked away as smoothly as the hits to leg. Two drives off Shine in one over whisked the total up to 300. Of the 89 required, 87 were scored in less than an hour; and then came disaster. With the atmosphere un-bearably tense, G.O. jumped out in his excitement to drive Cobbold for the winning hit; he just touched the ball, and was easily caught by Mitchell in the Slips.

As G.O. came in from the wicket the most famous Pavilion in the world accorded him the distinction that only the very few, such as Bradman and Hammond, have known in our time, of the members rising and taking off their hats to the incoming batsman. The game, however, was not over. Two runs were still required, Cobden's immortal hat-trick was still in memory and *The Sporting Life* observed, 'Those who had noticed Waddy's wild excitement at the top of the Pavilion as the score rose and his side's success became certain, had some fears for his steadiness as he walked to the wickets, and perhaps it was well, that not much was required of him.'

He scored a single, and Bardswell made the winning hit. 'Then the storm of popular enthusiasm broke in downright earnest,' relates *The DailyTelegraph*. 'As if by magic the whole of the ring dissolved and melted into one swarm of shouting, cheering, jostling partisans who rushed to the Pavilion after the departing cricketers and loudly called for "Smith" and "Leveson-Gower." It was a wonderful scene, coming at the close of an extremely remark-able match.'

Extremely remarkable was just about the correct description chosen. For if ever a match had everything that goes to make up cricket, this was it. Not only was there G.O.'s truly heroic innings with the story-book ending. There was the pathetic failure of W.G. Grace junior with whom *The Morning Post* commiserated: 'But for the failure of a usually sure pair of hands those of Mr Trott, the present Australian captain - the same fate would have befallen his great father in the England and Australia match at the Oval six years ago and then the whole country would have mourned.' There was the sensational action on the field which caused the change in the laws; superb fielding which saved countless runs and supported splendid bowling: subtle nuances in the weather and the wicket - suppose it had not rained on the Friday night? - and above all else, the razorkeen desire to win, not at all costs, but cleanly and fairly, within the laws and spirit of the game. As the popular *Daily Mail* told its readers for the price of a half-penny on Monday morning: 'It was magnificent, and it was cricket. There was no bad fielding on the Cambridge side, no breakdown of the bowling, no loss of spirit in the attack. Nor was there any rash and lucky batting to help Oxford to a dubious victory. By correct and resolute cricket the Oxford batsmen gradually wiped off the balance against them. ' Yet the triumph of one man in the game was also the triumph of eleven men. For if a single feature transcended the whole play, it was that Oxford, in Leveson-Gower's words, 'had precious little bowling,' and conventional fielding would have

given them no chance; 'the game was won by the work of the eleven in combination.' The *Morning Post* echoed these, words: 'It is a long time since two such fine fielding sides have been sent up from the Universities'., and *Cricket: A Weekly Record of the Game* noted: 'In ordinary years Burnup, Wilson and Druce would all have easily made their hundred, but so many hits, which were well worth four, were made into singles by extraordinary cleverness on the part of the field.'

On G.O., *The Morning Post* concluded: 'With his innings of 132 Mr G.O. Smith takes a far higher position in the cricket world than he has ever held before. On his general record at Oxford he cannot be classed among the great batsmen who have appeared in the University match, but,it is perfectly safe to say that no one on a big occasion could have played with finer judgment. Watchful and patient to a degree while the Cambridge bowling had to be worn down, he hit out with splendid power as soon as victory was fairly in sight.' Yet the last words on G.O.'s Varsity cricket and his four glorious hours are, most appropriately, those of the player in the match who gained the highest cricketing honours, Sir Pelham Warner. For, in his *Lord's 1787-1945, he* wrote:

'As long as there is a history of Oxford and Cambridge cricket the name of G.O. Smith will be emblazoned on its rolls. 'The full scores were:

CAMBRIDGE

First Innings			Second Innings	
C.J.Burnup, c Mordaunt, b Hartley	80		c and b Hartley	11
W.G.Grace, jun., b Hartley	0		b Cunliffe	0
H.H.Marriott, c Warner, b Hartley	16		b Cunliffe	1
N.F.Druce, c Smith, b Cunliffe	14		c Pilkington, b Waddy	72
C.E.M.Wilson, c Cunliffe, b Hartley	80		st Lewis, b Hartley	2
W.McG. Hemingway, c and b Hartley	26		b Cunliffe	12
F.Mitchell, c Leveson-Gower, b Hartley	26		b Cunliffe	4
G.L. Jessop, c Mordaunt, b Hartley	0		st Lewis, b Hartley	19
E.H. Bray, c Pilkington, b Cunliffe	49		c Lewis, b Waddy	41
P.W. Cobbold, b Hartley	10		not out	23
E.B. Shine, not out	10		c Hartley, b Waddy	16
B 4, lb 1, w 2, nb 1	8		B 5, w 1, nb 5	11
Total	319		Total	212

BOWLING ANALYSIS

	First Innings				Second Innings			
	0.	M.	R.	W.	0.	M.	R.	W.
Cunliffe	55	25	87	2	33	11	93	4
Hartley	59.5	I 3	161	8	30	3	78	3
Waddy	24	10	35	0	11.3	3	28	3
Pilkington	29	19	24	0	3	1	2	0
Leveson-Gower	2	0	4	0				

Cunliffe 5 no-balls, Leveson-Gower and Waddy l wide each, Hartley 1 wide and 1 no-ball.

OXFORD

First Innings		*Second Innings*	
P.F. Warner, run out	10	run out	17
G.J. Mordaunt, b Jessop	26	b Jessop	9
H.K. Foster, b Wilson	11	c and b Cobbold	34
G.O. Smith, c Bray, b Wilson	37	c Mitchell, b Cobbold	132
C.C. Pilkington, b Jessop	4	c and b Jessop	44
H.D.G. Leveson-Gower, b Jessop	26	c Bray, b Shine	41
G.R. Bardswell, c and b Cobbold	9	not out	33
P.S. Waddy, st Bray, b Cobbold	0	not out	1
J.C. Hartley, c Marriott, b Wilson	43		
F,H.E. Cunliffe, b Shine	12		
R.P. Lewis, not out	0		
B 12, lb 4, nb 8	24	B 6, lb 6, w 6, nb 1	19
Total	202	Total (for 6 wickets)	330

BOWLING ANALYSIS

	First Innings				Second Innings			
	0.	M.	R.	W.	0.	M.	R.	W.
Jessop .	37	15	75	3	30	8	98	2
Wilson	37	19	48	3	42	20	50	0
Shine	12.3	4	29	1	20	9	41	1
Cobbold	11	2	26	2	44.4	7	96	2
Burnup					2	0	3	0
Druce .					7	2	I I	0
Mitchell					2	1	12	0

Shine 8 no-balls, Cobbold 1 no-ball and 3 wides, Burnup 2 wides, Mitchell 1 wide.

'After the 'Varsity match [as G.O. Smith wrote to me], I played a few matches for Surrey, but with no success and as I knew I could not play serious cricket after that year I refused to go on with the County. Arthur Dunn had asked W.J. Oakley and myself to join him at Ludgrove and that meant no serious cricket in the future, though both Oakley and myself played football until Arthur Dunn's death.'

Nevertheless, when Leveson-Gower was told of G.O.'s death in 1943 he recalled in the 1944 edition of *Wisden* that 'Joe' was a good bat and 'I persuaded him to play against the Australians for Surrey at the Oval. Always modest, 'G.O. said, "I'm not good enough, I'll make two noughts," and sure enough he did.' He was hardly more successful in the innings he played for the County against Middlesex and Kent in that year. At a less exacting level, however, he did appear subsequently on a few occasions for Hertfordshire in the Minor Counties Competition, and made numerous runs for the Charterhouse Friars right up to the beginning of the First World War.

Yet his cricket career virtually ended at Lord's with his Varsity match successes. It is idle to speculate how far he might have travelled in rivalling R.E. Foster, who played for Oxford in three of the next four Varsity soccer and cricket matches and hit a century in his last: then went on to gain alongside G.O. several of his five full international soccer caps before setting up, in 1903, the record score of 287 for an Englishman in Australia, a record that has remained unbroken.

R.E.Forster

Certainly G.O.'s university record was in keeping with his schoolboy promise. In his four Oxford innings which included his 51 not out in 1895, G.O. had scored 222 runs with an average of 74. This was not surpassed for the Varsity match until R.W.V. Robins averaged 77.75 between 1926 and 1928, and the Nawab of Pataudi went even better with 91.40 over the period from 1928-30.

One of G.O.'s Oxford soccer colleagues, Sir E. Farquhar Buzzard, an eminent neurologist, wrote a memoir on G.O. in *The Carthusian:* 'Both as a boy and a man, G.O. was distinguished for his modesty and perhaps handicapped to a slight extent by his diffidence and shyness. It was unwise, however, for an opposing bowler to allow G.O. to overcome his nervousness at the beginning of an innings at cricket because the latter did not take very long to gain his self-confidence and, having done so, he was most difficult to dislodge and could be relied on to make runs at a very creditable pace.'

Another basis for that creditable pace can be seen in Herbert Strudwick's *Twenty-five Years Behind the Stumps.* The great Surrey and England wicket-keeper records there that only one man was faster between the wickets than Albert Knight of Leicestershire, 'and that was G.O. Smith, who occasionally turned out for London County.' Anyone who could gain such an opinion clearly enjoyed his cricket, and G.O. certainly did, as some of his letters to me have indicated. Indeed, R.C. Robertson Glasgow has told us that he had the pleasure of meeting G.O. more than once, and in his last years when living in the New Forest it was of cricket that he talked most.

On those London County occasions in between international soccer matches at the Crystal Palace, G.O. would have frequently come across the *only* sportsman besides himself known to the public by initials alone, W.G. Grace. After his withdrawal from the Gloucestershire side W.G. formed and captained the short-lived London County Cricket Club whose ground adjoined the soccer arena at the Crystal Palace; and in confirming that the champion did not see his own achievement in the Varsity match, G.O. expanded in the following way:

'I don't think W.G. was present in the 1896 Varsity Match on the Saturday: his own son bagged his brace on Friday evening and I think that finished his interest in the game. However I was lucky enough to know him well as I saw him often at the Crystal Palace when we played Corinthian matches there and he was generally present as he was the manager and captain of the London County Side. Incidentally, I missed him in the deep on my first appearance at Lord's for Oxford v. M.C.C. I have always been a great admirer of W.G., not only as the greatest of cricketers but in many other ways besides. He was a rough diamond, perhaps, but the diamond predominated and for those who knew him well he was a jovial, kindly friend.'

Although he shares with W.G. that unique recognition by initials alone, there could be no question of roughness in G.O.'s manner and appearance. W.G., a huge bear of a man, first impressed my mind when at school I pictured him - a biblical figure re-incarnated in cricketers' clothing, as removed from the twentieth century as was his kindred spirit of the eighteenth, Dr Johnson, remote from his own. G.O., on the other hand, standing barely five feet ten inches, lean and clean shaven when the faces of many of his contemporaries were hirsute to excess, had the manner and appearance of our own mid-twentieth century world.

G.O. added to his university sporting attainments a thirdclass Honours degree in the History School. Even more than this might have been achieved at another college, for the rule of 'The New Foundation,' Keble, created in only 1870, was in its early days supposed to be 'plain living and high thinking.' At that period, 'the *living,*' suggested one of Oxford's most distinguished historians, Sir John Marriott, 'was certainly cheap and plain; the *thinking,* if high, was certainly not conspicuously reflected by university distinctions.'

Armed, therefore, with his B.A., double Blues and international soccer caps, G.O. went down suitably equipped to join the staff of Ludgrove, a preparatory school barely four years old. He never married, and there his reputation grew until to-day he is still regarded as the greatest centre-forward in the history of Association football. There also he played his part in the growth of the school to its present stature as one of the outstanding preparatory schools in the nation's educational framework.

WITH ARTHUR DUNN AND LUDGROVE

Ludgrove School was founded in 1892 by Arthur Dunn at Cockfosters, near Barnet in Hertfordshire, with one pupil. When Dunn died there suddenly of a heart attack ten years later at the tragically early age of 41, the list of vacancies was full for almost another ten years. Within that short span he and his colleagues had built Ludgrove into one of the main preparatory establishments for his old school, Eton College. For the next thirty years after Dunn's death, firstly G.O. and W.J. Oakley together, and then G.O. alone, carried on the head-mastership. One suspects that it was of G.O. whom Sir Osbert Sitwell was thinking when he wrote that what finally converted both of his parents to Ludgrove as a preparatory school was 'the discovery that the headmaster was the most famous dribbler in England.'

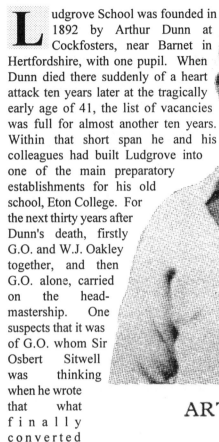

ARTHUR DUNN

County - Yorkshire - cricket sides, which included such characters as George Macaulay, Emmott Robinson and Percy Holmes. Barber followed W.J. Oakley on to the staff at Ludgrove after Shrewsbury and Oxford, and since the 1930s he has carried on his predecessors' tradition of wearing Corinthian colours while continuing with his staff to supply Eton and other schools with scholars and athletes.

About the time I was corresponding with G.O. I must have come across the writings of Sir Shane Leslie, for in June, 1942, G.O. wrote:

'When I went to Ludgrove in 1896 to join Arthur Dunn, Shane Leslie was top of the Third Division, which I taught. I therefore knew him well and have read *Men Were Different* and also *A File of Memory,* which is good, though it might not appeal to everyone.'

To-day, Cockfosters is mainly known as the northern terminus for the Piccadilly line of London's underground railway; yet its residents still recall the school run by Association footballers for entrants to the most famous and fashionable public school in the world. But evacuation, as at many lesser and greater schools, stepped into life at Ludgrove; and it never returned from its war-time home at Wokingham. There it thrives now, under the headmastership of A.T. Barber, who, in the late 1920s,' captained the Oxford University soccer and cricket elevens before leading his

In a book not mentioned by G.O., however, *The End of a Chapter,* published during the First World War, Sir Shane Leslie throws an interesting sidelight on Ludgrove as seen through the eyes of a pupil. 'I went to Ludgrove, one of a score of private schools preparing for Eton. It was under Arthur Dunn, captain of the English eleven. He was assisted by a staff of gentlemen athletes ' who posed for the illustrations of the *Badminton Book of Football.* There was no suspicion of pedagogue among them, and they became the subjects of our sincere hero worship. They included "Joe" Smith, another of England's captains, who saved Oxford from defeat in the most famous of cricket encounters with Cambridge. Arthur Dunn taught us to play football as honourably as the game of life, to recite the Kings of Judah and Israel, to love God and to hate Harrow. He died in his prime as the result of football strain - a bright and lovable memory touching "muscular christianity" at its highest.'

Clearly Arthur Dunn was a remarkable man. His daughter, the Hon. Mrs Andrew Shirley, has told us that after Ludgrove and sport two other great enthusiasms existed in his life: music and Eton; and his passion for music was doubtless the reason for Cecil Sharp becoming music-master at the school during his attempts to revive English folk-songs and dancing.

Dunn was on the short side, but, as the late F.B. Wilson recorded in *Sporting Pie,* he was also 'desperately quick, wonderfully strong and certain on his feet, and a wonderful dribbler. He was at his very best on treacherous ground and the worse the soup the more easily he slipped over the top of it.' Barely a year after obtaining an F.A. Cup winner's medal with the Old Etonians against Blackburn Rovers he was one of England's two centre-forwards - in accordance with the team formation of those days - against Ireland in 1883 and 1884. With the eclipse of the amateurs from the F.A. Cup, Dunn disappeared from England's team until 1892. Recalled in March of that year to captain the side - a mixture of amateurs and professionals - he played at left-back and England beat Wales by 2-0 at Wrexham. A month later he was the sole amateur survivor of that team in the otherwise professional England side which played Scotland in Glasgow, and was again captain from the left-back position, Dunn's team against Scotland, labelled the 'Old Crocks' by Scottish journalists, were inspired to a display of forward combination such as james Catton, writing in the mid- 1920s, had never seen equalled. Within ten seconds England were a goal up - surely the quickest goal ever scored in a home international. From the kick-off by John Southworth of Blackburn Rovers, Goodall slipped the ball to his

partner, William Isiah Bassett, king of nineteenth-century outside-rights, on the right-wing. The return pass came into the left, and Everton's Edgar Chadwick, running on to it, dribbled round the veteran Walter Arnott at right-back to finish a perfect movement. Three more goals came within the next quarter of an hour. Scotland never replied, and with Dennis Hodgetts from Aston Villa on England's left-wing, the five professional forwards and their colleagues left their amateur captain with as bright a football memory of his international days as his contemporaries had of him.

As G.O. commented in a later letter:

'"The Country Vicar," oddly enough, wrote to me some weeks ago and asked me about Arthur Dunn. He couldn't believe that he played back and forward against Scotland, but I put him right about that. Certainly a unique achievement and one that will never, I imagine, be equalled.'

Certainly the achievement has never been equalled for England, although Jack Froggatt in our own time has come near to doing so. After appearing for England at outside-left, he returned to the national colours as an attacking centre-half, one of the very few seen since the 1930s. Johnny Carey of Manchester United, however, easily surpassed this, for he played for Eire in no less than seven positions, from centre forward to full-back!

It hardly comes as a surprise, in view of Dunn's football versatility, to learn that as a cricketer he was ambidextrous and bowled right- and left-handed almost equally well. Nearly ten years after his remarkable come-back Arthur Dunn died in the night of 19th February, 1902. He will always be remembered, in the words of 'Pa' Jackson, not only 'as a perfect footballer, but also as a perfect man.'

Of his death G.O. wrote to me forty years later:

'That is why Oakley and I gave up international football at that time. We were called upon to take up Arthur Dunn's work at Ludgrove suddenly and could not get away on Saturdays, so really serious football became a thing of the past. I think we might have gone on for some years, as we were neither of us thirty years old, but I dare say that it was better to retire than to be shelved.'

G.O. and Oakley were no doubt lucky to be in a position that allowed so philosophic an approach to selecting their time for retirement. The professional who chooses to earn his living at a game can never approach the problem of retiring from the detached viewpoint of these two schoolmaster internationals. For the sad picture of the professional footballer who is obliged to overstay his playing time in the game is all too common.

Only from international sides, however, did G.O. and Oakley withdraw their support. Both continued their predecessor's practice of taking a team to Eton to play the Field Game, Dunn's old school's exclusive brand of football rooted in the dribbling code; both went on playing when they could for the Corinthians and their respective Old Boys' clubs in the Arthur Dunn Cup Competition. In the first Final of 1902 the Old Carthusians and Old Salopians shared the trophy jointly, the cricket season preventing the continuation of two drawn games. Then the Old Carthusians, as may have been expected, went on to win it for the next three.

The trophy was presented a month after Dunn died, by R.C. Gosling, with the simple inscription, "'In Memoriam." The Arthur Dunn Challenge Cup.' Since then most of the leading Corinthians have appeared in the competition and amongst the finalists, and since the Second World War Pegasus players such as Pawson and Doggart (Old Wykehamists), Shearwood (Old Salopians), Tanner (Old Carthusians) and Carr (Old Reptonians) have done so, too. Indeed, Pawson played in the 1953 Dunn Final only a week before helping Pegasus to their second F.A. Amateur Cup triumph at Wembley.

Shortly before he died, Dunn himself had advocated the formation of an 'Old Boys' association, but never lived to pursue the idea. How far he would have approved the limitations which the competition's rules now place upon the number of entrants must always remain a matter of conjecture. The proposals that were made as the competition approached its jubilee in 1952 for widening the scope were received with disfavour. Yet many of the early names such as Brighton, Felsted, Harrow and Rossall have now dropped out; and *Country Life* was constrained to comment in November of 1952:

'There seems much to be said for the movement to extend the entries for the Arthur Dunn Cup. Those Soccer enthusiasts who are alarmed by the encroachment of the Rugby game on their preserves among the public schools should certainly be in favour of it. At present the number of competing schools is confined to sixteen, and it is proposed that it should become thirty-two. This would involve only one more round, and an amount of travelling which should not be prohibitive, especially if, as has been suggested, the first round were played on a zonal basis. The doubling of the number of teams would increase the interest taken in the competition, now somewhat limited; it would be especially welcome to the schools of the north and would be good for the amateur game in general. The original rules referred to "public schools", and that is apt to involve a rather embarrassing question of definition; but it is always possible to confine invitations to the schools represented on the Headmasters' Conference, and to insist too much on any narrower rule is out of keeping with the spirit of the times. The Halford Hewitt Cup for golfing old boys has gained in popularity and friendliness by a generous policy in this respect.'

What G.O. would have thought of this we shall now never know. What we do know is that, despite the eclipse of his class of amateur from the F.A. Cup and international elevens, his sheer ability and charm never allowed him to be 'out of keeping with the spirit of the times.'

The professional footballers of his day, for all their qualities on the field both in England and with Her Majesty's Forces in South Africa, would hardly have drawn from C.B. Fry the compliments he paid to the professional in 1939: 'The modern professional teams, most of them so far as I have seen, have an altogether different mind [from those in the early days of professionalism]. But then they come from a more cultivated class. When the Arsenal players stay at the Grand Hotel at Brighton you would not distinguish between them and the generality of other leisured young men.' In Fry's own day, when the F.A. wanted the leading hotel in Birmingham to accommodate G.O. and the-ten professionals under his command for the international against Scotland in 1899, it had to obtain cast-iron assurances of good behaviour from London before the hotel management would grant their request.

Yet these were the men whom G.O. and Oakley in their years following Oxford would leave their colleagues at Ludgrove to join on Saturday afternoons: slip into an England shirt alongside them, and then return to their hero-worshipping boys. G.O.'s pupils, apart from any who later claimed to have been educated at school during the holidays, were not alone in their admiration. For *Gibson and Pickford* have written of G.O.: 'Hell was beloved of all professional players with whom he came in contact and when he captained English international teams no man found the paid player try harder.'

The selectors, representing mainly professional clubs, first appointed G.O. as captain after the Scottish *debacle* of 1896. and so he remained whenever he played for England except when Wreford Brown returned to centre-half against Scotland in 1898. The reaction of the public was summarised in *The Sportsman* after the choice of players for the first international of the 1897 season, against Ireland: 'No more happy selection could possibly have been made in selecting that brilliant player, G.O. Smith, to play centre-forward and to act as captain. Under his command the side is certain to be kept well in hand.'

It was kept sufficiently well in hand so that all but one of the games in that season (a 1-2 defeat by Scotland) and the next two seasons were won. In the last of those three seasons, 1899, England reached its highest total in an international for the second time against Ireland, winning at Sunderland by 13-2 (the first game of the series between the two countries at Belfast in 1882 having resulted in a 13-0 English win). Not for another fifty years did England's players again reach double figures in a full international, when Lawton, Mortensen, Matthews and Finney piled on ten goals between them against the goalless Portuguese at the sun-drenched Estoril Stadium at Lisbon in 1947. Two hundred miles farther north at Oporto stands a monument in the centre of the city, erected by a public subscription that raised £20,000 to commemorate the local club's 3-2 victory over the Arsenal during the Football League Champions' close-season tour of 1948! It is hardly likely that the Portuguese had heard of football in its modern guise in 1899, to say nothing of Woolwich Arsenal, the Corinthians or G.O. Smith. The Irishmen were not so fortunate. As G.O. wrote to me in 1942 of that occasion:

'I remember the game well as for an international match it was very one-sided. I was lucky enough to get four goals, Settle got three, Bloomer and Frank Forman two each, and Athersmith and Fred Forman one each. The match is perhaps mostly to be remembered by the fact that Bloomer of all people failed to score from a penalty kick.'

If Bloomer, the great Steve Bloomer, could miss a penalty in an international match, modern experts can take comfort when following this one bad example. For Bloomer was the goal getter *par excellence*: and for this reason it does not really matter whether he scored 350 or 450 goals in his career. It is nevertheless worth noting that in the days when first 30 and then 38 League games were played each season he scored officially 352 goals. This remained the record aggregate until Everton's 'Dixie' Dean, in the days of 42 League games per season, passed it in 1937 and ended his career, in 1939, with 379.

More important, however, Bloomer usually got the goal that mattered, and especially against the Scots who feared him more than any other forward except G.O. In ten matches against them he scored eight times. Perhaps it is now an old-fashioned view, but he firmly believed that whether you counted it a good shot or not, there was never a bad shot that scored.

The essence of his genius was refined to this end, usually with low slashing drives or volleys based upon his own precept: heel up, toe down. Since he was a genius it is not surprising that G.O. should write in 1943:

'Bloomer, like McColl of Scotland, was a most brilliant individualist and always worth a place as a magnificent shot, but he was not easy to play with, and personally I would much sooner have played with other inside-rights. However, he was a match-winner if ever there was one.'

He could not win his most coveted prize, however, a winners' medal, in either of the Cup-Finals in which he appeared just before 1900. In one of those Finals - that of 1898 - his Napoleonic features met their Waterloo when another genius, Ernest Needham, the 'Prince of Half-Backs,' turned up for Sheffield United. G.O. was here content to observe laconically:

'The best half-back was Ernest Needham.'

When I replied in 1942 to suggest the claims of Arthur Grimsdell, and from the successful Spurs' sides of the early 1920s, the great predecessor of the recent Wales and Tottenham Hotspur captain, Burgess, G.O. came back:

'I am afraid I can't say anything about Grimsdell as I never saw him play, but it would take a great deal to persuade me that he was the equal of Needham, whom I look upon as the greatest of half-backs, though there were many others who were very good. I played with and against Needham constantly, so I know his worth from both points of view and I can well believe that he could make even a Bloomer innocuous.'

Thus *The Times* reported on the Cup-Final of 1898, 'Where Bloomer would usually have outwitted an average half-back, here was Needham, by his tackling and persistency in never giving up a man,

constantly insisting upon his disclosing his game.' Bloomer's style of play, however, was not unlike that of another pale-faced wizard, Stanley Mortensen, at his electric best, but over less sustained periods than that symbol of perpetual motion. Probably he was most dangerous when showing no apparent interest in the game: then presto! he smelt a chance, chased it, and if his instinct said shoot, he did so, with the results inscribed in the record books. Both Bloomer and his mentor, Johnny Goodall, thought G.O. so easy to play with, and a man without petty pride; and G.O. once told James Catton, 'It was only necessary to say "Steve," and before his name had died on my lips the ball was in the net.'

When Bloomer returned to Britain between the Wars, after being interned at the Kaiser's pleasure and having coached in Canada, he had only one reply to what he thought of English games: the forwards did not shoot enough. What he would have said of the explanation, in *The Football Association Bulletin,* for the failure of the England players in the World Soccer Cup Competition at Rio in 1950 -'unbelievably bad shooting and ... we have lost the art of hitting a ball first time' - is perhaps unprintable. On the other hand, what he would have thought of the Hungarian players at Wembley Stadium in the last months of 1953 would have been most illuminating.

When that record score against Ireland in 1899 was compiled, however, Bloomer does not appear to have had a hand in any of G.O.'s four goals. They all came by way of passes from the wings. Yet this is hardly surprising, for as ever throughout that period G.O. was once more the perfect centre forward, the two wings pivoting with perfect precision and balance around him. As *The Times* put it: 'Of a brilliant front rank G.O. Smith in the centre stood out prominently, once more emphasising the fact that in this position he has no superior in England. His judgment in passing to his wings, whom he kept together admirably, was splendid, while his shooting was hard, low and frequent.' Accordingly the goals were spread among the whole attack.

It meant something, too, to have stood out among those brilliant professional forwards. Aston Villa's W. Charles Athersmith, for example, played a dozen times at outside-right for England between 1892 and 1900, when for a part of that time Billy Bassett of West Bromwich Albion was available for that position: the problem of having a Matthews and a Finney around at the same time is not new. The success of Athersmith lay in his easy combination with any inside partner, Bloomer for England or John Devey with the Villa, as well as his ability to sprint with the ball as neatly as he could without it on the track. He also gained caps against Scotland, Wales and Ireland in the same season as he won Cup and League medals in Villa's wonderful 'Double' year, 1897, a record which may never be equalled. His feat of running down the wing in a mackintosh during a League match, holding an umbrella, may also never be repeated.

On the left-wing Fred Forman, who played with G.O. in all three internationals of the 1899 season, did so with dash and intelligence, but he lacked the spark of greatness which his brother Frank, with his first-time tackling and pin-point kicking, displayed at right- and centre-half for Nottingham Forest and England. The other forward, Jack Settle from Bury, at inside-left, had the joy of scoring three goals - against Ireland in his first international. Shortly afterwards he moved a few miles south-west across the Lancashire hinterland to Everton. There with his shooting - so hard for so small a man - he formed a memorable left-wing partnership with H.P. Hardman, an amateur who played for England's full international side. While with Everton, Settle gained five more caps, and was on winning (v. Newcastle United in 1906) and losing (v. Sheffield Wednesday in 1907) F.A. Cup-Final sides. He also acquired a momentary notoriety at the time of the transfer of his *services* (the essence of the transaction) to Everton, for it was estimated that Everton's fee of £400 was then a record!

Of the other professional players in that record-scoring England team, Hillman, the goalkeeper, went from Burnley to Manchester City and gained a Cup winners' medal in the first all-Lancashire

Final, against Bolton Wanderers in 1904. Phil Bach, the right-back, moved from Sunderland to captain Reading; Williams, West Bromwich Albion's fearless left-back, departed from the game altogether at the age of twenty-four with six caps and the footballer's occupational disease, a displaced cartilage (its removal then being unknown); but the wonderful half-back line of Frank Forman, Needham and Crabtree remained loyal to their clubs throughout their careers while receiving caps in other positions for England. It was for Needham's club, Sheffield United, that Richard Sparling's *Official History,* published after the Second World War, suggests that G.O. and Wreford Brown both offered to play in the last days of the 1897-98 season, when the F.A. Cup came within reach of Bramall Lane. But the directors decided to go through and win with their own staff under the captaincy of Needham. Yet G.O. in one of his letters wrote:

'I don't remember being asked to play for a League side, and certainly would not have done so, as I had not time except for Corinthian and Old Carthusian games.'

That G.O., with his continuous Carthusian and Corinthian associations, could blend so superbly with the northern professionals is all the more remarkable when it is realised that the heat between the professional and amateur administrators, which burst into flames around 1907, was now smouldering with each successive season. The international teams were chosen by a Selection Committee appointed by the F.A. Council consisting of a large majority of representatives of professional districts. 'These gentlemen,' as 'Pa' Jackson wrote in his *Association Football,* 'although undoubtedly selecting the players impartially and to the best of their abilities, see nothing but professional football and are only associated with that form of the game, so that insensibly they favour professionals to the exclusion of amateurs.

'The aggressiveness of the professional element asserted itself in many ways. Not content with almost filling the international teams with professionals, it did all in its power to reduce the one or two amateurs who did play to the level of professionals. All were taken to the same hotel, all were expected to travel together, and all were asked to feed together. Until this year (1898) the amateurs had resisted the last request, but in Glasgow, on the occasion of the match between England and Scotland, the two amateurs, rather than appear to be exclusive, or run the chance of making themselves unpopular with the "pros," consented to lunch with them on the day of the match. One of these gentlemen asked the waiter for some potatoes. "Can't have any," was the reply. "What do you mean?" indignantly asked the amateur. "Mr - (the councillor in charge of the team) has given orders what you may have, and you can't have anything else.'"

As events turned out, it was afterwards explained that these orders had been intended to apply only to professionals. The team, and particularly the two amateurs, who were of course, G.O. and Oakley - Wreford Brown, the captain, was eating with the F.A. officials - so far from allowing such stupidity to upset their game, caused Alcock to record in *The Football Annual* that the Scotsmen, with their full side, 'for once were quite outplayed.' Indeed, certain Scottish critics suggested that for the only time in his career G.O. played with almost too much dash, at times amounting to recklessness. One cannot help wondering whether G.O. was in the same mood as George Gunn, the brilliant Nottinghamshire batsman of the 1920s, at the end of a game against Kent at Trent Bridge. Going in on the last day with all the time in the world to score the necessary runs for victory, Gunn hit the Kent bowlers all over Trent Bridge in double-quick time to win the match. Years afterwards Neville Cardus asked him why he had been so merciless in his treatment of the attack. 'Well, it was like this,' said Gunn, 'as I was going out to bat a Committee member said something rude to me; and the only people I could take it out of were the Kent bowlers. So I did.'

The fashion among professional cricketers, which lasted until 1939, of touching their caps and calling the skipper 'Sir,' prevailed among professional

footballers - or was expected to by 'Pa' Jackson - as long as the Gentlemen held their own with the Players. So he further complained of what was alleged to be a growing discourtesy shown by the professionally prejudiced F.A. to the amateurs at the end of the 1890-91 season, when the selection committee appointed one of the professionals as captain of the English team despite the inclusion in the side of amateurs! Throughout this growing ill-feeling G.O.'s example shone as a shining light on the less tolerant members of the F.A. Council. On the eve of his leading England to victory against Scotland at Birmingham in 1899 *The Sportsman* was writing, 'He forms one of the staff at Mr A.T.B. Dunn's school at Ludgrove, and the boys naturally regard him as a champion of champions. He is deservedly popular among both amateurs and the paid player, very unassuming and is a gentlemanly, generous foe.'

One of G.O.'s more regular professional foes and international colleagues of his early days, John Goodall, was the man who brought out Steve Bloomer. Goodall had played for the famous Preston 'Invincibles' when they had won the Cup and League in the same year, 1888: then he moved to Derby County and appeared in Derby's Cup-Final side of the late nineties. He gained fourteen caps, including eight against Scotland, and until he died during the recent war aged 78 he never hesitated to condemn the speed which has ironed the skill out of the modern game. When he died, Ivan Sharpe recorded: 'He has left a name in Association Football that no player can surpass - he was a pioneer of supreme skill and always his sportsmanship was of the highest standard.' I mentioned his passing to G.O. some months afterwards, and G.O.'s reply contained the following remarks:

'Many thanks for your letter and for the *Athletic News Football Annual. I* must have missed Johnnie Goodall's death in May and I am very sorry to bear the sad news. I played with him and against him on many occasions and he was good enough to dedicate his book on football to me. He was a great player and a great gentleman, and professional football owed him a great debt. I have always been proud to count myself his friend. I cordially agree with his views about all excessive training of modern days and I am sure that the game has greatly deteriorated and that skill and manoeuvres have given place to pace and speed.'

It was speed, too, that eliminated the university amateur entirely from professional football and hence from the public eye. Many of the Pegasus Cup players can hold their own in skill with all but a handful of their professional contemporaries. Pawson proved it when he capped a glorious display at outside-right for Charlton Athletic by scoring the winning goal against the Spurs in a First Division League game on Boxing Day, 1951, at White Hart Lane. Unfortunately the public and press focus their attention on the professional clubs, and the amateur player is submerged except upon Amateur Cup-Final day and sometimes - though all too rarely - when amateur internationals are played.

Even so, in many circles, the professional footballer himself is treated with disdain and disfavour. Boxing, with all its bestiality and boozy betting around the ringside, attracts the aristocracy and the mink coats. The decent clean-living professional footballer and the glorious game he plays are regarded as inferior. Should he don cricket's white garb and save Test Matches for his country he becomes every schoolboy's idol. Yet, as John Arlott, in his *Concerning Soccer* (a worthy book which failed to receive the attention it deserved), has so elegantly put it: 'Football, the craft ... can stir with the graceful, the dramatic and the epic,' - all qualities which are the quintessence of cricket.

Nevertheless the social position of the professional footballer in G.O.'s day may not have been entirely dissimilar from that of to-day. G.O.'s presence,

however, at centre-forward in the England team which recognised him as the greatest player in that position the game had then seen, did much to hold a nice balance between the amateur and the professional in the public eye for the benefit of the game. When he retired from the national side after the death of Arthur Dunn in 1902, that balance had shifted unrecognisably from the position existing when he entered big football barely a decade earlier. During that span of years, however, he had created a new record of twenty-one international appearances and built a reputation, now legendary, as the greatest of all centre-forwards. To what extent that legend has withstood the passing of half a century must now be examined.

Old Etonians defend their goal against Old Salopians in the 1952 Arthur Dunn Cup Final.

(Below) the Arthur Dunn Cup itself, first presented in the 1902/03 season.

(Above) Arthur Dunn's daughter, the Hon. Mrs. Andrew Shirley, hands the cup to G.H.G. Doggart, Captain of the victorious Old Wykehamists, 1950.

CHAPTER VI

THE GREATEST CENTRE-FORWARD?

In an obituary published by *Wisden* for 1944, Hubert Preston, the editor, wrote that G.O. 'earned the description, which lasts to the present time, of being the best centre-forward in the annals of the game.' Were this opinion not endorsed - so frequently by others, such a claim could be dismissed as extravagant. Indeed, a discussion of G.O. in these terms might be criticised as beating the air. Yet in the world of cricket, in some ways so vastly different now from what it was eighty years ago, who does not hazard to compare W.G. with Hobbs or Bradman - the greatest of the old with the greatest of the modern? The point is, of course, that the cricket of W.G., like the football played by G.O., was essentially the same as it is to-day.

Let us begin the evidence. The first witness is David Jack, one of the most famous and fascinating of modern inside forwards, and the son of an equally famous football personality, Robert Jack, at one time manager of Southend United and Plymouth Argyle. David Jack was a member of the great Arsenal side which did

G.O.Smith

more than any other to create and perpetuate the modern third-back game with its headache for modern centre-forwards. He was also the modern professional nearest to the Corinthians in style, rivalled perhaps only by Willie Watson of

Sunderland and Yorkshire, one of the very few 'double' internationals. In his book, *Soccer,* which appeared in 1934, Jack wrote:

'I have been brought up in a football atmosphere, taught to think and play football the whole day and every day, and compelled to listen for hours to the tales of fine old enthusiasts - who glorified the past at the expense of the present. Is it any wonder that I almost came to believe that there would never be another R.S. McColl (Glasgow Rangers, Newcastle United and Scotland), Johnny Goodall (Preston North End, Derby County and England), G.O. Smith (Corinthians and England) - and many other centre forewards whose names are inscribed in the book of fame? ... They were wonderful footballers no doubt, or otherwise their names would be forgotten, but they were playing at a time when defensive tactics - as we now see them - were unheard of, or at any rate, comparatively lax, combination was carried out more methodically, and individualism was encouraged. It would be absurd to suggest that a rejuvenated G.O. Smith, artistic footballer and prolific goal-scoring centre, would not be a shining light in the modern game, but it is not ridiculous to say that he would find it well-nigh 'Impossible to weave his way past defender after defender as reports credit him with doing so regularly in the good old days.'

74

Perhaps, like most leading witnesses, Jack has said too much. For, was the defensive position so very different in G.O.'s time? We have seen already how, in the 1880s, Wreford Brown had been shadowing the pro (W.B.A.) centre-forward excellently. Further, there has been handed down to us the story of G.O.'s famous amateur rival, R.S. McColl, whom Jack mentions. Finding himself opposed to a very attentive centre-half in an important game in Scotland, McColl enquired of his burly shadow why he did not occasionally leave him alone and 'play some football.' Back came the reply: 'I'm not here to play fitba'. I'm here to see that you don't play fitba'.'

It is a common fallacy to suppose that the ideas pervading defensive strategy to-day were unknown in G.O.'s time. Certainly there was one practical difference in tactics. Near their own goal the full-backs usually marked the inside-forwards while the wing-halves usually marked the outside-forwards. As play moved upfield with the wing-halves behind the attack, the regular modern defensive formation unfolded, the full-backs watching the wingers and the wing-halves retaining contact with the opposing inside-forwards.

Yet the rigidity of this modern style becomes necessary only so long as wingers hug the touch-lines and inside-forwards fumble with the ineffective subtleties of 'W' formations. Such rigidity is, moreover, almost exclusively domestic. Abroad, Austria and Uruguay, to take only two illustrations, have shown the possibilities of a reversion to the defensive tactics of G.O.'s day. With the growing emphasis on results, it is hardly surprising to find.

The Times writing after England's 2-1 victory over Scotland at Birmingham in 1899: 'Defence, in fact, is now brought up to such a pitch that in a match of Saturday's great class the smallness of the score is easily appreciated.' Barely half a dozen years later *Gibson and Pickford* suggest a continuation of the trend, when recording: 'In these days of close and chessboard tactics, when an agile line of half-backs - masters in every art and science of frustrating the attack - is accountable for so many ties ... the growing triumph of the defence seems irresistible.'

Is it so surprising then to learn that in the Cup-Final of 1896, Crawshaw, the Sheffield Wednesday captain and England's centre-half, withdrew his inside-left to half-back in defence, dropping back himself as far as possible to cover the goal, while the Wolves' forwards strove vainly to level a 2-1 deficit? The concept of the defensive centre-half or third-back, as he ought to be - and by many foreign teams is - called, clearly is not new.

It must be remembered that one of the many historical contributions to the game from the ancient universities came with the scientific and strategic organisation of teams. Thus in 1883 Cambridge University adapted the Scottish example of playing two half-backs and two full-backs, by turning one of the two centre-forwards into a centre-half and thereby becoming the first English side to play three half-backs. The emergence of the modern English formation therefore required only the withdrawal of the centre-half farther into the defence, in fact to the third-back position.

The year after that Cup-Final of 1896 C.B. Fry wrote in the Association Football section of *The Encyclopaedia of Sport and Games:*

'Sometimes, when a side is a goal or two ahead, and it is thought advisable to play a purely defensive game, a third-back is added by diminishing the number of forwards ... With regard to the shift of withdrawing a forward and putting an extra back, there is this much to be said: that three backs are extremely hard to get through ... But unless the players thus moved are versatile and capable of performing satisfactorily the duties of their altered positions ... it is certainly unwise to play a third-back, unless the extra man is a capable player in that position.'

Around that time two brothers named Chapman, born in Shropshire, became professional forwards. Harry Chapman gained League and Cup winners' medals with Sheffield Wednesday, still under Crawshaw's captaincy, in 1903 and 1907 respectively. His brother, Herbert, gained no medals with Tottenham Hotspur and the other clubs for whom he played with little or no distinction. In 1908 Herbert left the Spurs, his last club, to steer Northampton Town, Huddersfield Town and Arsenal to fantastic levels of sustained success. Both brothers would have been aware of the tactical possibilities which Fry discussed. All that Herbert Chapman did at Highbury in order to combat the changed circumstances caused by the revision of the off-side law in 1925, which required *two* and not *three* defenders between an attacker and the opposing goal line, was to dress up an old idea in red shirting. Others called the new position - made famous for Arsenal by Herbert Roberts 'policeman' or 'stopper' centre-half, whom G.O. is supposed never to have encountered!

The most famous of those stopper centre-halves in red shirting at Highbury after the Second World War was Leslie Compton, the Middlesex wicket-keeper. In 1951 he was paid a very great compliment by receiving his first full international soccer caps (v. Wales and Yugoslavia) at the remarkable age of thirty-eight. For when Neil Franklin emigrated from Stoke City to Bogota in 1950 after playing for England in all the twenty-six post-war internationals until his departure, Leslie Compton was generally regarded as his natural successor. Why? Not so much for his Arsenal-tutored defensive qualities alone; but he had spent seven or eight years at Highbury before the war understudying sufficiently as a footballer that superb pair of club and national defenders Male and Hapgood, to be selected at fullback for international Trial games while still an Arsenal reserve.

Yet by this lack of competition, what greater testimony was required for the decline in centre-half standards and quality since those G.O.

opposed, men such as Crawshaw and Scotland's James Cowan of the Villa or Alex Raisbeck of Liverpool? They all had more fusion of defence and attack in their little toes than most modern centre-halves possess in their two clumsy feet. So when Compton, or rather his Arsenal style, was found wanting at centre-half, the only alternative for England was - another centre-half? As we have seen, this was Froggatt, their outside-left! He was followed, in recent times, by two wing halves, Johnson and Wright. The next logical step is clearly the conversion of one of England's many able goalkeepers into this troublesome position! Is it perhaps, then, too much to hope for a return to the conditions of G.O.'s day, when 'Pa' Jackson was writing: 'The centre half-back is the most important man in the team. He must always watch the opposing centre forward, and ... be able to play anywhere and do anything that can be done at football.'

Centre-halves certainly tried to do most things to G.O. in his early days. The amateur as well as professional defences had a tendency to rush his light frame off the ball before he could control it properly. So he was thrown back to develop other qualities, and one can now see the first of the reasons which underline his fame and greatness.

'What W.N. Cobbold was to the dribbling game, G.O. Smith was to the passing game,' wrote his great Corinthian and cricket contemporary, R.E. Foster, shortly after G.O.'s retirement. 'In fact it may be said that he was the pioneer of the present system, and certainly by far the ablest exponent of it ... He would receive the ball and draw the field in pursuit of him towards the left-wing, and when he saw an opening he would send one of his long low passes to the extreme outside-right, who knew his captain's methods well enough to be on the alert to steal a march from his opposing half-back; many a goal was scored in this way, the scheme being all the more successful as it was unsuspected by the enemy.' Three or four years later, in 1907, these remarks were corroborated by the famous James Crabtree of Aston Villa, one of G.O.'s England colleagues who wrote in *Gibson and*

Pickford: 'The wonderful skill and dexterity with which men like Bloomer and G.O. Smith habitually slip the ball across to an unmarked comrade represents one of the greatest advances which has been made in football.' Apparently this was an early feature of his play, for F. Street, his first University captain, has written in *Fifty years of Sport: 'At* Oxford the most remarkable feature of his game was the way in which he fed his wings, drawing the defence in the direction of one wing, and then placing the ball with extraordinary precision at the very feet of the other - unmarked - winger.'

It was only natural that to assist his remarkable technique G.O. took care of his material equipment. For when I enquired of him what type of boots he wore, he replied:

'I always wore ordinary brown boots at football with a more or less pointed toe and very thin stockings. To my mind it is difficult to make delicate passes and to shoot with the rather clumsy square-toed boots that the professionals use.'

Similar conclusions now seem to have been reached by the more progressive of modern professionals. For the famous Irish international, Peter Doherty, has experimented with canvas lacrosse boots; and special lightweight boots were made for England's players in view of the exceptionally hard grounds upon which the World Cup Competition was played at Rio in 1950. Surely one may well ask whether there is anything essential that is not new in football.

If greatness is achieved or thrust on one by grasping opportunity when it knocks, then G.O., unknowingly or other, donned the mantle this way. He reached the soccer scene when the combination play which had superseded the dribbling game in the seventies and eighties was being consolidated. At that stage in the game's history when the amateurs could easily ,oppose and defeat the professionals, the differences in status produced differing styles of play.

The small sticky pitches of the industrial north upon which professional British soccer originated shaped the patterns which became associated with northern and majority of professional clubs - a constant pass and repassing between forwards until an opening could be found. The object was to tire out the defenders or so out manoeuvre them that gradually the ball would be worked nearer to the goal-mouth until the opportunity for a shot would occur. More often than not the ball was worked so near that the opportunity never occurred with defenders nipping in to spoil it all - as Newcastle United were eventually to find to their cost in the course of five unsuccessful Cup-Finals at the Crystal Palace between 1905 and 1911. But on the wider, harder grounds of southern England the amateurs developed first their dribbling and later that dashing, zestful attacking style which the Corinthians personified and 'Pa' Jackson in *Association Football* described as 'passing forward on the run. When one forward gets the ball he dribbles it as fast as he can, all the other forwards getting into line and keeping pace with him. Directly he is threatened by an opponent he passes well forward, but out of reach of his adversary, to such a point as one of his fellow-forwards may reach while still going full speed, and he in turn does the same. If this is done cleverly, the whole of the forward line will every now and then come clean through the defence and have the goal at their mercy.'

When G.O. arrived the time was ripe for unification. With his slide-rule precision on dry or sticky turf, he was able by long and short passes to place the ball, greasy, heavy or light, for his colleagues to run on to it. He developed to perfection his predecessors' tactics by blending them firmly within a flexible framework of attack that facilitated assaults from the most unexpected of angles; and then ultimately he introduced them to the professionals, whether playing in opposition for the Corinthians or as their leader for England. It is therefore hardly surprising that G.O. wrote:

'Individualism must be sacrificed to combination, and any tendency towards selfish play must be suppressed. "Union is strength" is not a bad motto for forward play.'

Soccer being essentially a team game, G.O. could not have reached his perfection without being surrounded by players of the highest class and supported by the finest inside-forwards in the land throughout his career, with all of whom he blended superbly. The most experienced of these, Johnny Goodall, reasoned that G.O. was the finest player he ever saw because he was such a master of doing the right thing at the right moment. One of those moments saw a peach of a goal against Ireland during G.O.'s first year of captaining England in 1897. Bloomer received the ball, and after taking it downfield, passed to his captain. G.O. made 'a tricky dribble,' so the report runs, and then he returned it back to his inside-right, but on the *left* side. For Bloomer had run round between G.O. and Aston Villa's Fred Wheldon at inside-left; and in the words of the day, he secured 'a fine opening of which he promptly availed himself.'

'Bloomer [as G.O. wrote] was undoubtedly the most brilliant inside-right of my day, though not very easy to play with. The best insides I remember were: R.C. Gosling, J.G. Veitch, R.E. Foster, S.H. Day and Johnny Goodall of Derby County.'

Goodall, of course, had been England's inside-right and captain upon G.O.'s first appearance against Scotland at Glasgow in 1894. His *protégé,* Bloomer, was in that position seven years later upon G.O.'s last appearance against Scotland at Crystal Palace in 1901. Before that span Goodall had been Preston North End's centre-forward when they had won the Cup and League in 1889. But as G.O. wrote:

'I never saw Johnny Goodall in the centre. I played with him many times, but he was always inside-right or inside-left. Though not so brilliant individually as Bloomer, he was much easier to play with and there was no suspicion of selfishness about his play. I am sure he must have been a great centre.'

Indeed he was hailed as the finest centre of his day and played for England and the Football League in that position before G.O. got under way. Technically he may not have had G.O.'s scientific precision, but he did possess the power of getting the best out of all the other members of the team. Certainly he got the best out of G.O. and Bloomer in their rise to greatness, and later did the same with lesser talents when he became team manager at Watford.

(Left) R.E.Foster (Below) R.C.Gosling

Other professional inside-forwards occasionally turned out for England with G.O. between them, Fred Wheldon and Edgar Chadwick being two of the most outstanding. They opposed each other when Wheldon's two goals helped Aston Villa to beat Everton by 3-2 in one of the most memorable of Cup-Finals, and so give the Villa the first part of their elusive 'Double' in 1897. Sir Frederick Wall has told us, in his *Fifty Years of Football*, 'On Everton's left there were Edgar Chadwick and Milward, than whom I never saw a better wing. Chadwick, with the footwork of a juggler in his control of the ball, and perfect in his passing and positional play, was probably as great a master as "Nuts" Cobbold, whose dribbling has become legendary. Milward was very dangerous, being strong, swift and a shot. He used to middle the ball so well.' G.O., however, could

'remember A. Milward, though rather vaguely. He played for many years on the left-wing with Chadwick for Everton and played for England v. Wales and Scotland in 1890-91 and again in 1897.'

Yet in 1897, against Scotland, G.O. had been Milward's captain. Clearly Milward had not carved a niche in G.O.'s memory as deep as that left by Corinthian insides who were all, except for Veitch, great cricketers too.

John Veitch, a tall 'ivory-faced hero with a black moustache,' as C.B. Fry recalled him, is perhaps the least remembered of them all. Perhaps on account of his unreliability he played only once for England, v. Wales, in the Corinthians' game of 1895. He was nevertheless a brilliant dribbler in the best Westminster tradition, with a deadly shot that brought him 60 goals in 68 tradition, with games for the Corinthians, a better average than G.O.'s. He spent four years in the Cambridge XI with G.H. Cotterill, and when, for the Corinthians, G.O. appeared between these two giants not unlike Douglas Reid of Portsmouth, among the moderns, in build, the combination struck Fry as magnificent. Another Cambridge contemporary of Veitch and Cotterill whom G.O. included among the best insides he remembered was R.C. Gosling.

Well over six feet in height and weighing nearly thirteen stone, he left his mark at both inside-right and inside-left, with his speed, passing and shooting from all angles that underline the dribbling skill he had acquired from Eton's Field Game. His unselfishness and finesse no doubt gave him the wonderful knack of knowing how to keep his line together, a quality which England's selectors have unhappily found wanting in nearly all the inside-forwards with whom they have experimented since the Second World War. Gosling's play, as Sir Frederick Wall recalled for us, was the very refinement of football, and effective football, too. Had any other club than the Old Etonians claimed his service beyond England and the Corinthians he would have been exalted at football in the manner reserved by cricket idolators for Lionel Palairet, Reggie Spooner and Victor Trumper. Yet in the summers, after his three years in the Cambridge XI (he was dismissed only once in three Varsity matches!) -1888-89-90 - alongside Stanley Jackson, Sammy Woods and Gregor MacGregor, Gosling played sufficiently for Essex to prepare that part of the world for the Ashtons some thirty years later.

Gosling was one of four brothers who had played at Lord's for Eton against Harrow, as well as for the Old Etonians at soccer; and like the Ashtons after him he contributed greatly towards the administrative affairs of his County, for he became a Justice of the Peace and High Sheriff of Essex.

Little removed in style and appearance from Gosling was Reginal Erskine Foster, of whom Fry wrote: 'His feet had, as it were, the Oxford accent.' Dying from diabetes at the tragically early age of thirty-six before Banting discovered insulin, Foster left behind the record which has lasted until our own day of the highest Test score for an England batsman in Australia, namely 287.

Schooled in the graceful Malvern style evolved by C. Toppin, Foster has been called, by no less a master than Jessop, 'the English Trumper,' and even Trumper with his greatest innings of 185 not out could not save that Test Match at Sydney in

1903 which Foster's record innings helped so much to win. In addition to his 287, however, Foster's fielding contributed greatly to England's victory, for in the first innings he fell over and caught Trumper brilliantly left-handed in the slips when the Australian had scored a single. But this was hardly surprising for as a slip-fielder Foster ranks with the greatest Lohmann, Tunnicliffe, Braund, Chapman, Hammond, Constantine and Miller.

This genius of a batsman mixed magnificent off-drives with superb late-cuts; and his grand yet graceful strokes were as powerful as his shots with either foot from any range or angle at a speed surpassed only by G.O. With his brilliant dribbling and constructive improvisations he was, as C.B. Fry put it: more typically Corinthian in his play than G.O. ... He will be remembered, like Brann, rather as a great batsman than as a great forward; but his football is as undeniable as his cricket.' Among the five international soccer caps that Foster gained, one at least forced Bloomer out of the England team. But injuries and business calls - he was a stockbroker - limited his appearances for England. In his last international, against Wales in 1902, he captained ten professionals. Five years later he captained England's cricketers against the South African 'googly' elevens. Thus he became the only man ever to have captained England's professionals at both her national games. In this it is likely that Foster will remain forever unique. As G.O. wrote to me:

' "Tip" Foster's early death was indeed a tragedy. He was a great cricketer with all the strokes, and a very fine slip. As a footballer I rank him very high; he was not quite as easy to play with as R.C. Gosling, or S.H. Day, but he was more brilliant and I put him next to Bloomer. I knew him very well and he was one of the best.'

Probably he was the greatest Corinthian and Cricketer of them all.

Only a shade inferior, in individual skill and genius, was S.H. Day. He really arrived just as

G.O. withdrew from the international scene, but probably combined more easily than any of the others. He was the reason for what G.O. described as a....

'rather funny episode on a foreign tour for Corinthians in 1904. We had travelled thousands of miles - had played matches in Budapest, Vienna, Prague and Leipzig, and had been entertained royally. We arrived in Paris for the last match against France at the *Pac des Princes,* most of us being either crippled or worn out. The Frenchmen played hard and with twenty-three minutes to go were leading by 4-2. Sam Day had been playing at outside-right, as he was lame, however, I put him next to me, as a last chance, and by the end of the game we won 11-4.'

In 1906 S.H. Day played at inside-right with another Corinthian, S.S. Harris, at inside-left, in all three home internationals alongside three different professional centre-forwards, Albert Shepherd, then of Bolton Wanderers later of Newcastle United, Arthur Brown of Sheffield United and Alfred Common of Middlesbrough. He packed a deadly shot in accordance with the traditional concept of inside-forward play, and in that 1906 season he scored the only goal against Wales. His lack of weight, which nearly cost him his football caps, gave him at both football and cricket a neatness and fleetness of movement best seen in R.W.V. Robins, a great Corinthian and Cricketer of our own day. Yet the shadows of his dashing style will perhaps be more lasting on Kentish cricket fields where he sparkled, and though he never played cricket for England, he was, as C.B. Fry opined, 'up to England form as a batsman.'

With Day, Foster and so many others providing such versatility in support, how could G.O. fail to reach the heights. A typical comment appears in Corbett's *Annals of the Corinthian Football Club* of their 8-3 win in a mud-heap at Molyneux over Wolverhampton Wanderers, then in the lower half of the First Division table, at the end of 1900: 'The combination and passing of the three inside-forwards, R.E. Foster, G.O. Smith and C.F. Ryder, was one of the best performances of the

Corinthians during the G.O. Smith period of the club's existence.' Amongst the greatest modern sides Arsenal had David Jack and Alex James at inside-forward before the Second World War, and Derby County won the Cup after that War with Carter and Doherty; but neither pair found a regular centre-forward of their own class between them. The greatest of modern centre-forwards, Tommy Lawton, at Everton had Alex Stevenson and Stanley Bentham beside him, but only Stevenson was capped and can be considered of the highest grade. By the time Lawton reached Chelsea after the War, Tommy Walker and Len Goulden had passed their zenith, and one will never forget the Victory international at Hampden Park in 1946 when the undoubted craft and skill of Shackleton and Hagan beside him could not blend, and England's centre-forward was left to forage alone.

In one respect alone does G.O. suffer in comparison with the other great centre-forwards, namely, in the matter of heading, in which Lawton, of course, has excelled. Sir Frederick Wall set down in *Fifty Years of Football* 'a statement that may be considered startling, but as my opinion is honest, 1 am not concerned if it does not agree with the views of others. G.O. Smith and Woodward were both great players, but the Tottenham and Chelsea forward was the better. Why was he the better footballer? Woodward was the more versatile, the more consistent and cleverer with his heading.'

The last point even G.O. himself would hardly have denied. In 1942 he wrote to me:

'I am, of course, a "laudator temporis acti," but even allowing for that I consider the two main faults of modern football are the incessant amount of indiscriminate kicking by backs and heading (by forwards).

Backs and half-backs have to use their heads at times, but, if forwards have to, there is in my opinion something wrong with the side. Whenever possible the ball should be kept on the ground and

any forward in the flourishing days of the Corinthians who did not do so would have found himself left out of the side. High shots are rarely effective, and the low cross shot is the one that goalkeepers dread most.'

Vivian Woodward had to be cleverer with his heading than G.O. for he played constantly alongside professionals or non-Corinthian amateurs when amateur internationals began in 1906; but Wall rated him G.O.'s superior as a *footballer,* not as a centre-forward. Woodford's frail physique, though no slighter than G.O.'s, could not stand the buffetings received against professional and international opposition, and this required his moving to the more spacious opportunities at inside-forward, where he picked up many of his sixty full and amateur representative honours. Perhaps the final word on G.O. and Woodward was best said by *Gibson and Pickford* at the time of Woodward's peak at centre-forward: 'he, was a happy blend of G.O. Smith and W.N. Cobbold, without possessing all the genius of the one or the other.'

Yet for all the support G.O. found it would have been as useful as an orchestra without a leader and conductor had he not possessed the technical skill for adapting it. Let C.B. Fry sum up this facet of G.O.'s greatness with words he composed for his own *Magazine* and Corbett's *Annals of the Corinthian Football* Club:

'The secret of his consummate skill in football, his adroitness in trapping and controlling the ball, his mastery in dribbling, his precision in passing and deftness in shooting, was an altogether uncommon neatness of foot. It was by his balance that, without being a sprinter, he moved so quickly; his speed on a field with a ball consisted of quickness in starting, in turning, in stopping and in changing his paces. By his own quick change of balance he upset that of a would-be tackler; got him stuck on the wrong leg two yards out of reach. By quick change of balance he feinted, without swerving from his bee-line of progress; by balance he arranged in a twinkling for his lightning shot through a two-foot space. By balance he moved always unruffled and fluent. He never sprawled feet wide apart, never let any bias of motion take him out of action. His neatness of foot gave him more obvious virtues - cleverness and quickness, a foot so light in running, so heavy, by accurate timing, to drive his shot. Over and above, he had an uncommon instinct, that of the genius half-back, for the future whereabouts of the ball, and his own special instinct for the whereabouts of self and friends, and the clear passages between. He'd eyes all round his shirt had G.O. Most unselfish of players, he got most of his many goals by his own individual effort. Just his own final turn of the ball made good the chance, though the midfield leading up was done by pass and repass. And no forward was ever more artfully adept at drawing his opponents before passing.'

Shortly after Fry first wrote these words, Alfred Common, whose professional services at £4 per week were the subject of that first £1,000 transfer fee, in 1905 to Middlesbrough, likened G.O.'s play to Paderewski's pianistic genius when he wrote in *Spalding's Football Guide* on 'how to play centre-forward':

'The greatest artist is the man who conceals his art G.O. Smith was one of those conjurors whose tricks looked so simple that the merest tyro believed he could perform them. Yet therein lay the perfection of his art. Its very simplicity was the outcome of studied practice. The best footballers are those who give strict attention to training. To excel you must be fit ... The excellence of a G.O. Smith is the excellence of a finished artist, of a man who gave thought and study to the rudimentary principles of forward play.'

Yet the qualities creating G.O.'s technique and style required some deeper spring from within the man himself. The secret, if secret it be, is seen in the sympathy and sensitivity which pervaded his features and allowed him to blend harmoniously with players of all character, of differing styles of play and, more significantly, from differing homes and backgrounds. Years later at Highbury a similar sympathy and sensitivity enabled Herbert Chapman and Tom Whittaker to reach down within eleven players and lift them to unprecedented levels of sustained success.

When G.O.'s great friend, Oakley, was knocked senseless in the Scotland international at Glasgow in 1900 the reports were unanimous in noticing that not only was the full-back rendered comparatively useless; but that the majority of the side were unnerved, and especially G.O. For the only time in his international career G.O. played far below his normal form and could scarcely do anything useful; and when the remainder of the team departed for the south after the game, G.O. stayed on to nurse his friend until he was well enough to travel back to Ludgrove after the week-end.

A season later, in 1900-01, before the internationals got under way, G.O.'s mother died. So he withdrew from the England trials under the pretext of 'flu, and when his selection was inevitable he notified the F.A. that he would not be available for any further football that season. In his absence Wales were beaten 6-0 and Ireland 3-0. But neither Beats of Wolverhampton Wanderers nor Hedley of Sheffield United could fill his place to the satisfaction of the selectors. So, much against his own wishes, G.O. was persuaded to link up in March at the Crystal Palace with Bloomer and Foster once again, for a 2-2 draw with Scotland - the same result as on his first appearance, and, as it turned out, for the last time in the domestic championship.

Six months later, at the beginning of the following season, he led England's amateurs on Saturday, 21st September, 1901, to their 12-0 victory against Germany in England's first international against a foreign country. But before all the home internationals - in March and April in those days - could be played in the second half of the season, in 1902, including the Scotland match at Ibrox Park, Glasgow, with its disastrous collapse of one of the stands, Arthur Dunn had died on 19th February at

Ludgrove, and international football saw G.O. no more.

G.O.'s Carthusian, Corinthian and Oxford colleague, as Sir E. Farquhar Buzzard, touched on this human element in G.O.'s character when he wrote in *The Carthusian* during 1944: 'With all his reserve and nervous temperament G.O. was universally popular, both on and off the field.' Off the field he was described by James Catton as 'the quietest, mildest man who ever deceived a pair of heavy backs and crashed the ball into the net.' Indeed, he struck Catton at their first meeting in the Crystal Palace grounds as rather frail in physique, gentle in manner and kind in disposition.' Slightly over middle height 'with a winsome face that bore traces of the pale cast of thought, as '*Gibson and Pickford* put it, this man with the most common of names typified the finest characteristics of his people, unassuming and composed until aroused to action.

'To see him walk quietly on to the field with his hands in his pockets,' continued *Gibson and Pickford,* 'and watch the fine lines of an intellectual face, one wondered why the student ventured into the arena of football. But watch him on the ball with opposing professionals - maybe the best in the land - in full cry after him, and you saw a veritable king amongst athletes.'

Because G.O. wore his crown so naturally the professionally biased selectors had no alternative but to persist with him as England's centre-forward until he withdrew his services for reasons which recall the comment in *The Carthusian* on his schooldays: 'He was almost too conscientious.' Clearly G.O. had many more years of play left when Arthur Dunn's untimely death forced his premature retirement from the international scene at the age of twenty-nine; but, as we have already seen, his work at Ludgrove was thereafter to command his undivided attention.

In the years that have followed, the hall of centre-forward fame has inherited imperishable memories. For the traditional position of the centre-forward as the spearhead of the attack suggests a thrill and glamour that no other position in the- team has ever shared. Nevertheless, no one has ever arrived to overthrow G.O. as the greatest of them all. For like W.G., he is immortal.

After Vivian Woodward's succession to and abdication from G.O.'s throne the selectors found it as difficult to find their successors as those of a later decade were to discover upon their unnecessary dismissal from England's team of Tommy Lawton. For a year or two the pace and drive of George Hilsdon fired England's elevens before he burned himself out, somehow in keeping with the unpredictability of his club, Chelsea, then the most recently founded, in 1905. Bert Freeman played for England and Everton as well as scoring the goal which gave Burnley the Cup in 1914; and in that year and the one before England selected Harry Hampton after he had helped Aston Villa to a League Championship (1910) and two F.A. Cup victories (1905 and 1913) with that same courageous dash and skill which terrified goalkeepers, blended his fellow forwards and later became associated with another leader from the same club, Trevor Ford.

Between the two World Wars the legions of centre-forwards come marching down the years. Jack Cock of Chelsea; Billy Walker, Pongo Waring and Dai Astley with Aston Villa; Vic Watson from West Ham United; Joe Bradford at Birmingham; Billy Rawlings at Southampton; Norman Bullock at Bury; Ted Harper and George Hunt with the Spurs; Frank Osborne with the Spurs and Fulham; Jimmy Hampson for Blackpool; George Camsell and Micky Fenton with Middlesbrough; Jack Bowers of Derby County; Bobby Gurney with Sunderland; Ted Drake of Arsenal; Hughie Gallacher with Newcastle United and Chelsea; Jimmy McGrory from Glasgow Celtic, Gallacher's great rival for Scotland and the successor to G.O.'s contemporary, R.S. McColl; the two Freddies, Tilson with Manchester City, Steele with Stoke City; and of course, literally as well as metaphorically, above them all, 'Dixie' Dean and Tommy Lawton at Everton.

THE GREATEST CENTRE – FORWARD?

G.O. SMITH

V.J. WOODWARD

'DIXIE' DEAN

TOMMY LAWTON

GREAT DEFENDERS

A.M. WALTERS   W.R. MOON   P.M. WALTERS

L.V. LODGE   G.B. RAIKES   W.J. OAKLEY

GREAT ATTACKERS

BILLY BASSETT   STEVE BLOOMER   JOHN GOODALL

Each club and each connoisseur can nominate a favourite. In 1948, for example, the memoirs, *Behind the Scenes in First class Football,* were published of Leslie Knighton, a famous modern manager who had been in command at Arsenal, Birmingham, Huddersfield Town and Manchester City before he brought Hughie Gallacher, one of the greatest of modern centre-forwards, to Chelsea. The book contains a chapter headed 'Best Ever' that deals with the everlasting topic it suggests, and one paragraph commences:

'Let's go through the greatest centre-forwards. Has there ever been a better than G.O. Smith or R.S. McColl, both amateurs and on the £15,000 to £20,000 mark if they were playing to-day? McColl turned pro. later for Newcastle United, but was at his best as an amateur. Dixie Dean of Everton - one of those men who deserved more football notice than he got - a football marvel; Vivian Woodward, quicksilver leader of Spurs and Chelsea; Hughie Gallacher whom no hands or feet ever could keep out, on his day. Camsell (Middlesbrough), Hampton (Villa), Hilsdon (Chelsea), Lawton (Notts County)? No, none, even of these. Joe Bradford of Birmingham? No, not even Joe. If I have to say what I think, the palm goes to G.O. Smith, tireless attacker, and above all, peerless pivot of a line.'

Yet when the final assessment is made linking G.O.'s day with the tactical and legislative changes that have led to the present background to the game, perhaps Lawton alone may be G.O.'s greatest challenger. For in one way or another all of the others lacked one or more of G.O.'s essential qualities. Lawton, on the other hand, like his great mentor at Everton, Dean, has become a legend in his own time, especially for the subtle grace and thrust of his headwork: and after his loss of international favour because of the transfer of his services from Chelsea to Notts County in their Third Division days, England played nearly a dozen centre-forwards in half a dozen years without finding a regular successor.

Every conceivable permutation was tried by the selectors, from the verve and zest of jackie Milburn with Newcastle United and Nat Lofthouse for Bolton Wanderers to the roaming tactics of Roy Bentley at Chelsea and jack Rowley for Manchester United, with the variations of Stanley Mortensen for Blackpool in the inside-forward positions: and the result has been a situation as unsettled as it was certain when Lawton was at his peak. Yet, as Ivan Sharpe has pointed out in his *40 Years in Football:* 'Tom Lawton could shoot with great power and accuracy, but he could not seize a chance and slash the ball into the net so quickly as this perky little Scotsman,' Hughie Gallacher. From that alone, apart from Lawton's appearances between inside forwards who do not rank with those alongside G. O., it may be judged that G.O. can resist this challenge, however real it may be.

In finally relating G.O.'s position to his contemporaries, however, the most illuminating indication of his significance may be seen from the imaginatively conceived Chart of 'Leading Centre-Forwards, 1872-1950' that appears in *The F.A. YearBook, 1950-51.* There, set down in five columns and tabulated opposite each year can be found over the period of seventy seasons the centre-forward in every England home international side, Football League XI against the Scottish League, and F.A. Cup-winning side. G.O. does not appear in the Cup-Final lists, since of the clubs he played for, Oxford University and the Old Carthusians, past winners of the trophy, had dropped out of the competition and the Corinthians were not to enter for another thirty years. Nor does he appear for the Football League which had then just commenced and has always relied upon players from the professional clubs comprising membership of the League. Yet although such names as Goodall, Southworth, Devey, Beats and Hedley roll down the League and Cup lists there is an unparalleled block of G.O. Smiths in the International column, as can be seen from the reproduction which follows........

Season Ending	England v. Scotland	England v. Wales	England v. Ireland	Football League v. Scottish League	F.A. Cup Winners
1891	F.Geary *Everton*	John Southworth *Notts F.*	T.Lindley	-	John Southwood *Blackburn R.*
1892	John Southworth	A.E. Henfrey *Corinthians*	J.Devey *Aston V.*	J.Goodall *Derby Co.*	T. Nicholls *West Brom A.*
1893	G.H. Cotterill *Old Brightonians*	J. Goodall	G.H.Cotterill*	John Southworth	J.H. Butcher *Wolves*
1894	G.O. Smith	G.O. Smith	J. Davey	J. Devey	A. Logan *Notts Co.*
1895	J. Goodall	G.O. Smith	J. Goodall	J. Devey	J. Devey *Aston V.*
1896	G.O. Smith	G.O. Smith	G.O. Smith	J. Goodall	L. Bell *Sheffield Wes.*
1897	G.O. Smith	G.O. Smith	G.O. Smith	J. Devey	W. Campbell *Aston V.*
1898	G.O. Smith	G.O. Smith	G.O. Smith	W.M. Beats *Wolves*	L. Benbow *Notts F.*
1899	G.O. Smith	G.O. Smith	G.O. Smith	W. Toman *Burnley*	G.A. Hendley *Sheffield U.*
1900	G.O. Smith	G.O. Smith	G.O. Smith	G.A. Hedley	J. McLuckie *Bury*
1901	G.O. Smith	W.M. Beats	G.A. Hedley	S. Raybould *Liverpool*	A. Brown *Tottenham H.*

*G.O. Smith played at inside-right

No other centre-forward in the pattern has such a record for consistency.

Comparisons, however, are odious. They defy logic, too. So the position may be regarded as most aptly posed, appropriately, by the modern game's foremost historian, Geoffrey Green, better known as *The Times* Association Football Correspondent. For in his *Soccer: The World Game* he writes of G.O.: 'How would he have compared with the Dixie Deans and Tommy Lawtons of this world, not only clever with their feet but sheer artists with the deadly accuracy of their heading? It is a question that can never satisfactorily be answered. Perhaps, though, we should not ask it. We should not be disbelievers.'

Greatness is always a relative factor, and G.O. stood out in an age of giants. It is not without significance that his last appearances after his retirement from the international scene were not far removed in time from those of W.G., whose last important games took place at the Oval in 1908. 'W.G. Grace, The Great Cricketer,' to quote the simple wording of his Memorial Gate at Lord's, passed on at the age of sixty-seven in the First World War. G.O., The Greatest Centre-Forward, died at seventy-one in the Second World War. W.G.'s period in cricket overlapped nearly the whole of all the Corinthian days before and after G.O.'s era. Yet when the only two sportsmen ever to be known to the British public by their initials alone retired from the scene, they closed a golden chapter in a Golden Age.

CHAPTER VII

THE GOLDEN AGE: 1890-1914

The younger generation will be itching to challenge my statement that ... 1900 to 1914 was the golden age of football,' wrote Ivan Sharpe in *The Sunday Chronicle* during the early days of the Second World War; but, as he went on, 'the golden age is not measured by the size of crowds, the noise and the excitement. The play's still the thing - the standard of play.' So at the end of that war Neville Cardus wrote in *English Cricket:* 'The years extending from 1890-1914 witnessed the Golden Age of batsmanship. The circumstances so much favoured batsmanship that the technique of stroke-play and footwork developed at a pace which outran and outwitted every bowler not of the highest class.' Yet, he acknowledged in the same volume, 'There were bowlers too. There can be no great batting without great bowling.' And seven years after the end of that war Ivan Sharpe had seen nothing to prevent a reiteration of his view in his *40 -Years in Football:* 'It was the golden age of football because, from 1900 to 1914, Newcastle United, Aston Villa, Manchester United, Everton, Sunderland, Blackburn Rovers, were all near their peak. Safety play had not arrived.' Teams went out to attack.'

It was attack which brought a magic to the name of Aston Villa even before 1900 which remained undimmed by their later decline. Although in 1953 Arsenal gained their seventh League Championship, thus surpassing the Villa's six titles, the Villa still remain the only club to have also won six F.A. Cup-Finals, including the historic 'double' in 1897. Unhappily their last League success was achieved in 1912, and their last F.A. Cup victory was in 1920 at Stamford Bridge. Is it any wonder that their reputation is now but a faded memory of more spacious days? Nevertheless, when I asked G.O. to overcome his modesty and consider what may have been his outstanding performance, he replied:

'About the best performance achieved by me I am absolutely defeated as I played in hundreds of Corinthian matches, etc. and it is difficult to make a choice. However, I remember with pleasure getting the winning goal against Aston Villa for the Sheriff of London Shield in the season 1899-1900. It was the first time the Shield was won, and Aston Villa were a very fine side.'

They were, indeed. The League Championship was carried off in all but two of that and the previous six seasons, not to mention a couple of Cup-Final wins. The finest traits of Scotland's traditional short-passing and dribbling artistry were brought by players from that land, and this was merged in the long-passing game which their neighbours from West Bromwich, with a candour reserved for close rivals and a parochialism which ignored the Corinthians and Preston North End, hinted had been copied from them.

Against the Corinthians the Villa were without James Cowan and Crabtree, who had injured himself in training, their places being taken by Wilkes and Mann: and the Corinthians were without Wreford Brown, England's centre-half and captain against Scotland twelve months earlier. Otherwise both clubs were well represented, and lined up as follows:

ASTON VILLA
George

Spencer   Evans

Bowrnan   Wilkes   Mann

Athersmith   Devey   Garraty   Wheldon   Smith

●

B.O. Corbett   G.C. Vassall

G.P. Wilson   G.O.S.   R.E.Foster

H. Vickers   R.R. Barker   B. Middleditch

W.J. Oakley   C.B. Fry

W. Campbell

CORINTHIANS

Although only Fry, Oakley and G.O. were then internationals, all the others except Campbell and Vassall were to join them. Spencer and all the Villa forwards, except Garraty, had already played for England, and Garraty with George and Wilkes were later capped, too.

CORINTHIANS 1896 – WITH FOUNDER 'PA' JACKSON

ENGLAND *v.* SCOTLAND – CRYSTAL PALACE, 1897

Team – (Back, l. to r.): Crawshaw, W.J. Oakley, Robinson, Needham, Spencer.
(Front): Reynolds, Athersmith, Bloomer, G.O. Smith (Capt.), Chadwick, Milward.

On a rain-sodden pitch at the Crystal Palace Cup-Final and international ground, progress on the wings assured the greatest success. So in the ten minutes before half-time Walter Garraty headed home a lovely centre from Stephen Smith on the left wing. Four minutes later G.O. from mid-field passed the ball to his outside-right. Vassall dribbled down the wing and, drawing the half- and back, centred superbly for Foster to pick his spot to equalise. In the second-half play swung to and fro with G.O. pulling out shots from all ranges as if determined to win the game. Twelve minutes from time he again found himself with the ball in mid-field, suspiciously near off-side, while the Villa backs were lying well up. On this occasion he passed out to the left-wing after 'a dodgy run.' Corbett took the ball down, slipped it back to G.O., and with an unstoppable left-foot cross shot into the corner of the net he won the game. A cutting from the scrapbook which Corbett kindly lent me told me that 'the victory was one which was well deserved, but there was just the question as to whether the amateur captain was not in the first instance off-side. The shot by which, however, he ultimately scored after the ball had been passed back to him fully merited success, and the ovation he received at the close from the crowd fully proved how much his brilliant play had been appreciated.'

The magnitude of this achievement can be measured only if Pegasus were to repeat it against Arsenal, Aston Villa's successors to success, or other modern masters such as Manchester United, Tottenham Hotspur or West Bromwich Albion. Sir Thomas (later Lord) Dewar, 1897, had offered the Sheriff of London Shield for competition between the best amateur and the best professional clubs of the previous season, the proceeds going to various charities. To-day its equivalent is the F.A. Charity Shield for which the Football League Champions and F.A. Cup winners are usually invited to compete. The Corinthians, together with Queen's Park, Glasgow, were undoubtedly the outstanding amateur clubs of the period and in order to enter for the Sheriff of London Shield, a competition of one match, the Corinthians had to alter their strict rule that the club should not compete for any challenge cup or prizes of any description whatever. The first two years of the competition

had seen the Corinthians v. Sheffield United and Queen's Park v. Aston Villa in drawn matches, so not until this game, as G.O. pointed out, was the Shield won by any club. Nevertheless one of the greatest all round Corinthian triumphs of this Golden Age was away from the soccer and cricket fields seven years before this Villa game during G.O.'s last year at Charterhouse.

In 1892 the Corinthians threw down a challenge and offered to meet any other club at football, cricket and athletic sports, the proceeds to go to charity. It was accepted by Corinth's counterpart in the rugby world, the Barbarian Rugby Football Club. At cricket the Ba-Ba's - as the Barbarians are affectionately known - won by four wickets. Quite naturally the Corinthians romped home at Association football by 6-1, and they squeezed a victory in the athletics by one point. Then, in the words of a contemporary newspaper: 'certainly as a surprise to everyone,' they beat the Barbarians at their own game by 14 points (2 goals and 2 tries) to 12 (2 goals and 1 try). C.B. Fry who played in that game for the Corinthians, and had also played for the Barbarians, has recalled that there were no half-measures about this game. It was won because the defence and running of the Corinthians' back division was as good as that of the Barbarians, and because the soccer forwards outclassed their opponents with the ball on the hard turf in the open. In *Life Worth Living* Fry has written, 'The Rugby world was inclined to regard the whole thing as a freak and a lark. I can assure you it was a very proper and first-rate rugger match.' Norman Creek, in his *A History of the Corinthian Football Club* graciously observes: 'The Barbarians lost much by courteously not claiming penalties for breaches of the rules, especially in the early part of the game.' Equally graciously does O.L. Owen, the Rugby football correspondent of *The Times,* suggest in his foreword to *Barbarian Records* (compiled by Emile de Lissa): 'It may well be that the success of the fast and powerful Corinthian forwards as well as backs led to the speeding up of Rugby forward play.'

Yet while the Corinthians spread their talents over many fields of interest, their professional rivals trained on towards a monopoly of the honours. West Bromwich Albion, with Billy Bassett at outside-right, followed their neighbours from Aston with two F.A. Cup victories. Both Nottingham clubs, the County and the Forest, took home the trophy once each over five years. Derby County, thanks to Bloomer, reached three Finals, but missed the Cup. Sunderland never got there at all with their 'team of all the talents,' but won four League Championships. Both Sheffield Clubs, United and the Wednesday, picked up the League as well as the Cup; and Everton and Liverpool and both Manchester clubs, United and City, between them did likewise for those parts of Lancashire. Indeed, Manchester United anticipated their great constructive teams under the managership of Matt Busby after the Second World War, with the magnificent half-back line of Duckworth, Roberts and Bell to support a daring set of forwards - Meredith, Halse, Turnbull (James), Turnbull ('Sandy'), and Wall - all of whom could dribble and shoot on the run and take the risk of losing the ball in a bold frontal attack instead of passing closely into a concerted defence.

For all these great sides, however, only one team matched the Corinthians and the Villa as the greatest names in football: Newcastle United. Between 1904 and 1912 they won three League Championships; made five unsuccessful Cup-Final appearances at the Crystal Palace, and could win the trophy only away from the festival atmosphere which the Palace engendered by scoring twice without reply against 'Battling' Barnsley from the Second Division in a replay at Everton. Barnsley themselves, be it noted, were successful two years later at West Bromwich Albion's expense, and with their admirable tackling and healthy robustness deservedly merited their nickname.

Yet no greater contrast can have existed to the Barnsley style of play than Newcastle's. Over this period of Edwardian gaiety with its sombre portents for the future, they really united a perfect blend of Scottish, Irish and English internationals into a balanced team unit. In their F.A. Cup successes of 1951 and 1952, Newcastle added to a similar collection a Welsh international and George Robledo of Chile. As may be expected, the keynote to success lay in the magnificent half-back lines: Gardner, Aitken and McWilliam in their early triumphs, and later Veitch, Low and McWilliam - the same Peter McWilliam who was

to bring his Newcastle and Scots touch as one of the game's greatest managers to the famous Tottenham Hotspur side immediately after the First World War, and nearly twenty years later was to prepare the way for the successes following the Second World War achieved largely by players he introduced at White Hart Lane.

Behind these great halves were first Kingsley and then Lawrence in goal and McCombie, McCracken, Carr or Whitson at full-back. Combining with them all in front lay a quintet of brilliant forwards, dribbling, passing and controlling the ball with impeccable harmony. Their only defect, and a serious one at that, was an over-elaboration of tone colouring through the reception of the traditional short passing Scottish game that had been the theme for the Villa's success a decade earlier in the 1890s. They worked with superb skill the Scottish tactical import of the three inside game, as the forward trio in the centre would merge in taking the ball downfield, a formation which would perhaps pay small dividends against the later trend of massed defences, based on the rigid stopper centre-half.

The strategy to which the players' brilliant talents were harnessed was nevertheless the perfect execution of the fundamental principles of all good football: the ball on the ground and movement towards the opposing goal, not away from it. At centre-half there was a *footballer,* be he Alex Aitken, Colin Veitch or Wilfred Low (father of Norman Low, modern player and manager), radiating attack from the pivotal position of the team instead of merely plugging the goal hole like a bath-stop. Newcastle's players, as did all the great footballers of this era, saw to it within the natural order of things, and not as a messianic revelation that modern tacticians would appear to proclaim, that they should make and let the ball do the work with the controlled pass, long or short, to a team-mate or open space for a colleague to run on to it, as have the players of Manchester United, Tottenham Hotspur and West Bromwich Albion in our own time. Even if we bear in mind their shortcomings, they emphasised the tradition evolved by the Corinthians and the Lancashire and Midland professional sides of attacking the opposing goal instead of negatively defending one's own, which must always be the classic way of

CORINTHIANS *v.* ASTON VILLA – 1901

Teams – CORINTHIANS (*Back, l. to r.*): B.O. Corbett, H. Thwaites, C.F. Ryder, H. Vickers, R.G. Wright, L.J. Moon. (*Middle*): B. Middleditch, R.E. Foster, W.J. Oakley, C.B. Fry. (*Front*): G.E. Wilkinson.

ASTON VILLA (*Back, l. to r.*): Johnson, George, Evans, Crabtree, Smith. (*Middle*): Devey, Athersmith, Bowman, Cowan. (*Front*): Wilkes, Garraty.

ENGLAND *v.* AUSTRALIA – EDGBASTON, 1902

Team – (*Back, l. to r.*): Hirst, Lilley, Lockwood, Braund, Rhodes, Tyldesley. (*Front*): C.B. Fry, F.S. Jackson, A.C. MacLaren (Capt.), K.S. Ranjitsinhji, G.L. Jessop.

playing the game. So *Gibson and Pickford* were constrained to write of such international forwards as Rutherford, Howie, Orr, Gosnell, Speedie, Shepherd, Higgins, Appleyard, Wilson and the great R.S. McColl in the twilight of his career, if they 'could shoot goals as well as they can load and aim for them, the last word on football would be theirs.'

That last word during this period, however, appropriately seems to have been supplied by the Corinthians. On 5th March, 1904, the F.A. Cup-holders, Bury, came to the Queen's Club, Kensington, to meet the amateurs for the Sheriff of London Shield. The previous season had seen Bury establish the record F.A. Cup-Final score of 6-0, unbroken after over half a century, though poor Derby County greatly missed the absent Bloomer and suffered a mishap to their goalkeeper during the game.

Of that conquering Bury side all except the inside-left, Joseph Leeming, turned out on that windy afternoon, and the inside right, Wood, crossed over to inside-left to let in Swarm. The Corinthians had hoped that G.O., who was still playing occasionally for them and the Old Carthusians, would turn out and captain the side, but he could not. The teams therefore lined up as follows:

CORINTHIANS

T.S. Rowlandson

Rev.W.Blackburn   W.U. Timmis

H. Vickers   M. Morgan-Owen   H.A. Lowe

G.C. Vassall   B.O. Corbett

S.H. Day   G.S. Harris   S.S. Harris

⬤

Plant   Wood   Sagar   Swann   Richards

Ross   Thorpe   Johnston

McEwan   Lindsay

Monteith

BURY

CORINTHIANS *v.* BURY – 1904 – 10-3

Team – (*Back, l. to r.*): S.S. Harris, T.S. Rowlandson, Rev. W. Blackburn, H.A. Lowe. (*Middle*): W.U. Timmis, G.C. Vassall, M. Morgan-Owen, B.O. Corbett, H. Vickers. (*Front*): G.S. Harris, S.H. Day.

G.O.'s presence certainly appeared desirable, for Norman Creek tells us, 'The prowess of the Club had so deteriorated by 1904 that before the Charity Shield match with Bury, it was seriously debated whether the Cambridge University XI should be given the preference over the Corinthians.' That preference undoubtedly looked justified within a quarter of an hour from the start. For playing against the stiff wind, the Corinthians found themselves two goals down. R.E. Foster's international partner, Charles Sagar, and Plant, had beaten Rowlandson and the decline seemed set to continue. Then, as if by some magician's touch, the Corinthians somehow clicked.

The forwards swung into action, finding their men with dashing rushes in the true Corinthian dribbling and passing style which the professionals' defence could not counter. Yet this was the same Bury defence that had emulated the Preston 'Invincibles' in not conceding a goal as it fought through the rounds of the Cup. In less than ten minutes from their reverses G.S. Harris reduced the lead and Day snatched it with two fine shots. S.S. Harris notched another goal before half-time, and the Corinthians lead then 4-2.

In the second-half Bury held out for a quarter of an hour. Thereafter the Corinthian bombardment prevailed; and with their forwards in full cry the halves and backs could devote themselves solely to breaking up the not infrequent Bury attacks. S.S. Harris scored a hat-trick, and G.S. Harris his second goal. Bury never gave up the hunt and came once more through the deputy, Swarm, who had a fine match. Then the Harrises each scored once more to set up double figures. The Corinthians had beaten the Cup-holders by 10-3, and the famous old name was redeemed.

At this distance of time it is of interest to note that all the goals in the game, except Plant's for Bury, came from the inside-forwards. The Bastin-Brook type of goal-scoring winger had not yet arrived, although Meredith's unorthodoxy was occasionally anticipating it. Certainly the Corinthians stuck to the technique - which precludes off-side decisions - of the ball being taken to the corner flag before the centre was made, normally backwards along the ground for the insides to run on to. This technique,

as played by the Corinthians, was explained to me half a century after the game by B.O. Corbett (who was capped against Wales in 1901) with his walking-stick on the carpet of the lounge in his manor house set among Dorset's Purbeck Hills. Corbett's fast raids, and those of Vassall in that memorable match certainly achieved their object. To these raids was added the Scottish-Newcastle tactic of working the 'three insides.' So S.S. Harris scored five goals, G.S. Harris three and S.H. Day two.

Despite the sparkle of the forwards, the result was nonetheless a triumph of team-work harnessed to individual skill. G.O. implied this when he wrote to me:

'I am sorry to say I never saw the Corinthians v. Bury match, but I have always been told the C.F.C. side outdid themselves and played a wonderful game. They must have done, as I should put few, if any, in the best Corinthian side of all time. However, I should imagine it will stand as the greatest performance in C.F.C. annals.'

It was certainly on a par with the triple defeats handed out to Blackburn Rovers at the beginning - 1884 (8-1) and 1885 (6-0) and end - 1924 (1-0) - of that great club's greatest age. Yet perhaps the most remarkable feature of the game was the Corinthians' superiority in speed. Eight months after the Bury match, in November 1904, a similar Corinthian side by 11-3 whipped Manchester United, then lying around third position in the Second Division 3 before winning promotion a season later, in 1906. Once more the superior pace of the amateurs especially in the second half - as well as their superior skill, turned the scales, and again the victory reflected the forward strength of Corinth at this period.

All the forwards who played against Bury, except Vassall, were or became internationals, and loyalty to his University alone, as has been seen, prevented Vassall from joining them. Rowlandson and Timmis also played in amateur internationals for England, while Morgan-Owen obtained eleven caps for Wales and the compliment from Norman Creek, the club's Modern historian, of being the greatest Corinthian of this Edwardian period.

Morgan-Owen, one of the last great Old Salopian footballers, moved back to centre-half after playing at centre-forward for Oxford, and it was appropriate that his school, Shrewsbury, should have provided K.A. Shearwood for the centre-half position in the Pegasus Amateur Cup-winning teams both in 1951 and 1953. When it is realised that in front of Shearwood for Pegasus there nearly always appeared at centre foreword another Oxford Carthusian, J.D.P. Tanner, the perpetuation of the Corinthian lineage in the new creation becomes apparent.

The Corinthians of this latter period of the Golden Age reflected the spirit of the times. Despite the Queen's death in 1901, Victorian England lived until 1914, for these were the days that have been described in Frederick Willis' delightful memories of Edwardian London, 101 *Jubilee Road*, as the 'Victorian After-glow.' The golden sovereign, symbolic of a golden age, was a stepping-stone to the comfort and security its very name implies, and was not to be reckoned in silver dollar equivalents. Income tax was a shilling in the £, whisky was 3s. a bottle and the £1,000 transfer fee in 1905 for Alfred Common from Sunderland to Middlesbrough created a record which shook the world far harder than did the £34,000 cheque paid by Sheffield Wednesday to Notts County forty-six years later, in 1951, for Jack Sewell, who till then had hardly been considered for international honours. So in 1942 G.O. touched a nostalgic note when he wrote to me:

'It is very sad that amateur football and amateur cricket have deteriorated so much. I think the nineties were the golden age of sport and I don't fancy their like will ever be seen again. The reason to a large extent is £.s.d., especially as regards cricket. It is a great pity, but the old days have gone, and though I have no word to say against professionals, the absence of amateurs is a great pity.'

There were amateurs apart from the Corinthians who could be seen in England's full and amateur international football teams in the Golden Age. Herbert Smith of Reading, Ivan Sharpe of Derby County and R.M. Hawkes of Luton Town, were just a few, with Woodward and Hardman who held the stage.

In the summers at cricket there were so many amateurs of quality that only one recognised professional batsman found his way into what is generally acknowledged as the greatest

England Test cricket XI of this century. At Edgbaston, Birmingham, in 1902, A. C. MacLaren led into the field against the Australians: C.B. Fry, Tyldesley, K.S. Ranjitsinhji, F.S. Jackson, Braund, G.L. Jessop, Hirst, Lockwood, Lilley and Rhodes. They did not win, for the rain did that. But it was the presence of such bowlers as Rhodes, Lockwood, Hirst and the all-rounders Braund and Jackson that caused G.O. to write in his next letter:

'I am afraid that modern cricket has deteriorated very much. Where there is one good batsman now, there were many more in the nineties, and the modern batsman has to face a poor set of bowlers these days. I allow that Hobbs, Woolley, Patsy Hendren, Hammond and Sutcliffe were very fine players, but their vast total of runs was made against very poor stuff. After Grace and Ranji I put Trumper, though there were hosts of others like MacLaren, Jackson, etc., and they had to face bowlers like George Lohmann, J.T. Hearne, Lockwood, Richardson, Mead, Briggs, Peel, Peate, Hirst and many others like Martin of Kent. Too busy to write more.'

Hobbs, of course, had commenced his career during the heights of the Golden Age. Yet had G.O. not been too busy to write more he could have gone on to point out that at that period accurate fast bowlers were to be found in almost every county side up and down the land; and at the other end to start the bowling with them were less explosive but no less effective attackers with the slower and subtler ball. Colin Blythe, of immortal Kentish memory, opened with Arthur Fielder; Arthur Hallam with Tom Wass for Notts, Walter Mead with Kortright, Buckenham and 'Sailor' Young for Essex; and of course for Yorkshire there were George Hirst swerving the ball, Schofield Haigh varying extremes of pace and Wilfred Rhodes conjuring left-hand leg-breaks, a formidable enough trio for any kind of cricket eleven at any state of the game's history.

Against them all, or rather because of them, upon wickets fairly balanced, appeared the men who with and after Ranji, Fry and Jessop created the 'Golden Age of Batting.'

Yet even the Golden Age had troubles not unlike our own. Drawn games and the l.b.w. law produced their annual agitation, and the Editor of *Wisden* suggested under his 'Notes' in 1904: 'I am not alone in thinking that nowadays we have too many matches. In my opinion, bowling and fielding would be better if the leading players were not so constantly kept at full tension six days a week. Not many years ago the leading bowlers were able to vary their serious cricket with a holiday match now and then and the relief did them good. Now they are hard at it from the first week in May till the first week in September, and in fine summers are apt to get stale.' So are the modern players, and identical conclusions appeared under the Editor's pen in *Wisden* for 1949. The solution to the problem remains to be solved, though, and after I had written at length on the topic to *The Cricketer*, G.O. commented in 1943:

'I think your suggestion about Divisions in County Cricket is a good one. As things are, Hampshire v. Yorkshire is a farce and very many other matches as well. With two Divisions there would, I think, be much more keenness ... which would, I believe, make the game much more interesting to onlookers and the counties themselves. It would, I feel sure, give an incentive to teams like Hampshire etc. to have some definite object to strive for. At the moment they have only to hope to avoid defeat as much as possible.'

By 1911 the position described in 1904 in the Golden Age had not changed, for the Editor of *Wisden* was writing again: 'I am strongly of the opinion that we have now too much county cricket, but there is an obvious danger in cutting down programmes.' Whether this was the reason, or whether it was merely the lean years following the fat years we shall never know, but, 'while the standard of cricket was slowly but surely rising from about 1875 until its zenith between 1885 and 1905, it was unmistakably on the wane during the five years immediately preceding the outbreak of war.' This was the opinion of E.H.D. Sewell, in 1915, and he was certainly no detractor of the

Golden Age. During the early days of the Second World War he came out with a vitriolic attack on modern cricket that caused G.O. to write to me in September 1942:

'Have you read *Cricket Under Fire* [described in a review in *The Cricketer* as "Modern" Cricket under Fire] by E.H.D. Sewell? I just write this line to say that I have never met Sewell, though he must have been an exact contemporary of mine I always thought of him as a cricket reporter, but I imagine he must have played some good innings in his time. He starts off one chapter - " 'Laudator temporis acti' and why not, pray." A badly written book in some ways, but interesting, and bears out the conclusion that the present day standard is much below that of the old days.'

Was G.O. justified in that conclusion? It is hardly likely that he would have altered it had he lived. The essence of the genius which made the period and personalities of the stage G.O. bestrode lay in their adherence to first principles in the games they played. In the summer of 1950 when the West Indies cricketers with their cavalier styles and calypsos were winning their first Tests in England and England's footballers were being unceremoniously bumped out of the World Cup Competition in South America, the difference between winners and losers in each case was merely the application of first principles of play on the one hand and their absence on the other. Five years earlier, in the autumn of 1945, after the Moscow Dynamo Club had opened British eyes with the incisiveness of its forward play, J.G. Orange, a former Casuals footballer, summed it all up in a lucid article in the London *Evening News*. He pointed out with regard to the Dynamo's football alone that the superiority they exerted over our own players was obtained by exactly the sort of football which we in this country started to teach the world forty years beforehand, and which we had not lived up to ourselves because of the third-back defensive strategy and its accompanying vices.

Those vices of safety and negative play to the detriment of attack were not beyond destruction; and when the League Championship drew near to Tottenham Hotspur in 1951 while the club's professional players were coaching the Oxford and

Cambridge University sides for their own triumph as Pegasus, Ivan Sharpe recorded at Easter of the Spurs: 'They are the team with the purest and most exemplary style for twenty years.' Yet the essence of that style, the short pass building up from defence to attack, was inherently an adaptation of those first principles of play which gave to the period now under review its title. When the Hungarians at Wembley in 1953 merged it with the long-passing game and a technique of ball control that modern eyes had never believed possible, the Golden Age had returned for one enduring afternoon. That England's unbeaten record of ninety years dissolved in the haze surrounding Wembley Stadium that day was merely incidental. For the conquerors from Central Europe warmly and spontaneously acknowledged their gratitude and indebtedness to the famous English coach of the Austrians who had shaken England to the narrowest of 4-3 victories at Stamford Bridge twenty years earlier in 1933 - one Jimmy Hogan. And where and when had Hogan learned his football? Why, with Bolton Wanderers, Fulham and other clubs before 1914, in the Golden Age, of course.

In addition to Hogan's contribution, however, the Corinthians had also left their mark in Hungary. For barely a month after their triumph against Bury in 1904 the Club undertook its first continental tour. An invitation was accepted from the Magyar Athletic Club of Budapest to play seven matches to be arranged by them. The first three games were won by 6-0, 9-0 and 12-0, but, Corbett's *Annals of the Corinthian Football Club* points out, 'in spite of this huge total, in no game did our opponents relax their efforts, but went their hardest from start to finish. This I think, speaks well for the future of the game in Hungary. If, as our captain mentioned at the farewell banquet given by the city that evening, they were ready to take a beating in a thoroughly sportsmanlike manner, they were also ready to take a few hints from a team with a far greater experience of the game, and when the Corinthians next had the good fortune to visit Budapest they would have to be prepared to play on considerably more even terms.' The Corinthians never returned to Budapest. Fifty years later, however, almost to the day, England did - and lost 1-7. The Association football correspondent of *The Times,* Geoffrey Green, reported home:

'These Hungarians have probably achieved at this point of time as great a mastery over a football as any team in history. By a perfect mixture of the short Continental game and the long pass English style they have found the best of two worlds.'

Yet a few years before the Corinthians played Bury, 'Pa' Jackson had written, in his Association Football:

'No team had really mastered the secret of passing slightly forward on the run, and of close passing combined with a soupçon of dribbling, until the Corinthians gave an exhibition of the utility of these combinations by beating the then almost invincible Blackburn Rovers by eight goals to one at Blackburn ... The Preston North End team were the first to profit by the example of the Corinthians and their extraordinary success during 1887-89 was in great measure due to this factor.'

But when the men of Corinth flourished and 'Proud' Preston achieved the 'Double,' no more than a dozen clubs played in the only division of the Football League, and a bare 100 to 150 clubs entered for the F.A. Cup with only three proper rounds required before the Semi-Final. By the time the Corinthians beat Bury in 1904 the League had grown to 36 clubs in two divisions and nearly 300 clubs participated in the Qualifying, Intermediate and Proper rounds of the Cup. By the end of the Golden Age four more clubs had joined the League, and over 600 battled through the Divisional, Qualifying (six rounds) and Proper (four rounds) before the Semi-Final ties of the Cup.

Yet even a Golden Age unfortunately cannot endure for ever, and, as at cricket, a downward trend could be seen in football standards from about 1910 or 1912, towards the end of the great Newcastle era. The reason, however, if not necessarily the trend itself, can be traced to a specific date a few years earlier - 1907.

Although the Corinthians as well as the ancient Universities had played the leading professional clubs to the mutual benefit and enjoyment of both from the commencement of modern soccer, there were still not a few bitter enemies of professionalism as such, while the paid players and their clubs devoted their attentions to trophies and overtaking the amateurs in international honours. Growing transfer fees and foul play fed by the lust for competition successes and increased gate monies added fuel to the fire of those who, not unlike their 'ruggah-the-man's game' counterparts of to-day, decried professional soccer as the hallmark of social and athletic inferiority. The spark that lit the powder which blew the lid completely off was a ruling on 31st May, 1907, from headquarters at the professionally controlled Football Association. In effect this required every county and district amateur association that was in membership with the F.A., and from which the professionals were entirely excluded, to admit as members of those mainly provincial associations all clubs within their areas, whether amateur or professional.

Many amateur interests took the view that if this ruling were enforced it could mean that as growing professional bodies would expand their connections with the amateur world, the unpaid player and his club could eventually come under professional control. Not unnaturally it was felt that professional sources should be excluded from any control of the amateur game.

The quarrel was not with the professional player who had always commanded the respect and often the admiration of the amateur footballer, but with the professors' myopic administrators. No compromise appears to have been possible, and after the adoption of the rule by the F.A., the ancient Universities, old Public School clubs and prominent players, encouraged by the support of the Corinthians, which undoubtedly turned the scales, decided to break away and in the same year they formed the Amateur Football Association. Lord Alverstone, then Lord Chief justice of England and president of the Surrey County Cricket Club, became its first president and another well-known legal figure, H. Hughes-Onslow, its first secretary. With recognition of the organisation refused by the F.A., to whom the majority of amateur and, of course, all professional clubs in the country remained loyal, the rebels were left to play among themselves and to conduct their own affairs.

At first the secession was hailed in *The Times* as resulting in such a recrudescence of zeal for the purely recreative side of the winter game as has astonished even the promoters of the new governing body and more its detractors.' But slowly the effect was seen to be doing more harm than good. Reduced to playing with strictly amateur sides, the Corinthians soon lost their ability and the public's attention, as well as their places at the side of the professionals in England's full international elevens. Against their chief opponents, the Universities and lesser amateur sides, the toughness for sharpening their traditional forward play that professional defenders such as Needham and others had supplied could now never be obtained. Likewise, many of the leading professional teams, missing the refreshing combat and spirit of the cream of amateur talent, now found their playing standards and manners sometimes suffering to such an extent that the Cup-Final of 1913 between Aston Villa and Sunderland, which had promised so much, was to be more remembered for its brawn than skill and the subsequent disciplinary action against the referee and a player from each side.

The result of the 'split' upon the fortunes of the Corinthians of the future, however, was even more disastrous. By 1910 the really great Public School and University players of recent years comparable with those of G.O.'s day could be counted on the fingers of one hand. A contributor to *The Times* in that year wrote: 'The only present playing members who are worthy of inclusion in the roll of honour indeed are S.H. Day, S.S. Harris, M. Morgan-Owen, G.C. Vassall, R.A. Young and, possibly, C. E. Brisley. And of these only Young and Brisley have come to the fore during the past three seasons.' As it was, Brisley, one of the few outstanding footballers from Lancing College, never realised the heights that he had promised and sadly lost his life in the First World War. Young had a distinguished batting and wicket-keeping career for Repton, to keep wicket Cambridge and Sussex which he interrupted to keep wicket - wearing glasses - for England v. Australia in the winter of 1907-08 under A.O. Jones' captaincy only months after gaining an amateur soccer cap for England v. Holland at outside-right. Yet he played no further games for the Corinthians after 1912.

Between 1910 and 1914 the only other players of real note to come to the front with the Corinthians were, from Oxford, F.W.H. Nicholas of Forest

School, A.H.G. Kerry of Oxford High School, and the cricketers G.N. Foster of Malvern and Miles Howell of Repton, all of them England amateur soccer internationals at some time or another; and from Cambridge, Lieutenant Harold G. Bache (not to be confused with Aston Villa's Joseph Bache), a centre-forward from King Edward's, Birmingham, with fine dribbling and shooting powers who showed great skill for West Bromwich Albion before he fell in France in 1916. There was also from Cambridge the incomparable Max Woosnam, a Canon's son and a Wykehamist, who played for Cambridge at four different games, was its twelfth man at cricket and represented England at tennis with Lycett and at soccer with the professionals. All of these players, except Bache, overlapped the next period. But alone they could never fill the places of those who had retired, and there were now no professional rivals with whom to compete in play and for honours against whom they could test their standards and styles.

The eventual effect of the 'split,' however, lay deeper still. In 1905 one of the Corinthian heroes of the Bury game, and the previous season's soccer captain at Cambridge, Stanley (S.S.) Harris, the last great Old Westminster footballer, recorded his feelings with what may be regarded as a dash of Victorian sentimentality even though the feeling can still be found among the nation's schools, if not its colleges:

'To belong to a club which is able to confine itself to the 'Varsities and public schools, and yet be, year after year, the first amateur club in the land, is an honour of which one may feel justly proud. It is no wonder that footballers who have met in rivalry on the field at Queen's in the 'Varsity match join together after and strain every nerve to keep the Corinthians in the position they have always held.

When one is at school there is the feeling that the sense of pride in one's school can never be surpassed; when the schoolboy goes to the 'Varsity he finds that love of his school is swallowed up in an altogether stronger feeling - a sentiment almost of reverence - towards his University; it is a feeling which nerves him to do all things for the honour of alma mater. Then the 'Varsity man goes down, and the feeling is carried on with regard to the Corinthian F.C. They know that they have the honour to be members of a club without rival, and their one desire is to help it to retain that position.'

The disappearance of the Corinthians from the public gaze after the 'split,' however, left no outstanding amateur models for emulation among the game's patrons except for those internationals such as Woodward and Sharpe who alone could be seen in the professional and England's teams. Accordingly, many schools small in mind, tradition and size, regarded the time as opportune for changing their winter game from soccer to the then more socially-fashionable rugby. They ignored the attitude of those guardians of the English Public School tradition: Eton, Winchester, Charterhouse, Westminster, Shrewsbury, Repton, Malvern, Bradfield, Lancing, Brentwood, Forest, Aldenham, Ardingly, Chigwell, Wellingborough and Highgate (a convert from rugby to soccer!) who all remained firm in their adherence to the pure football game, and some of whom continued their excursions in the Arthur Dunn Cup Competition and their supply of soccer among other Blues to Oxford and Cambridge. So whatever the rugby game may have gained in quantity, it could have appreciated by little, if at all, in social quality. Finally, in April of 1914, shortly after the return of the amateur rebels to the F.A., the appearance of King George V wearing Lancashire's red in his buttonhole to see Burnley defeat Liverpool at the first Cup-Final attended by a reigning monarch swept the game's social detractors from their vantage points, although they have continued to snipe at it ever since.

The re-entry of the rebels to the parent fold had become inevitable as less than half a dozen years of conditions under the 'split' had exposed an impasse that grew more obvious with each successive season. Under the Corinthians' and older Universities' leadership peace negotiations with the F.A. were commenced. In February of 1914 the breach was healed with the malcontents embraced once more within the F.A.'s fold. By then, of course, we know now that the union was too late to be of value in amateur spheres. This was the last Corinthian season under the old regime. When the players lined up again in 1919 after the intervening holocaust, the position of the amateur in both football and cricket was ultimately to reflect the changed conditions. The Golden Age was over; and so, too, not long afterwards, was the Glory that was Corinth.

_____

99

THE GLORY THAT WAS CORINTH

When the Corinthians and English cricket picked up the threads in 1919 the links with the past were yet to be snapped. The reactions to Victorian and Edwardian inhibition flowed freely in the period now identified with the Bright Young Thing and Jazz; and the economic and social consequences of two World Wars that by 1950 had resulted in high taxation, a technological mind and a universal specialisation so as to grind the amateur out of all spheres of activity were not so potent immediately after 1918.

Amateur sportsmen still abounded to carry on the standards and traditions from before 1914. The sportsmen may not have been as rich in general quality as they had been in G.O.'s day and in the Golden Age. They were sufficient in number, however, to maintain the blue-blood stream of English cricket while fresh supplies were being pumped in from the Public Schools and Universities, where men, matured with war experience, together with schoolboy Freshmen could still find the leisure and money to aspire to Blues and good degrees, and then sometimes apply both in posts that permitted incursions upon the public field.

In cricket, at least, there was then hardly any change to make the general standard of the game superficially different from what had existed before the war. A myopic experiment adopted at Lancashire's instigation of playing two-day county matches was hastily abandoned in the summer of its trial during 1919, and Glamorganshire joined the County Cricket Championship in 1921. But these were matters of form rather than of substance. The balance of the county elevens had started to shift from amateurs to professionals around the second half of King Edward VII's reign when the first ominous shots were being fired in the battle for modern social reform; the swing over was not completed until the social revolution following 1945.

In the summer of 1926, for example, of over two hundred cricketers who appear under the first-class batting averages of the 1927 *Wisden,* headed as one may expect by Jack Hobbs, 47 per cent were amateurs. By 1936 the percentage from a similar number had dropped to 35, and in 1950, even including the semi-professional administrator, the percentage was down to 27, a drop of 20 per cent in twenty years. In 1900 the percentage was just over 50, only slightly higher than in 1926. So if the blackout of 1939 saw a totally different position in the numbers and status of the amateur cricketer from what it had been in 1914, the eclipse after 1919 was a gradual, almost imperceptible process. Players of the calibre of P.G.H. Fender, J.N. Crawford and D.J. Knight of Surrey, P.F. Warner and F.T. Mann of Middlesex, J.C. White, P.R. Johnson and J. Daniell of Somerset, E.R. Wilson with Yorkshire and R.H. Spooner with Lancashire had all survived the war and were to play during the whole or part of the 1920s.

With the Corinthians, however, the prospects and position were bleaker. Thanks to the 'split' and the natural retirement of a footballer at least ten years earlier than a cricketer, they had to look back nearly twenty years for a supply of names with which to conjure. Amateur footballers of outstanding ability there had been before the men who had won for England, or rather the United Kingdom (not Great Britain in those days), two Olympic Games soccer tournaments in 1908 and 1912.

There was no question as to who was the leading footballing nation in those years. But outstanding players such as Ivan Sharpe, Rev. K.R.G. Hunt, V.J. Woodward, R.M. Hawkes, A.E. Knight, H.P. Hardman, R.C. Brebner, A. Berry and H.A. Walden nearly all preferred to wear the England shirt from Football League and other non-Corinthian ranks. Whether or not they were ever invited to play for the Corinthians would have been academic at that time, for the 'split' would have precluded most of them from following the example of C.B. Fry and S.S. Harris who assisted amateur as well as professional clubs.

There was, however, a very small core of experienced and tried men to form a basis for the Corinthians when they too picked up the threads in 1919. The cricket blues, G.N. Foster and J.S.F. Morrison, as well as I.E. Snell, had played for the club before the war; and K.R.G. Hunt and A.E. Knight forsook Wolverhampton Wanderers and Portsmouth respectively to serve it. Unfortunately these additions were partially offset by the departure of the brilliant Max Woosnam who threw in his lot with Chelsea and then, when business took him north, with Manchester City, and England, until a broken leg prematurely ended the career of a really great centre-half. It was, therefore, to the Universities at Oxford and Cambridge to which the Corinthians looked for their future. During the 1920s Oxford produced D.R. Jardine, G.T.S. Stevens and E.R.T. Holmes, and Cambridge sent out G.O. Allen, the Ashton brothers and A.P.F. Chapman, some of the greatest University cricketers of all time. In football, too, the ancient Universities produced players of the highest calibre and Corinth did not therefore look entirely in vain.

The 1920s produced a line of Corinthians ready and able to carry on the traditions of, G.O.'s era in a manner that many consider resulted in the greatest Corinthian era of all. Such a claim, of course, is almost as equivocal as that which holds that G.O. was the greatest centre-forward ever. But bearing in mind that the Corinthians of the 1920s had to contend with a better trained and tended professional opposition than did the players of G.O.'s era, the plea is not as extravagant as it may first appear.

When the war was over, the Football League was extended so that from the Second Division Chelsea were gratuitously elected to the First Division without any vote being taken. Arsenal joined them upon a committee's string-pulled decision, while Coventry City, West Ham United, Rotherham County and South Shields were elected to the Second Division, thereby increasing the first two Divisions of the League from 18 to 22 clubs, the present number. The two sections of the Third Division were formed in 1921 and 1922, and professional soccer geared itself for a twenty-year spell of increased speed and swiftly changing training and tactical methods that swept old standards from the field of play and the untrained out of opposition.

Before the War, Newcastle United had set the course for many future soccer successes by emphasising the modern trend of combined play to the exclusion of the individual dash and clan that Bassett, Bloomer and the Corinthians of the 1890s and before had employed. This modern style was to be seen in the results achieved by Burnley, Tottenham Hotspur, Liverpool and Huddersfield Town, the most successful of the immediate post-war sides. Not only had the professionals built a broader structure; within it they set up fresh records that made others all the keener to emulate and beat. Burnley won the second post-war League Championship in 1921 by surviving thirty successive League games without defeat, an achievement which has yet to be surpassed. In the same year Tottenham Hotspur won the F.A. Cup for the second time in their history. They were then still the only professional London or Southern club to break the Northern and Midlands monopoly, while twelve months earlier they had won the Second Division Championship with a total of 70 points, still a record for the First and Second Divisions of the League. The first Wembley Cup-Final in 1923, between Bolton Wanderers and West Ham United, and the fantastic crowds there showed the shape of things to come. Bolton Wanderers won the Cup on each of their three appearances at Wembley in seven years. Aston Villa had broken the old amateur Wanderers' record of five Cup wins by obtaining it for the sixth time when they defeated Huddersfield Town in 1920, while the Yorkshire Club, under the great Herbert Chapman, outshone them all by becoming the first team to win three successive League Championships. In the midst of all this, the off-side law was changed, in 1925, and in consequence so were tactics and all goal-scoring records.

In 1927 Cardiff City took the Cup out of England for the only time by beating Arsenal, who in turn went on to a purchased glory in the thirties, after Everton had won the Second and First Division Championships and the F.A. Cup in three successive years. Then came the gland treatments which Hitler's intervention alone prevented from turning the game into a laughing-stock and the players into guinea-pigs.

For ten years the Corinthians of the 1920s held their own in these changing circumstances and the ever-increasing tempo. What may rank against them in the final assessment, however, is the greater proportion of defeats suffered against the professional sides, often of a mediocre calibre, than those inflicted by the leading professors of G.O.'s day. But human qualities cannot be assessed in figures, even if doctors do so in calories. What mattered above all else was that even if the football fashions of the period were moving swiftly from individualism to combination for combination's sake so that the brilliant hallmarks of G.O.'s era were no more to be seen, the fighting spirit and personality and the courage and aggression that had always been associated with the Corinthians were on English fields again. Their gallant but vain efforts in the F.A. Cup Competition stirred the complacency of their detractors, the imagination of the public and the keenness of their opponents. Yet in doing so, the men of Corinth wrote what proved to be the penultimate chapter in their wonderful history.

During those first few years after 1918, G.N. Foster, K.R G. Hunt, C. Wreford Brown (who at last hung up his boots) and W.U. Timmis, a fine full-back of the post-period and also a valued secretary of the club, were, with others, in the vanguard of the crusade to revive the Club's fortunes. Unfortunately for them the Football League was now expanded to 22 clubs in each Division (G.O.'s day had seen first 16 and then 18 clubs in each of the only two Divisions). Therefore no Saturdays remained for the traditional friendly fixtures. Because of the difficulty in obtaining professional opposition and in order to give the Club the stimulus which was necessary to enable it

to rebuild its strength and public standing of the years before the AM 'split,' the strict rule of not competing for trophies (relaxed only upon charitable grounds for the Sheriff of London Shield) was now amended to permit the Club to participate in the F.A. Cup. The Club's popularity with League clubs and the public, and the lateness in starting its playing season, enabled the Corinthians to obtain exemption from the early rounds, and so enter the Competition at the same time as the leading Football League clubs.

The decision to enter for the F.A. Cup was not taken without dissent among the Club's older members and friends. An interesting example of this was shown by Roland Allen, the distinguished. sporting journalist, who wrote in his delightful sporting reminiscences *All in the Day's Sport*:

'My opinion was that it would be better for the much-desired revival of the Corinthians to be delayed indefinitely than that they should develop into just another of the Cup teams ... Year after year, with a few brilliant exceptions, the Corinthians were quickly bumped out of the competition by professional teams of varying degrees of efficiency. I could not and cannot see how all this helped towards recreating what the Corinthians had once meant to football ... The Corinthians have gone: at least they are now the Corinthians and Casuals. Queen's Park remain, as an all-amateur club, members of the Scottish League ... I still believe that the Corinthians alone could have achieved some resemblance to their former eminences without amalgamation and without the undistinguished interludes of their Cup chasing. We shall never know ...

The Corinthians wrote the greatest pages in their history in about forty years, during which they did not bother about cups. Their name lost a lot of its significance - let there be no mistake about this - during the period which included their Cup adventure. The Cup was never anything more than incidental to their revival. Perhaps the mistake was made of thinking that it might be used as the means.'

Roland Allen's opinion voiced the feelings of many, and while we shall now never know how far the Club might have gone without the Cup and amalgamation with the Casuals, one cannot help thinking that the final appraisal lies somewhere between Allen's view and the circumstances of the time. For the post-War period with that first Wembley Final saw the beginnings of the Cup mania which now sweeps the country throughout each season, and its effect is seen for better or for worse in almost every other sphere of sporting competition and rivalry. The knock-out cup competition principle is common to all. The F.A. Cup-Final, which is now on a par with the Derby, the Grand National and the Boat Race, as one of the sporting and social events of the year, was fast becoming in the 1920s the shop-window for football to attract its patrons. It was also a tangible stimulus to Corinth. Faced with more highly trained opponents than any previous Corinthian sides had tackled, the Club could never expect the parity of fitness that had prevailed from the time of 'Pa' Jackson until the end of G.O.'s day, for a Max Woosnam who could play with and against professionals without any special preparation comes, like a C.B. Fry, once in a generation. Hence the F.A. Cup gave the Corinthians, who took over as their headquarters the historic old Cup-Final ground at the Crystal Palace, a position in football's shop-window.

As a consequence the Public Schools amateurs who chiefly comprised the Club set up ground records at the time at Brighton, Norwich and Walsall. They drew crowds of 38,000, 42,000, 56,000 and 60,000 for the battles with Sheffield United, West Ham United, Newcastle United and Millwall. The old fighting spirit and verve that the amateurs displayed more than justified the means of the F.A. Cup as a reviver. Indeed, the average gate in the nineteen games from 1923 to 1933 was over 30,000.

But once the object of reviving the glory had been achieved, a graceful retirement from the Competition in favour of less strenuous encounters with the professionals and with other teams in mid-week the odd free Saturday would have avoided the final ignominy. For in 1934 the F.A. partially withdrew the Club's exemption, thus forcing it to compete at an earlier round than hitherto a run of defeats accumulated in the 1930s, and the Club in the end surrendered its identity. But a decline from success and glory has never been popular, and to be wise after the event is easily the most irresistible of temptations. Three cup victories in nineteen games does not amount to an outstanding record. Yet, as F.N.S. Creek in his *A History of the Corinthian Football Club* put it:

Cup-tie action at Crystal Palace

'it was only in three of their contests that the Corinthians were definitely outclassed - by West Bromwich Albion, Sheffield United (1925) [winners that year] and Manchester City (a replay). [In 1926, that year, beaten finalists.] All the other games produced hard struggles, and in the ties against such first-class sides as Blackburn Rovers, Newcastle United, Manchester City and Sheffield United (1932), the amateurs fully held their own. For the Corinthians' comparative lack of success, two reasons - one negative and one positive - stand out above all others; the weak headwork of the amateurs, and the superlatively steady goal-keeping of the professionals. The feeble heading has not been confined to the forwards, who, however, have not headed a single goal of the twenty-three they have scored.

Yet, whatever the results, it is certain that the entry of the Corinthians into the Cup competition has resulted in increased interest in amateur football. It cannot be denied that the great struggles with Brighton, Blackburn Rovers, Manchester City, Newcastle United, Millwall and Sheffield United raised immense enthusiasm throughout the country. The magnificent contest with Newcastle United was broadcast by the B.B.C. Finally, it can be said with certainty that the admission of the Club into the national competition has not in any way weakened its happy relations with the professional clubs. Rather has it strengthened them; and it is a pleasing fact that to-day the League clubs, great and small, are always keen to play the Corinthians whenever a suitable opportunity occurs.'

The later thirties were a sad sequel to the glories of the twenties. As the tempo and intensity of the professional game increased further and the third-back defensive strategy came to rule the day with the 'W' formation and roving inside forward of the Alex James type replacing the five-in-a-row frontal attack, the fruits of that post-war period were now beyond the reach of amateurs. Nevertheless while the twenties lasted, the flames were rekindled in the hearts of the traditionalists and die-hard supporters, and memories were stored for a new generation which was never to see the famous club at its greatest again.

Can one ever forget that famous defence of Howard Baker, 'Baishe' Bower and John Morrison; those famous forwards R.G.C. Jenkins, A. E. Taylor, Walter Robins, Graham Doggart, Norman Creek and Lieutenant Hegan; or Harvey Chadder, Freddie Ewer, Tommy Whewell, L.B. Blaxland, C.B.G. Hunter or Robin Moulsdale at half, and the late, lamented and unforgettable Claude Ashton everywhere? There were not a few among even the most long-standing and long-suffering professional supporters who could not have minded the amateurs conquering at the expense of the professional favourites. It was not so much a matter of David against Goliath as the idea of seeing young men in their prime playing for the joy of the game against others sometimes, but not always, more skilful, but paid to be so. The story might have been told again in a lower key in relation to organised amateur soccer twenty years later after 1945, if the Corinthians had been in existence, even though the gap between competitive professionalism and amateurism is now even greater than what it was in the 1920s. For, matured with the War years, as were not a few of the Corinthians of the 1920s, John Tanner, Tony Pawson, Ken Shearwood, Denis Saunders and Ben Brown of Oxford, and Doug Insole, Hubert Doggart and Ralph Cowan from Cambridge could well have formed the core for a revival of Corinth. But, as we shall see, they formed the core of a new club which has filled the gap left by the Corinthians and brought fresh lustre and glory to Oxford and Cambridge soccer.

It should not be overlooked, moreover, that these Corinthians of the 1920s, inheriting the tradition of their predecessors, also played their parts for England in full international matches. B. Howard Baker appeared in goal for England as well as the Football League. A.G. Bower played five times for his country at right- or left-back in the days of Smart of Aston Villa, Clay of Tottenham Hotspur, Wadsworth of Huddersfield Town and Warney Cresswell, then of Sunderland, and captained the side against Belgium and Wales. Claude Ashton for one fleeting afternoon stood in G.O.'s shoes as captain and centre-forward of England's full side, against Ireland in 1925, and the dashing K.E.

Hegan with four full caps, not to mention countless amateur representative honours alongside many of his fellow Corinthians, was in direct line with E.C. Bambridge and B.O. Corbett in the Club's tradition of outstanding left-wingers. These four could surely take their place amongst the greatest giants in any Corinthian hall of fame.

Howard Baker, in keeping with the tradition of those earlier Corinthians, Oakley and Fry, was a British jumping champion, on this occasion the high-jump, and his qualities here were seen in his goalkeeping and his treatment of rising shots. He played in full and amateur internationals for England, gaining his last full cap against Ireland in 1926, and he received an honour rarely granted to the unpaid player, when he played for the Football League against the Irish League in 1925. His black goalkeeping jersey ribbed with white, together with his spectacular and debonair fielding of the ball and his hefty kicking for Everton and Chelsea as well as the Corinthians, made him one of the most colourful as well as popular sights on modern soccer grounds in the 1920s. Norman Creeks tells us that 'From 1922 until 1931 he was the Corinthians' regular goalkeeper, and his total number of appearances, 176, is the highest reached by any member of the Club.' He also represented England at athletics in the Olympic Games of 1912 and 1920, and somehow managed to excel at tennis, water-polo and high-diving. No wonder he kicked a ball the length of the field in the Blackburn Rovers and Millwall Cup-Ties, to mention but two occasions that bring his feat to mind.

Bower and Morrison followed their Charterhouse predecessors, the brothers Walters, in forming once more an Old Carthusian full-back pair. Bower, like P.M. Walters, had failed to get his First Eleven colours at school, but went on to obtain honours similar to, if fewer than, those that P.M. obtained when there were fewer professionals with whom to compete. Standing a good six feet high and perfectly built for a back, Bower will always be remembered for his courageous tackling and headwork and for his positional play. In particular, the way in which he mastered Hughie Gallacher,

the great Scottish and Newcastle United centre-forward, comes to mind, on the few occasions when that 'will o' the wisp' slipped A. H. Chadder at centre-half during the most famous of Corinthian Cup-Ties against Newcastle United in 1927. Morrison was a triple-Blue, at cricket, golf and soccer. He captained Cambridge at cricket in 1919 when Miles Howell, the Oxford captain, was also a Corinthian; and if he had done nothing else apart from gaining an amateur soccer cap he will never be forgotten for the barrier he presented to the Blackburn Rovers' forwards who were striving desperately for the equaliser that never came, in the First Round of the Cup in 1924 at the Crystal Palace.

The game of 1927 against Newcastle United, however, perhaps symbolised the Corinthians' play of this period. As *The Times* account of the game so aptly put it: 'It is not the heavy shoulder charge of itself that kills - it is the pace and what, for the moment may be called the rigour of the game.' If there was not the same direct line for goal from the wings that had existed in G.O.'s day, the Corinthians of this period still possessed that distinctness about their forward play which distinguished it from the stereotyped style of the professionals. Even before the off-side law was changed to its present form, the position of the centre-forward lying upfield for a snap goal as the spearhead of the attack generally prepared a monotonous path towards the centre of the playing arena. During this period of the Corinthian twilight, the old five-in-a-line frontal attack of the forwards mixing close- and long-passing with the half-backs in support, still prevailed. Once they resorted to the 'W' formation and the third-back strategy in the thirties, their distinctive style went, and with it their reputation. Yet in 1933, Norman Creek in his *A History of the Corinthian Football Club* spoke approvingly of the changes in tactics in the game as a whole which followed the altered offside law, because 'Play is now much faster, more goals are scored and there are fewer drawn games.' But it was faster play that was killing the Corinthians and, as Goodall and G.O. realised, was gradually killing football too.

Against the then League leaders and ultimate Champions for 1927, Newcastle United, at their best, the Corinthians deservedly led at half-time by a grand goal scored by Claude Ashton playing in this game at inside-left, a goal that followed a centre from his wing partner Hegan, who had drawn the defence after a perfect cross-kick by Creek. They held on to their lead until a quarter of an hour from the end. Until then it looked as if Newcastle might not break their hoodoo of never having won a cup game at the Crystal, Palace. With each succeeding moment in that second half, the atmosphere became more electric and eventually, as *The Times* put it, 'the professional team turned in their desperation to what the boxers call the "rough stuff" - some of it fair enough, but some of it decidedly not.' Fourteen minutes from the end Newcastle were awarded a free-kick from which they found the Corinthian net off the shoulder of a Corinthian defender, Howard Baker being left hopelessly unsighted - a lucky equalising goal.

In the remaining few minutes R.G.C. Jenkins, the amateurs' centre forward, retired hurt, and against ten Corinthians, two of whom were injured, the professionals took their chances and won by 3-1. Thus the Champions-elect prevailed against the cream of amateur soccer, but only just. The ghosts around the Palace towers and the crested Corinthian shirts had nearly saved the day.

The teams lined up as follows:

CORINTHIANS

B.Howard Baker

A.G. Bower			A.E. Knight	
J.R.B. Moulsdale		A.H. Chadder	F.H. Ewer	
A.E. Taylor	F.N.S. Creek	R.G.C. Jenkins	C.T. Ashton	K.E. Hegan

●

Seymour	McDonald	Gallacher	McKay	Urwin
	Gibson	Spencer	R. McKenzie	
	Hudspeth		Maitland	

Wilson

NEWCASTLE UNITED

Ashton's goal in this game was only one of over one hundred that he scored for the Corinthians and he played at one time or another in every position on the field, including goalkeeper; indeed, in the victory over Blackburn Rovers, he had been at centre-half, and an outstandingly good one at that, frustrating the efforts of Ted Harper, who was two years later to play for England against Scotland and then set up goal-scoring records for the time with Blackburn, Tottenham Hotspur and Preston North End. Claude Ashton was the only Corinthian to play in all of the Club's first eighteen Cup-Ties, by far the most memorable ones. Perhaps his best football was at wing-half-back, but his versatility and his appetite for goals indicated the complete all-round footballer, which he undoubtedly was, even though he suffered from the traditional Corinthian weakness of poor headwork, which was not up to the standard of ball-control with his feet. He played in over a dozen amateur international games as well as the full international against Ireland in 1925, when, although he combined well with Aston Villa's' Billy Walker, who was at inside-left, he did not strike his best form.

At Winchester Ashton had captained the College at almost every game he played, and at Cambridge, where he was captain of cricket in 1923 (his brothers had been captain in succession in the two previous years) he also won a hockey Blue in the same year, in addition to soccer Blues in 1920 and 1921. On going down he always added strength as

THE GLORY THAT WAS CORINTH
CENTURION GOALSCORERS

A.G. DOGGART

F.N.S. CREEK

C.T. ASHTON

CAPTAINS COURAGEOUS

A.G. Bower (Corinthians and England) greets Fred Keenor (Cardiff City and Wales) – 1927.

A.T. Barber (Oxford Univ. and Yorkshire C.C.C.) with Billy Walker (Aston Villa and England) – 1929.

well as colour to the Essex batting on the few occasions when he could appear until 1938, and as may be expected, he was a most attractive batsman with a lovely cover-drive and superb footwork as well as being a glorious fieldsman in any position. Though wars inure to disaster and bereavement, it still came as a profound shock to learn in 1942 that Acting Squadron-Leader C.T. Ashton had been killed at the age of forty-one whilst on active service, in an air crash that also caused the death of his fellow Old Wykehamist and another Cambridge soccer captain, Squadron-Leader R. de W.K. Winlaw.

Ashton's brothers, Gilbert and Hubert, spent less time with the Corinthians, although both were powerful Cambridge forwards. Hubert also won a hockey Blue, scored a, truly faultless century in the 1881 Varsity cricket match in the year of Gilbert's captaincy, and then a year later unselfishly deprived himself of another, when captain, by declaring the Cambridge innings closed when he was 90 not out. Years later he returned from Burma to follow R.C. Gosling, an earlier Corinthian inside-forward, as High Sheriff of Essex, and in 1950 he was elected to Parliament as well as the Member for Chelmsford. Not since the days of the Studds in 1881 had three brothers played in the same Cambridge Cricket XI in one year, as did the Ashtons exactly forty years later in 1921; and in playing at soccer also, in 1920, they set up a fraternal record which is hardly likely to be equalled.

Their successor for sheer individual versatility may well be G.H.G. Doggart, another Old Wykehamist, who has gathered four post-Second World War Cambridge Blues and would appear to have inherited his games' sense from his father, A.G. Doggart, the Ashtons' cricketing and soccer contemporary. Doggart senior played twice for Cambridge at cricket and soccer, and at inside-left he was one of the most consistent Corinthian forwards in one position. At inside-left he not only obtained amateur international caps but captained England's full side - which included Moss of Aston Villa, Creswell of Sunderland and Seddon of Bolton Wanderers - against Belgium at Antwerp in

November 1923. His careful batting assisted not inconsiderably towards Cambridge's two innings defeats of Oxford in 1921 and 1922, and he afterwards played occasionally for Middlesex. But he comes more readily to mind as a Corinthian. Both he and Creek were to join Claude Ashton in being the only Corinthians to emulate in scoring a century of goals for the Club, and some of Doggart's were indeed memorable. There was one in a Cup-Tie at Norwich just before 1930 that was out of the Cobbold dribbling book, and another, right out of the blue, shook the Blackburn netting and the Rovers from the Cup in 1924. After representing his University on the F.A. Council for eighteen years, Doggart became a Vice-President of the Association in 1950.

F.N.S. Creek was another full, as well as amateur, international of those days. Slightly built, appearing almost too frail to oppose professional defences, he had Woodward's knack of balance and avoiding hard knocks; and like that earlier and greater amateur he started in the centre, where he obtained his Blue at Cambridge, and then turned to a position less vulnerable for injuries - inside-right - in the Cup-Ties. He holds the Club's scoring record of ten goals in one match, against the Army, although it is probably not comparable as an individual performance with Stanley Harris' five goals against Bury in 1904. Besides writing an indispensable history of the Corinthians he has produced attractive manuals on soccer and cricket, and is often to be heard as a B.B.C. commentator. In the Second World War he added an M.B.E. to the M.C. he received in the First, and has now returned actively to the game as Assistant Director of Coaching at the F.A. and England's amateur team manager.

F.H. Ewer and Frank Hartley also obtained full caps against continental teams of this period, as well as amateur honours. Ewer was a left-half like 'the man of iron,' Wilf Copping of Leeds United and Arsenal fame, with tons of pluck and courage, and he completed a memorable tri-angle with Doggart and Hegan. Hartley was an inside-forward of a direct rather than a stylish type who was the only regular Corinthian one can recall who turned professional (appropriately enough, perhaps, with Tottenham Hotspur). Arthur E. Knight played at right- and left-back in the early Corinthian Cup-Ties after captaining Portsmouth. He appeared in the 1912 and 1920 United Kingdom Olympic Games soccer sides, as well as in a 'Victory' international against Wales in 1919 and nearly thirty amateur internationals. He was not far behind Jesse Pennington of West Bromwich Albion in positional play, and perhaps was his superior in tackling and certainly his equal in heading. J. G. Knight, a smaller full-back, and of a slightly later vintage, who sometimes played at centre-half, also gained amateur international honours.

So did C.B.G. Hunter and A.H. Chadder who were as good centre-halves as most professionals in the days when a player in that position was expected to be a footballer, and Chadder also played at back and forward in the Cup-Ties. Lieutenant F.W.H. Nicholas, A.E. Taylor, R.G.C. Jenkins on the right, and A.T. Davies on the left, were other wingers to be capped, while R.W.V. Robins , of course, gained all the cricket honours about the time of his Cup-Tie appearances. J.R.B. Moulsdale, a skilful wing-half and the only well known Corinthian from the Quaker school at Bootham's, York, gained a full and numerous amateur caps for Wales, while B.C.A. Patchitt was one of the last Old Carthusian Corinthians to gain a full cap for England, against Sweden, twice in 1923.

The Corinthians of this era, therefore, were still a national asset, in more ways than one, but representatively in the main for only amateur occasions. In the thirty years from G.O.'s time, the professionals had so improved their standards as well as squeeze the amateurs from the full international sides, except against the continental pupils who were then in their soccer infancy.

If the Newcastle game was symbolic of the Corinthians' play in these days, the Millwall matches of 1930 signified their spirit, bound up with the guts and pluck of one of them who played for more than half the second game with a broken leg. In the first struggle at Crystal Palace before 40,000 spectators, the Corinthians twice fought back to draw level after being a goal down. R.W.V. Robins equalised that first goal, the all important one, in a Cup-Tie which had been scored by Jimmy Forsythe, and Claude Ashton, now at centre-forward, saved the day in the last minute after Phillips had put the professionals once more in the lead. It was not good fortune, however, that let the Corinthians live again, but magnificent all-round football in atrocious conditions with the ball on the ground, superbly controlled.

The outstanding forward afield, however, for pace and style was undoubtedly Hegan, and when the replay took place four days later at New Cross, the Army officer found himself as direct a target as the ball. He may well have been excused for believing himself in a commando raid instead of a Cup-Tie, for he was so roughly treated and knocked about that he found out afterwards that he had played throughout the last 85 minutes with a broken tibia! Even then the policy of playing the star opposing forward instead of the ball did not pay immediate dividends. Millwall drew level, after another goal by Robins, which followed a run by Hegan while his pace was still not appreciably impaired; and when extra time of half an hour was played, the final period found the amateurs with even Hegan, by some anatomical miracle, swarming round the Millwall goal.

With the Corinthians' outside-left in hospital, the teams lined up at Stamford Bridge for the third match in ten days. At half-time the score was 1-1; indeed, if the amateurs had taken all their chances they could well have established a lead. But in the second half, with Bower limping and Robins lame, the effect of the professionals' training and tactics took its toll. The Corinthians' battered defence cracked, four goals were surrendered and the score of 5-1 registered Millwall's superiority as the better and more effective team of the day, although not necessarily as well as the better footballers.

The three games were watched by 140,000 people, including 60,000 at Chelsea, but as *The Times* put it after that match:

'It has to be admitted that not a little of the play of Millwall was of a nature not likely to attract fresh followers. Twice the referee had to speak to members of the Millwall defence for their tactics, and one at least of their players must be considered lucky that he did not have to retire from the game before it was ended. Yet on the whole it was a clean and fast game, so far as the referee could see, but there are ways and means of impeding and polling an opponent which cannot be seen but which can be felt by the player.'

The presence of these crowds at a game between amateurs and a professional team third from the bottom in the Second Division in itself indicated the Corinthians' appeal to the public in 1930. A year later under vile conditions on the frost bound pitch to which they could not adapt themselves with the facility of their opponents, they fell 1-3 to Port Vale, then midway in the Second Division. In 1932, 30,000 at Bramall Lane saw a Corinthian side that had never played together before go down by 1-2 to Sheffield United, who had just beaten Arsenal twice at Christmas and were fourth in the First Division. A draw would have been fairer and also the result Jimmy Dunne, the Irish international, later of Arsenal, had not scored for Sheffield United first and then headed the winning goal; and in 1933 the Corinthians lost undeservedly by 0-2 to West Ham United (eventual semi-finalists who in turn were beaten by the eventual winners, Everton), on the day that Walsall by the same score amazed Arsenal and everyone else except, perhaps, themselves. But the slide was now well on. Bower, Baker, Doggart and Ewer had dropped out, Hartley had turned professional, and the varsities and public schools somehow never seemed to supply the Corinthians' ranks with sufficient talent at one and the same time to fill the retiring places permanently.

It is true that W.H.L. Lister of Lancashire and H.M. Garland-Wells of Surrey, both county cricket captains, and R.S. Grant, captain of the 1939 West Indies touring side, as well as W.H. Webster, A.H. Fabian, W.T. Whewell and A.H. Woolcock obtained their amateur international caps as well as their Blues; that E.D.R. Shearer gained many caps

for England and went to Brussels with the 1936 Great Britain Olympic Games soccer side, and that A.T. Barber Of Yorkshire and B.H. Valentine of Kent - two more county cricket captains - J.S.O. Haslewood, the golfer, and G.A. Strasser and J.L.T. Guise were other talented Varsity footballers. Yet the grammar schools were gently edging the traditional names from the annual Varsity match team lists although not from the Public School fixture lists; and when representatives of the two schools combined at University the lowering standards of the traditional other talented Varsity schools retarded the progress of the less fashionable. Hence, around the period shortly before 1939, Varsity soccer standards slumped badly, and as Roland Alien put it in *All in the Day's* Sport:

'Soccer at English universities and public schools, as far as I saw any of it - and I eventually gave up going out of my way to do so - was a travesty of the game. The annual University soccer match was an undignified scramble, in vivid contrast to the rugby match at Twickenham, the Boat Race, the boxing and the athletics, all of which reached and maintained a high standard ...

The loss of prestige which the Corinthians suffered had, in my opinion, not the remotest connection with the drift of the public schools away from soccer. The attitude of the schools and universities towards soccer was wrong. They did not think that a thing worth doing at all was worth doing well.'

Perhaps they had forsaken soccer for tea and tennis with the ladies, and motoring and golf thrown in as added counterattractions. The differences down the years was seen when I mentioned to G.O. 'Pa' jackson's *Sporting Days and Sporting Ways*. He replied:

'I have read one of "Pa" Jackson's books, but I don't think it was the one you mention. Personally I don't consider him an interesting writer and as you say, his accounts of tennis left me cold. That game, though it has its uses, was frowned on in my day.'

Sincere attempts to raise the standard of soccer in the schools and colleges in which the game was born were also frowned upon and the effect of this was felt after the First World War in the 1930s. Money cheerfully dissipated on inadequate cricket coaching was never considered for guidance on the winter game; or perhaps the ageing games-master saw therein a challenge to his fading power. Whatever may have been the reason, the Corinthians' sources of recruits of quality in effect dried up. Further, that loss of prestige, described by Roland Alien, was something entirely different from the Corinthians' virtual disappearance from the public eye before 1914 - they just could not cope now with the professional opposition; and while outstanding individual players would rise to the surface in the universities and schools and ultimately with the Corinthians, there was never the time or opportunity to mould them once more into a successful team. The third-back system and the tension of the Cup and League games were now accelerating the professional's speed and training to leave the recreational Corinthian amateur farther and farther behind in the race for fitness. Amateur soccer, with its own network of League and Cup competition was now organised smoothly and completely over the whole country. The old seams of talent were running out, and the glory that was Corinth was crumbling

The Football Association withdrew the Club's exemption from the third round of the F.A. Cup after the defeat by West Ham United in 1933; many of the smaller League clubs were now openly resenting this favourable treatment which was now certainly not justified as it had been ten years earlier, and for the season of 1933-34 the Corinthians held aloof from the Competition. They came back for the season of 1934-35 and were granted exemption until the first round, along with all the Third Division clubs. How, indeed, were the mighty now fallen! In less than five years the glories of the twenties were but a legend alongside G.O. in Corinthian and soccer history, and from the multitudes who had seen the Millwall battles, a mere handful dotted the terraces to see a once great side.

I shall never forget a dull November afternoon in 1937 at the White City, itself a legacy of Edwardian London, when the Corinthians, themselves then nothing more than a legacy in name of Victorian and Edwardian soccer, made their final F.A. Cup appearance in London, against Southend United. Any resemblance to the old greatness, even of the twenties, had completely gone. A miserable crowd of 2,000 sprinkled round the empty stadium gave an eerie atmosphere to what resembled a memorial service rather than any parade of soccer talent, or at least of amateur soccer talent, by what had once been the country's premier amateur club. As the thumps of the ball echoed round the deserted stands, with the occasional whisper, 'Play up Corinth,' filtering through the murky air like some haunting cry that one snatches to retain but always slides away, the forward-line of the Third Division team, then under the management of David Jack, showed clearer shades of the combined Corinthian forward style than their ghostly opponents who bore the famous name. Yet even among the ruins one could pick out the sinuous dribbles of L.C. Thornton at inside-forward, the daring enterprise in goal of A.H. 'Bertie' Woolcock in his yellow sweater - he had no chance at all with either of the two Southend goals that won the game - and Tommy Whewell, the captain, at full-back, struggling to keep alight the flicker from more spacious days. It was not to be; and last of the playing Corinthians they were, for with Claude Ashton, they never came through the Second World War alive.

Yet during the decline there were great amateur footballers holding their own among the professionals. Bernard Joy, like so many Corinthians of this period, was a schoolmaster. After gaining an Amateur Cup winner's medal with the Casuals in 1936 at centre-half as well as about a dozen England amateur caps and also a full one v. Belgium, he won a League Championship medal with the Arsenal in their 1938 side. There were also other amateur internationals: J.C. Burns at right-half with Q.P.R. and Brentford; A.H. Gibbons with Tottenham Hotspur and other clubs as well as the R.A.F.; Maurice Edelston with Brentford before he moved to Reading where he became a professional; and W.W. Parr, another war casualty with Blackpool. Yet only Joy of these was a Corinthian and there are no more who spring readily to mind as regular performers with the professionals. It is not entirely otiose to wonder why these and other amateurs were not regularly members of the Corinthians. For as Norman Creek pointed out in 1937 in *Association Football,* the younger universities had been progressing steadily, and:

'If only the Corinthians had widened their outlook and made more use of the talent at these smaller universities, that famous amateur side need never have fallen to its present lowly estate.'

This apart, the chief reason for the Corinthians' decline was, of course, the professionals' speed and intensity that after the 1920s dominated the game. Not far behind can be seen the drying up in quality of the sources of recruitment; and finally another cause can be considered from a higher plane entirely.

Thanks to the fanatical nationalism that the 1930s produced in Europe, international soccer was elevated by the totalitarian countries from its natural place in the fixture lists as well as a friendly link between nations to the lofty status of national honour and prestige alongside science and art. The bonuses that Mussolini dangled before his players, including exemption from military service, if they could beat England at Highbury in 1933, resulted in the battle which Hapgood, England's captain on that day, has recorded, 'as the dirtiest game I ever played in.' Stanley Matthews, who was at outside-right called it 'the roughest in which I have ever taken part'; and the England team at Berlin in 1938 had to start their game against Germany by giving the Nazi salute before successfully resisting by six goals to three a specially trained team's vain efforts to win glory for the Third Reich.

With England's players thrown on to the defensive, even against the less belligerent countries, in an attempt to resist these unnaturally incited onslaughts on their country's soccer prestige, the international soccer arena became no place for the amateur. The professional alone could stand the fire and fury of these games. The heat at the top was felt all the wa y down the scales of the public game, especially as the League and Cup competitions were turning defences into safety-curtains.

Although A.H. Fabian, the Old Cholmeleian and Cantab, appeared with Barker, Bowers and the late Tom Cooper among others in Derby County's Semi-Final side that was beaten 3-2 by Manchester City in 1933; and Bernard Joy of both the Corinthians and the Casuals played at centre-half with Sagar of Everton and Arsenal's Male and Hapgood in the England team that lost 2-3 to Belgium at Brussels in 1936, this kind of player certainly became the exception rather than the rule. Over thirty years had passed since G.O. and ten other amateurs had beaten Germany 12-0 in the first home international against a foreign country, in 1901. In 1930 the cream of England's professionals could force only a 3-3 draw against Germany in Berlin. When the continental countries grew up at soccer there was no longer any place for the Corinthians and other amateurs in the higher reaches.

The signs of the amateur times were reflected in June of 1937 by the decision that the Corinthians could no longer carry on by themselves. It was decided that the Corinthians should join with the Casuals and the two clubs should run under a joint executive committee for at least the next three seasons. The Casuals had been founded a few months after the Corinthians, for those, some had unkindly said, who could not gain membership of the senior and more famous club. Nevertheless, down the years it had always been a nursery or graduation school for the Corinthians and many of the great players of Corinth matured through the Casuals' ranks. With the Corinthians' increasing difficulty in finding sides of the required strength even for their rapidly diminishing reputation, the union with the Casuals was cemented by the amalgamation that took place in 1939 at the end of the last full season before the black-out. This merger, which created the present Corinthian-Casuals F.C., did not please everybody and G.O.

was not alone when he wrote to me in 1943: (Half a dozen years later, after the first Pegasus season in 1949, A.G. Doggart - the first Hon. Treasurer of Pegasus - was writing in *The Field:* 'There are many who must now be feeling some doubt as to the wisdom of a step they advocated in 1939 - namely the amalgamation of the Corinthians and the Casuals.')

'I was always against the amalgamation of the Corinthians and the Casuals and wish the former, if they had found themselves unable to carry on, had just retired from the game.' In reality they did retire. The identity and individuality of their famous white-crested shirts were swamped by the combination of chocolate and pink that had served the Casuals since their inception.

For the first time in its existence the name of Corinth became associated with the rigidity and monotony of regular League fixture lists - those of the Isthmian League.

No internationals became associated with the new formation until Pegasus supplied the talent; and when the threads were picked up after 1945 the Corinthian-Casuals seemed to spend their time in bolstering up the remainder of the League Table. Perhaps the War nullified any benefits from the union, just as the earlier struggle had retarded the recovery of amateur soccer after the 1907 'split' was healed. Yet just as the universities in the 1920s sent out their Blues to write fresh chapters of glory in the Corinthians' wonderful history, the maturity of the ex-servicemen after 1945 saw them prepared to do so again. But to what end? In the Isthmian League to hold up fifteen other clubs? Or in the extra-preliminary qualifying rounds of the F.A. Amateur Cup? Fortunately for football and the whole of British sport, however, a new Corinthian glory was rising once again in its traditional homes of learning and playing at the ancient universities. Only this time, not from the ruins of old, but on the outstretched wings of a new, exciting creature - Pegasus.

A wartime team: Corinthian-Casuals 2 The Army 0. November 1939
Left to right J.T. Barker, R.P. Wakeford, L.J. Kingston, R.V. Kingston, R.E. Palmer, Sgt F.G.I. Packington (Club Joint Secretary, referee), M.F. Coop, W. Whewell, A.G.M. Creed (in front), R.M. Hollis (behind), P.K. O'Brien, P.T. Collins.

CHAPTER IX

PEGASUS SPREADS ITS WINGS

Pegasus, the winged horse of classical mythology, swooped down into the world of Association football after the Second World War; and through the teachings of players from Tottenham Hotspur and other professional clubs it carried the game, now almost swamped by the waves of commerce and professionalism, once more to the heights created by the Corinthians. The affinities between Corinth and Pegasus, two of the three greatest amateur clubs in the history of soccer Queen's Park, Glasgow, being the third - are, of course, obvious. Yet as Roland Allen pointed out in his assessment of the 1951 F.A. Amateur Cup-Final between Pegasus and Bishop Auckland in the *Sunday Times*:

Dr H.W. THOMPSON
Founder of Pegasus.

'If any ghosts of Corinth were hovering over this green Wembley pitch sparkling in the sunshine, they no doubt would have approved of what Pegasus did, without seeing in them any threat of rivalry or any challenge aimed at removing the Corinthians from the niche they created for themselves.

Comparisons between Pegasus and the Corinthians are perhaps rather too obvious, and might be misleading. Although the title lingers on, the real Corinthians have gone.

It is not for Pegasus to attempt to recapture their glory. Pegasus have to create their own history in

a different sort of football world.' The different worlds of the two clubs saw different reasons for their existence, too.

It seems incredible that it is still not widely appreciated that 'Pa' Jackson founded the Corinthians to check the flow of soccer victories in favour of Scotland against England, and to give the best English players a certain measure of combination (see, for example, the curious explanation of the origin of the Corinthians given by Morris Marples in his *A History of Football*, 1954, pp. 171 and 223). Dr Thompson and his group of enthusiasts founded Pegasus to raise the standard of soccer at Oxford and Cambridge Universities and to check the flow of minor schools from Association to Rugby football. The achievement of these aims by Pegasus will finally explode the myth that any of the major public schools have been disloyal to the game they gave the world. As Dr H.W. Thompson, F.R.S., Fellow and Tutor of St John's College, Oxford, better known as 'Tommy,' put it on the eve of their first Wembley Final in 1951:

'Three years ago Pegasus F.C. was little more than a thought in the minds of a few Soccer enthusiasts at Oxford. While admiring the rising skill of the professional game, they saw with some dismay the effects of prejudice by others against it, for this prejudice was providing a channel for the flow to

Rugby football in many schools all over the country. Within a generation this might prove disastrous and damage our national prestige even in the world of International Soccer which this country has done so much to create, for without a veritable host of amateurs behind them, the professional ranks must surely dwindle ... So, in order to strike one modest blow in Soccer's cause, the founders of Pegasus at Oxford and Cambridge determined to experiment with a new club, strictly amateur, formed from members of the two Universities.' Here the formal comparison with the Corinthians ends.

Membership of Pegasus is exclusively restricted to members of the Oxford University Centaurs A.F.C. and the Cambridge University Falcons A.F.C. Corinth, at the outset, however, admitted internationals and F.A. Cup-Final players from the Old Boys Clubs and others who had not advanced to Oxford or Cambridge University; and the famous eleven against Bury in 1904, for example, contained five Oxford Blues, five Cambridge Blues and one non-University Reptonian, a fair reflection of the proportionate supply.

Like its classical namesake, Pegasus is something of a freak. It was born from the marriage of the Oxford Centaur - the man-headed horse - and the Cambridge Falcon - a bird - these being the two undergraduate Association football clubs at the Universities. Its name was born from the pre-war marriage of Dr Thompson to Miss Grace Penelope Stradling, an Oxford classics scholar, who supplied a title which her husband and his fellow founders had sought in vain. Can any other club which has achieved such fame and distinction have received its name in such a way? Mrs Thompson's contribution to the foundation of the club was recognised when Dr B.R. Brown. goalkeeper of the 1953 Cup-Final team, presented her with his winners medal. Finally, Pegasus must also be considered a freak because, for the first time in the history of the game, a leaf had been taken from cricket's book and a permanent and direct link effected between University talent and professional assistance.

At its birth the Pegasus players had all been coached by professional internationals and so have all their successors. Indeed, some of them had played with professional clubs, notably John Tanner with Huddersfield Town. To Cambridge came Don Welsh of Charlton Athletic, Frank Soo of Stoke City and Billy Nicholson of Tottenham Hotspur; Oxford welcomed Maurice Edelston of Reading, Lauric Scott of Arsenal, Len Goulden of Chelsea and Vic Buckingham of Tottenham Hotspur. These professionals, in their different ways, all prepared the way for the Club's spectacular Amateur Cup successes under the guidance of, firstly, Buckingham himself, and then George Ainsley, who had played with distinction before the War for Sunderland, Bolton Wanderers and Leeds United, as well as for England in South Africa.

For the Club's first fixture on Wednesday, 8th December 1948, played at Oxford's Iffley Road Running Ground, four days after the Varsity match, Arsenal sent down its full Football Combination side.

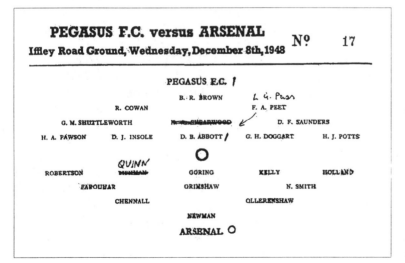

It was defeated by the only goal of the game headed by D.B. Abbott, the Cambridge Blue, from a centre by his fellow Wykehamist from Oxford, H.A. Pawson.

Later Arsenal allowed two of its players - Leslie Compton and Joe Mercer - to coach the Club, and has assisted with medical and training facilities. Charlton Athletic provided similar facilities and also the services at various times of its trainer Jimmy Trotter, who has acted for many years in that capacity for England's national side. The bonds with the Kent club have since been further strengthened. In April, 1952, the two clubs played at Maidstone for the benefit of a local player. On the eve of the Pegasus New Year tour of 1951-52 Pawson played for Charlton in a First Division League match. Chelsea, whose centre-half, Ron Greenwood, was Oxford's coach at the time, generously arranged a private trial for the Club behind closed doors in preparation for the Amateur Cup Semi-Final replay against Southall in 1953 at a time when their precarious position in the League Table gave them more pressing matters to worry over. Yet beyond those priceless benefits, without which Pegasus could never have reached the pinnacles of its dreams, one professional club stands out for the influence it has wielded on the achievements of Pegasus and the renaissance of University football after the Second World War - Tottenham Hotspur.

In his delightful *Football Facts and Fancies* Dr Percy Young wrote, just before the 1950s: 'We are generously agreed in the North and the Midlands that, if our own team must ever lose, there are certain teams from whom defeat is a privilege ... In the South Tottenham Hotspur, Chelsea, Plymouth Argyle, possibly Southampton.

As for Tottenham. They play at White Hart Lane, which suggests antiquity, if by accident. One recalls the White Hart Inn at Southwark, where Jack Cade stayed in the fifteenth century and where, four hundred years later, Mr. Pickwick met Sam Weller. Shakespeare's *King Henry IV* (Part I) allows to Harry Hotspur the prophetic,

O, let the hours be short,
Till fields and blows and grass applaud our sport.

Thus Tottenham Hotspur come to be associated with ancient rules of knightly prowess and knightly chivalry. Nor have they ever lacked in courage or chivalry.'

Forty years before that, at the period of the pre-1914 'Split,' *The Times,* always so well disposed to amateurs, referred to Tottenham Hotspur as 'a team which has never become altogether professionalised in its methods.' Nor did the passage of years make any difference; for the Spurs have always made room for the amateur who could reach their traditionally high standards. There is a continuous descent from the legendary Woodward after G.O.'s day, through the Corinthian Hartley of the 1920s down to the airman, A. H. Gibbons, just before the Second World War, and to-day the Finchley schoolmaster, George Robb. Thus in the second full University season after the foundation of Pegasus in 1948 there went to Cambridge as coach, Nicholson, the Spurs right-half who later played for England; to Oxford University went Buckingham, the Spurs own coach and stylish defender.

To both Universities free of charge from the directors of the Tottenham Hotspur Football and Athletic Company Limited - to give the full professional title - went the use of their ground at White Hart Lane for the Varsity match. To Pegasus, moreover, went the Spurs own adaptation of the classic Corinthian style with the close-ground passing. Shortly before the 1951 Amateur Cup-Final Tottenham Hotspur, fielding almost their League Championship eleven, staged a training match for Pegasus on the Spurs' nursery team's ground at Cheshunt, under the direct supervision of their manager Arthur Rowe; and Colin Weir, Oxford's captain in 1947, and reserve goalkeeper to Ben Brown in the 1951 Cup-Final, had played for Tottenham Hotspur. Once again, therefore, were the Gentlemen and the Players on the field together at Association Football, with full justification for the old adage of all the Players

PROFESSORS AND STUDENTS

Vic Buckingham, Spurs and Pegasus Coach, gives a tactics talk to Ron Burgess (Spurs Captain), Eddie Gibbins, John Dutchman and Les Bennett, while Arthur Willis advises John Maughan.

Wing - halves Denis Saunders (Pegasus Captain) and Billy Nicholson converse while right-wingers Tony Pawson and Sonny Walters listen to Arthur Rowe, Spurs Manager.

Alf Ramsey (right) guides Ralph Cowan.

being gentlemen and all the Gentlemen players. The wheel had turned full circle to bring back the fifty years from 1901 when G.O. had played his last game for England against Germany on the Tottenham Hotspur ground, so ending a career in the course of which there was no sign of the now regrettable gulf between Gentlemen and Players in football.

Yet the triumphs and thrills which have followed this reunion are all the more amazing when one recalls the circumstances prevailing before it was effected. The legacy of University football before the Second World War, as has been seen, was not one to be envied; and the first three Varsity matches at Dulwich Hamlet's ground, Champion Hill, after the War period gave little hope for improvement. At Oxford, Pawson had taken his dash and alacrity from Kentish cricket fields to centre-forward, and Tanner had followed G.O. in being capped in that position. From the Cambridge sides Guy Shuttleworth, first captain of Pegasus, received a cap, and Insole and Doggart Junior added to their cricket Blues, while Trevor Bailey at outside-right in 1947 showed his disrespect for Oxford by scoring the winning goal against them and for the *other* game played so diligently at his old school, so near to the Dulwich Hamlet ground.

Nevertheless, little justification appeared for the pious hope expressed in the programme for the last match on the Dulwich ground which trusted 'the time is not far distant when soccer will once again be as popular as rugger not only at the Universities, but at all Public Schools. They are both great games and we think there is room for both to be played and the scholars should have the opportunity of their choice.'

Strangely enough, even in G.O.'s day, on the eve of his day from the first moment to the last.' last Varsity match as captain, 1896, *The Times* suggested: 'If the Association game between the Universities scarcely commands the widespread interest devoted to the Rugby Union played before

Christmas, it yet attracts a good share of public attention, which is increased by the numerous visits of each of the teams to London grounds..

That attention following the Second World War was certainly increased seven months after Pegasus had been founded by the meeting of Oxford and Cambridge on Saturday, 4th December, 1948, at White Hart Lane, the famous Spurs ground in North London. A record post-war Varsity soccer match crowd of more than 10,000 turned up; and the players responded with one of the finest games played there that season, and even since the end of the War. Oxford won by 5-4. Seven of the goals stemmed from crisp, incisive attacking football, outstanding for the beautifully balanced Oxford assaults with Pawson and Potts flying down the wings with superb ball control, both delightfully served by their captain, Tanner, a veritable G.O. in the centre, and the scheming of Heritage and Rhys at inside-forward. Indeed, it was an attack every bit as attractive to watch as that of Leicester City just three months later comprising Griffiths, Revie, Lee, Chisholm and Adam, which, on the day that Russian Hero won the Grand National at 66-1 and Cambridge the Boat Race by half a length, swept a very surprised Portsmouth team out of the Semi-Final of the F.A. Cup and back to the sea from Highbury.

On that tingling December afternoon one could easily have let the years slip by to picture in the imagination the days at Queen's Club, with G.O. in the centre and Vassall Corbett on the wings for Oxford, and Insole's shooting and captain's heroics at inside-right for Cambridge as an enlarged edition of that earlier cricketing Cantab, S.H. Day. *The Observer* summed it all up perfectly the following morning in two sentences that could hardly have been applied to many supposedly high-class professional games in that season: 'Here was an exciting game of high attacking quality and above all, of first-class shooting. Attack, indeed, was the order of the day from the first moment to the last.'

Both teams contained a sprinkling of cricketers, Pawson, Potts, Tanner and Shearwood for Oxford, and Doggart and Insole for Cambridge in the manner of the great Varsity sides of the 1920s and earlier; and with Winchester, Charterhouse, Shrewsbury, Repton and Wellingborough supplying nine of the twenty-two players, a fair reflection of the manner in which the Grammar Schools had caught up with and overtaken the Public Schools at Association football was indicated. The teams lined up as follows:

OXFORD UNIVERSITY

Goal
R. LENTON
(Quarry Bank H.S. & St. Peter's Hall)

Backs

D.M. RICHARDS
(Salesian College, Battersea and Queen's)

L.G. PASS
(Glossop G.S. & Hertford)

Half-backs

J.R. TILLARD
(Winchester & Trinity)

K.A. SHEARWOOD
(Shrewsbury & Brasenose)

D.F. SAUNDERS
(Scarborough H.S. & Exeter)

Forwards

H.R.S. RHYS
(Shrewsbury & Wadham)

S.G. HERITAGE
(Holloway G.S. & Exeter)

H.A. PAWSON
(Winchester & Christ Church)

J.D.P. TANNER
(Charterhouse & Brasenose)

H.J. POTTS
(Stand G.S. & Keble)

●

E.W.N. JACKSON
(Chorlton H.S. & Queens)

T. McGURK
(St. Peter's College Glasgow & Christ's)

J.A. DUTCHMAN
(Cockburn H.S. & King's)

G.H.G. DOGGART
(Winchester & King's)

D.J. INSOLE
(Monoux G.S. & St. Catherine's)

Forwards

C. TYSON
(Darwen G.S. & Jesus)

R. COWAN
(Chorlton H.S. & Queens')

W.B. SHERET
(Wellingborough& St. Catherine's)

Half-backs

A.R. BUTTERFIELD
(Bolton G.S. & Caius)

M.H.H. BISHOP
(Repton & Clare)

Backs
M.J. HARDY
(Repton & St. Catherine's)
Goal

CAMBRIDGE UNIVERSITY

So was the way prepared for a fusion of the two teams on the playing fields as Pegasus for that first game against Arsenal at Oxford, four days later. Seven months earlier, Cambridge University footballers had accepted Dr Thompson's invitation to join forces with Oxford. Suggestions in this direction had been raised before the War; and even the entry of Oxford University alone for the F.A. Amateur Cup had been mooted by E.O.W. Hunt (Malvern) and P.H. Williams (Bradfield), two Brasenose College members of the Oxford University team which had toured Czechoslovakia in 1936-37. The difficulties of playing through the early qualifying rounds scheduled for before the Varsity match in December, however, as well as preparing for that annual fixture, proved insuperable. Now Dr Thompson, in discussion with members of the Oxford side in early 1948 while returning from a friendly match with Bournville Athletic in the Midlands, was to carry the idea a stage further.

On Sunday, 2nd May, 1948, a meeting took place between representatives of the Association Football Clubs of Oxford and Cambridge Universities, with members of the Corinthian Casuals in attendance, at the East India and Sports Club in St James's Square, London. This was the same Sports Club where, fifty-five years earlier, after G.O.'s first Varsity match, at the dinner given to both teams, Sir John Astley had remarked that, as an Old Etonian, he was glad to see that they played '*foot-* and not hand-ball' Now, exactly twenty-five years after the Corinthians' entry into the F.A. Cup in 1923, the Pegasus Football Club was formed. At a subsequent meeting of the Corinthian-Casuals Club it was unanimously agreed to give wholehearted support to the new creation. This was hardly surprising, for the mere amalgamation of the two famous names without anything else was not enough to attract the matured and experienced ex-service players from Oxford and Cambridge who preferred to spend their vacations and leisure after going down in playing for their Old Boys teams, Yorkshire Amateurs or any other club. Yet by the Casuals approval of Pegasus they acknowledged that the game would benefit most if the Universities united to form their own separate club. For the object of Pegasus, as stated in its Constitution, was and is: 'the encouragement and improvement of Association Football at the Universities of Oxford and Cambridge by the formation of a joint team.' No doubt the Casuals realised that without such encouragement and improvement the prospect for their own future was even bleaker than their post-War record indicated.

In principle Pegasus teams were to be selected from members in residence at either University, but the Constitution granted the Selection Committee a right to call upon players who were in residence during the previous season. Dr Thompson, the founder and guiding-light, became the first Honorary Secretary; the Rev. K.R.G.

Hunt, of Corinthian, Wolverhampton Wanderers and England fame, the first President; A.G. Doggart, the first Honorary Treasurer; and a Committee was to include the captains of the University football teams and the Secretaries of the Oxford Centaurs and Cambridge Falcons.

There was no money in the bank or in sight, and until matches were played funds could come only from the 2s. 6d. life subscription payable by the joining members. There was no local support to count upon as in other areas. There was, in fact, no visible means of support. But all the same there was something deeper, finer and purer, something more permanent, than all the public trappings usually associated with Association football clubs: something even more endurable and admirable than the professional monuments to these Victorian pioneers in the chapels, churches and schools, whose devotion to the game laid the foundations for Aston Villa, Preston North End, Tottenham Hotspur and their contemporaries in the Football League. 'I do not yet know the secret of Pegasus,' wrote J.P.W. Mallalieu, the Member of Parliament for Huddersfield, in *The Spectator* on the eve of the second Pegasus triumph in 1953. 'The members of the team are lucky if they see each other once a week, yet they have now, in only five years of life, reached Wembley twice.' Such a triumph nevertheless, as these pages will show, contains no secret.

For into a cynical world of false values and over-glamourised professionalism Pegasus brought an ideal, an ideal reflecting the true nature and spirit of Association football as a game, bringing healthy happiness and delight to its players and followers. This ideal burned brightly among its founders and lit a beacon in the hearts of all true lovers of the game which blazed throughout the land within months as the public became aware that the dying embers of soccer in the Universities had been rekindled and fanned into flame through the passion of a handful of devotees. Cambridge had joined her sister in the crusade for this apparently most hopeless of lost causes; and she has proudly shared the joy which has followed the realisation that once more the home of lost causes has seen the revival of an old one.

At the Club's formation it was hoped that it would take part in the F.A. Amateur Cup Competition, and that a means could be found to fit this in with the normal arrangements for the University season. In order to enter for this Competition, the regulations required that all clubs, whether members of, or affiliated directly to, the F.A. or County Associations, should have a registered ground. Pegasus had, of course, no ground of its own. The Grange Road pitch at Cambridge belongs to the Cambridge University Rugby Club and it would have been very difficult, if not impossible, to arrange fixtures there on Saturdays. The Oxford University Association football ground at the Iffley Road therefore emerged as the only possible venue, and this became the Club's registered ground, although the Club is in fact affiliated to the Cambridgeshire County F.A. as well as the Oxfordshire County F.A.

The Varsity match is not played until the beginning of December, and the preceding two months in the Michaelmas terms are required for the matches against the professional, amateur and representative teams for building up the University side, whose players are therefore not available till after the Varsity match. Therefore, without some exemption from the earlier rounds of the Cup played before December, nothing could really be done at all effectively. Members of the Club believed that not only had they the playing strength to justify such exemption, but also that the past record of the Universities of Oxford and Cambridge in the development of the game, at all times, warranted a request of this sort. Preliminary enquiries from the F.A. were not very hopeful, but a lengthy memorandum drawn up by Dr Thompson set out the case fully, and with the far-seeing help of Sir Stanley Rous, Secretary of the F.A., was considered by the F.A. Amateur Cup Committee. There was by no means unanimity, but it was decided to grant the Club exemption until the Fourth Qualifying Round, to be played at the end of November. Further, Pegasus was given

permission to ask its opponents, when known, to defer the game until early December, the week after the Varsity match. The generous help and wise counsel of the late Mr Harry J. Huband and the late Mr Andy Ralston meant very much to the Club at this critical time. At the same time, the playing record of the Corinthian-Casuals caused the F.A. Amateur Cup Committee to limit even further the exemptions hitherto granted to them in that Competition.

For that historic first F.A. Amateur Cup Pegasus were drawn *at home* to Enfield. But the Middlesex Club agreed to postpone the date *only* if the match were played on its own ground instead of at Oxford. The illogicality of this may seem curious, but force of circumstances left Pegasus no alternative but to agree.

The winged horse, therefore, prepared for its flight to the stars through the clouds of a Cup adventure. An Oxford science don from Yorkshire, with all that county's native grit and character, appropriately enough aided by an Old Carthusian, John Tanner, also from Yorkshire, who played a vital part both on and off the field, was in the foreground, and the background, too, leading and guiding the fervour and enthusiasm of students, some young, some more mature after their war experiences. Here was the world of science and careful planning harnessed to a faith in a mission that had been courageously undertaken though every omen for a successful fulfilment was dead against it. Yet the idealism of Dr Thompson and his players and assistants was merged with a realism that acknowledged the magnitude of their task. Providence and their own unquenchable spirit, the spirit of the Corinthians born again within them, were to see that they would not fail.

In the opening Cup-Tie, played only three days after the Club's first match, against Arsenal, Enfield met the fate their action had deserved. They lost 1-3, and, Pegasus set a future pattern by conceding the first goal, but eventually flying off with the spoils of victory. Tanner's goals in this match were a portent of things to come, for during the first six years of the Club's existence he was by far the most consistent goal-scorer. In 18 Cup-Ties he scored 20 goals. In the next two rounds, the First and Second of the Competition proper) Pegasus beat Smethwick Highfield from the Midlands 4-1, and Brentwood and Warley from Essex 2-1. Then in the Third Round Willington (Cup winners of the following year and defeated finalists in the last season before the war), were overcome by 3-2, and before one had realised it, 1949 was well under way and the Pegasus Club in its first season had reached the QuarterFinals of the F.A. Amateur Cup. The formidable Bromley side at Oxford were its reward.

Few of the Bromley supporters brought from Kent by special trains and coaches, with their rattles, bells and colours, could have expected the fight that their favourites, including five amateur internationals, were to encounter on that fine February afternoon. Before a crowd of over 11,000, a record for any University sporting event at Oxford, after the Athletic Club generously advanced its annual sports by a day to Friday, Pegasus ran their opponents to the narrowest of victories, by the odd goal of seven. The Pegasus performance against one of the most consistently successful amateur clubs in southern England since the War was truly amazing, and the result could easily have gone the other way. They took the lead twice, equalised to three-all and then surrendered the winning goal in the last five minutes through a defensive slip. Even the Rugby dons were cheering a grandstand finish with Pegasus shots hitting the post, the goal keeper, in fact everything except the back of the Bromley net. The wingers, Pawson and Potts, flying down the touchlines and sending over lovely centres or firing in at goal themselves nearly carried the day; and but for that, fatal defensive error, a penalty which might have been awarded to Pegasus and the questionable selection of a semi-fit Tanner, who was nevertheless among the scorers, Pegasus would surely have entered the Semi-Finals and perhaps the first F.A. Amateur Cup to be played at Wembley Stadium. Indeed, Bromley themselves were reported to have said after the game that Pegasus gave them their hardest fight on the road to Wembley. Their final tie with Romford was a damp squib compared with the fireworks that the Universities had set off against them, and without a doubt the shades of G.O., 'Tip' Foster and their fellow Corinthians must have gazed approvingly from the Elysian Fields at these stirrings in their ancestral home. The teams were as follows:

PEGASUS

B.R. BROWN
(Mexborough G.S. & Oxford)

R. COWAL   G. PASS
(Chorlton H.S. & Cambridge)   *(Glossop H.S. & Oxford)*

G.M. SHUTTLEWORTH   K.A. SHEARWOOD   D.F. SAUNDERS
(Q.E.G.S., Blackburn & Cambridge)   *(Shrewsbury & Oxford)*   *(Scarborough H.S. & Oxford)*

D.J. INSOLE   S.G. HERITAGE
(Monoux G.S. & Cambridge)   *(Holloway G.S. & Oxford)*

H.A. PAWSON   J.D.P. TANNER   H.J. POTTS
(Winchester & Oxford)   *(Charterhouse & Oxford)*   *(Stand G.S. & Oxford)*

●

M. RUDDY   R. DUNMALL   G.R. BROWN   A.H. HOOPER   C. MARTIN
E. FRIGHT   C.FULLER   T. FULLER
K.YENSON   D. CAMERON

T. CORNTHWAITE

BROMLEY

'Pegasus lost to Bromley,' wrote the former amateur international, Edgar Kail, in the *Daily Graphic,* their first defeat by a club side, 'but this is not the end of this gallant club - only the beginning.' *The Times* put it, 'by their display against a side of Bromley's calibre they have regained the prestige of University football.' Nor did they lose ground a season later, 1949-50, when they had to be content with winning what has been called the blue riband of Oxfordshire football, the Oxford Senior Cup. This time their F.A. Amateur Cup run was much shorter. In the First Round proper, to which exemption had now been granted on the strength of the previous season's record, they beat Erith and Belvedere 5-2 at the second attempt after achieving a splendid draw with virtually ten men on treacly turf in Kent. Against Walthamstow Avenue in Essex in the following round they scored first; but mistaken strategy caused Potts, their most dangerous forward, to be starved on the wing and Pegasus were out by 1-3. Yet once more the Corinthians' mark was left, for the Avenue supporters were loud in their praise of the Varsity boys' sportsmanship.

Despite all this, incredible as it may seem, opposition arose to the club from a small group of individuals who, in the words of a leading figure in amateur football circles, after the triumph of 1951, were 'suffering from an overdose of sour grapes.' So intense was this opposition that it was later recorded in *The Sporting Chronicle* (25th April, 1951) that Pegasus nearly had to disband in the January before its greatest triumph; and that the publication was considered of a report to show the difficulties which had confronted the club since its formation. Clearly the jealousy and greed for gold that are the essence of human nature abound in certain amateur soccer circles as they do in other spheres. Yet, apart from the feelings of leading amateur clubs whose own interests would obviously be affected by the progress of a new formation, friction with the Casuals was around the corner.

In the summer of 1950, before the season in which Pegasus first won the Amateur Cup, the original rule of the Club limiting playing members to those in residence and one year after was altered. In its place a rule was formulated which allowed older players to be chosen by the Selection Committee if required. It was also provided that the Casuals should have prior right to request services of any player who had been down for more than one year. If the rule had not been changed, the older players would all have had to withdraw without seeing any suitable substitutes among the former schoolboy freshmen to take their place. Had the rule been retained, players such as Brown, Pawson, Potts and Tanner would have been lost to University football and probably to England's amateur sides also. In the summer of 1950 players like Potts, Pawson, Tanner would have become ineligible and would not have played for the Casuals. The players themselves felt, as did many others, that it was wrong to exclude them from their own Club, and it was the general feeling of the Committee and Officers that Pegasus should conserve its forces and not waste them. (just how far the Casuals have wasted playing talent has been seen since 1950.) It was also felt that the best way to achieve success and command public interest was by this course. A year later, after the first Cup win, in the summer of 1951, the rule was finally altered to its present form: 'all members shall be eligible to play.'

If the Club had not decided to conserve its forces there is no doubt that the Pegasus crusade would have failed. Thereupon the supporters who had rallied to it from the factories in oxford and elsewhere, as well as the old Corinthian followers, would have returned to their memories and dreams, once more to await the call of another Jackson or Thompson.

Within this context a great friend and chronicler of the Club's fortunes, Geoffrey Green, Association football correspondent of *The Times,* when dealing with this matter in his colourful and effective *Soccer - The World Game,* would appear to have fallen from his usual accuracy in writing:

'The very real danger now exists that they may have forgotten their original object - to strengthen and keep University football itself in a flourishing state. Very soon, by extending their original playing qualification for the Club - a player in residence at the University and for one year after he had "gone down" - Pegasus cut across that older foundation the Casuals (the Corinthian-Casuals), who have always drawn their playing strength from ex-University players. By partly cutting off that source Pegasus have laid themselves open to criticism in some quarters.'

So does Geoffrey Green by writing this. For, as is well known, the Casuals (like the Corinthians) did not always form their teams from ex-University players; and by widening their original playing qualification Pegasus saved first their own club, then the cause for which it stood, and above all else, the good name of Association football which had at last discovered a medium for placing it within a correct perspective in the public's mind and eye. Those difficulties, obstacles and pinpricks to which the Club had been subjected throughout its short life must now await full disclosures by its members. Here, without emphasising the problems to be solved, one desires to record only its saga of success. For all those earlier justifications of the F.A.'s generosity in granting exemption to the Club until the preliminary rounds of the Amateur Cup Competition, though complete in themselves, fade into the background when one comes to the triumphs of 1951.

The Varsity match in December, 1950, again played at Tottenham without charge to the Universities, thanks to the generosity of the Hotspur Directors, resulted in a 0-0 draw; a successful New Year tour saw Pegasus gain two victories in the three games in Winchester, Salisbury and Jersey. The success of this tour was greatly due to the inspiration of the presence of the Club's coach, Vic Buckingham, who at that time was also the coach to his own club, Tottenham Hotspur. Nevertheless, there were few outside the Club's members and supporters who thought much of its chances in the Amateur Cup Competition of 1950-51.

Their step-brothers, the Corinthian-Casuals, had gone out in the earlier rounds, taking with them

D.J. Insole, and one or two others who would not now be eligible to play for Pegasus in the same competition. So when all but one of the players who eventually triumphed at Wembley went to Hampshire at the very doors of the current Football League Champions at Portsmouth and defeated Gosport Borough Athletic by 4-3 before a record crowd of nearly 3,500 they attracted little more attention in the amateur world than the raising of a few eyebrows. In the next round Slough Town at their Dolphin Stadium were unfortunate enough to find two heroes of that memorable Oxford 5-4 victory over Cambridge, Tanner and Pawson, back to their finest form. Well prompted by their captain, Saunders, at left-half, they scored the goals that took their side by 3-1 through to the Third Round. Again drawn away from home, this time to Brentwood and Warley, the, prospects of Pegasus, who found themselves at the last minute without Pawson and Shearwood, both unfit, were not highly favoured; and at half-time the jeremiahs seemed justified, for the home team scored twice without reply. But what had been done before could easily be done again. Cowan (whose place at full-back was taken by D.M. Richards, who had played for Oxford in the 1948 match) was outstanding at centre-half.

Threading their way through the puddles and mud, Pegasus hit back magnificently with two cracking drives from Potts, at outside-right for Pawson, and a cunning lob from a Cambridge recruit on the left-wing, Sutcliffe, to win the game. Another away draw followed - in the Quarter-Finals this time, at the ground of Oxford's town side, Oxford City. Injuries on this Town v. Gown occasion kept out Tanner and Pawson, but their Cambridge deputies, Laybourne and Sutcliffe, with Carr, saw to it that against expectations three goals came without reply, and here were Pegasus in the Semi-Finals drawn against Hendon, the leading southern amateur team of the year, with the best amateur defence in the country.

Before this match, and even the Final, few authorities held out much hope for Pegasus. But who of those present can forget these two memorable games against Hendon? Even without the Final at Wembley, these thrilling encounters alone would have set the seal on the Club's newly created fame, have written fresh glories on the scrolls of University sport, and established a Pegasus tradition to which the Corinthians themselves would have been proud to lay claim. In both these matches against Hendon, a goal down with seven minutes to go, Pegasus hit back against their more experienced opponents to save the day and then spread their wings to gain the twin towers of Wembley's battlements.

At Highbury the match suddenly flared up in a final breathtaking twenty minutes. First, Roy Stroud, the Hendon centre forward, from the left-hand corner of the penalty-box, took a twenty-yard drive that spelt goal directly the ball left his foot, and spurred on his colleagues for a second and decisive blow. But with only five minutes left, Dutchman sent Tanner away and there was the centre-forward dribbling from the right for goal and withstanding all tackles with that same balance and control which were the secret of G.O.'s play. Suddenly down he went, just outside the area: free-kick. Dutchman shot low, Tanner deflected, and Pegasus were level. Yet without one of the most phenomenal penalty saves Pegasus might never have fulfilled their destiny. For with two minutes to go, Avis fell to a clumsy tackle in the Pegasus area, and Referee Leafe had no option. The crowd stopped breathing, Adams shot head-high and hard, a yellow streak dived to its left, and Ben Brown had entered the gallery of heroes. But from the moment when he had pulled the ball out of the air in the opening minutes of the game with the agility of Evans keeping wicket for Kent or England, Brown had been reviving memories of that wonder line of distinguished Corinthian goalkeepers from Moon, Gay, Raikes and Rowlandson down to Howard Baker and Woolcock, in our own time.

By this memorable performance Brown played himself into the England amateur international side at Hampden Park a fortnight later, and subsequently he was selected for the Great Britain soccer party at the 1952 Olympic Games in Helsinki.

The replay, a week later during the Easter week-end, was, ironically, taken to Selhurst Park, the ground of the Crystal Palace Club, upon whose old Cup-Final ground at Sydenham so many Corinthian glories were achieved and so many Cup hopes dashed. But on this day when the Oxford Boat Race crew sank in the morning within three minutes of the start, something sensational might have been expected to happen, and happen it did. The Pegasus full-backs, Maughan (Oxford) and Cowan (Cambridge) switched positions in the manner of Oakley and Lodge of half a century earlier. Pawson, who had been unfit for the Highbury game was risked at outside-right, allowing Potts to cross over to the left against Hendon's captain, Lynch. Thus once more, with Tanner in the centre, the old Oxford three-pronged spearhead that had struck so forcibly against the Cambridge and Bromley defences was reshaped. The move worked, and with Carr at inside-left the attack took on a keener edge. Yet it was Hendon who scored first, six minutes after the kick-off, and once more Pegasus faced an uphill fight. Within a quarter of an hour, however, Pawson and Tanner cut swiftly through the left defensive flank in a manner befitting the most skilled of professionals or, shall we say, G.O. and Vassall, and Pawson equalised. Two minutes after the interval when the ball appeared to have passed over the line, the Pegasus defence relaxed, as had the Arsenal's against Newcastle in that famous Cup-Final nearly twenty years earlier - with equally disastrous consequences. So with Hendon defending confidently and the minutes ticking by, one onlooker in particular was miserably recalling the Crystal Palace as the graveyard of so many Corinthian Cup hopes in the past. Suddenly the right-back, Cowan, of the build and style of A.G. Bower, joined forces with his forwards and a great shot narrowly missed the goal.

This was just the spark required. The winged horse soared into attack, the ball flew to Dutchman, a first-time shot, and Pegasus were level once more. It had hardly seemed possible for the pattern of the earlier game to be repeated. Six minutes to go now. Could the defence hold out? The answer soon came. Before calmness could be simulated

('I'll take your umbrella, young man, till you get over your excitement,' said the lady in front whom I had accidentally hit on the head when Pawson scored), Tanner was through once more: a corner kick gained, Potts took aim, a Tanner flick down to Dutchman, another drive ... and Pegasus were at Wembley. In the moment of triumph, however, one could not help feeling a warm sympathy with Hendon for the Cup, if not quite at their lips, was at least within their reach, and had now been so peremptorily dashed away after two fine displays of clean sporting soccer. But the gods and skill were on the side of these young men from Oxford and Cambridge that day.

Now Pegasus had to meet the sternest opposition it had yet encountered, the most formidable in the history of the Amateur Cup, Bishop Auckland, from County Durham. Since their foundation in 1889 by Oxford and Cambridge students who were studying at the time under Bishop Lightfoot at Auckland Castle - a novel historic link with Pegasus - Bishop Auckland had created an unequalled record of having been in the Final on fourteen occasions and successful on seven; and in forty-eight seasons of the Competition they had reached the Semi Final on twenty-one occasions. Some twelve months earlier they had been defeated by their neighbours, Willington, at Wembley, before a mere 77,000 onlookers by four clear goals, in a game whose balance was not fairly reflected by the score, but was nevertheless memorable for its high quality. Now 'the Bishops' were there again with more supporters than those who had attended the all-Durham struggle in the previous season; experienced, steeped in the traditions of the Amateur Cup, and ready to meet a three-year-old thoroughbred. What greater test could fate have provided for Pegasus in the fulfilment of its mission and destiny?

The public certainly realised the significance of it all. Norman Ackland had told us on a number of occasions that his distinguished sports-journalist colleague, Ben Bennison, once declared, 'If Corinthians reached the Final it would have to be played on Epsom Downs!' Well, for this particular Final many more people applied for tickets than the

record 100,000 who were accommodated at Wembley - the maximum possible. On this, the most memorable of soccer Saturdays since that fabulous first Wembley Final in 1923, the sun came out in all its golden glory as if to bathe within its lustrous glow these heirs to the Corinthian traditions, who treated their opponents and the crowd to a beautiful display of cool, controlled attacking football, with a combination that the brilliantly individualistic cup-fighting Corinthians of the 1920s never attained.

Coached by Buckingham and etching their style within the framework of their individual personalities upon the simple Tottenham Hotspur principle of push and run, which in itself is an adaptation of the old Corinthian forward style, Pegasus on this one magnificent display consummated their earlier triumphs and set a new standard for University and schools soccer. They also gave fresh hope and faith, not only to their immediate followers within the narrow confines of the University walls, but to all lovers of the game who have helplessly seen its fair name besmirched by the financial circus tricks of some of the professional administrators, and its technique degraded by some of the professional tactics. As Dr Thompson wrote in the official programme of the match, it was 'a triumph for the Universities of Oxford and Cambridge, for both teams carry the light and dark blue colours of their foundation. The full cycle has been turned, and Pegasus may claim to have shown that student leadership, properly applied, is still a vital force.'

Right from the kick-off 'the Bishops' looked as if they mean to prove that 'vital force' in 1951 to be limited and the Pegasus conquests in the south to cause no qualms for County Durham. For nearly half an hour Pegasus were on the ropes. Yet those of us who had seen the two Semi-Finals could sense here a firmer confidence in the defensive play of the University players than had been evident in either Hendon game. Beautifully linked movements across the field out of the Tottenham Hotspur and traditional Corinthian copybook from the back to half and inside-forward and then to the opposite wing took the balance of the game to the

Auckland goal before half-time. The second half started as the first had left off, with Pegasus in full cry, and the goals came as just and expected reward against seasoned opponents who put their trust in the airborne pass that compared so crudely with the polished play of the victors.

Although Nimmins scored with an overhead kick three minutes from time, the result was by then a foregone conclusion. Two goals, one at the beginning and one at the end of that half, settled any lingering doubts that Pegasus would fly to triumph. Hardisty, captain of Bishop Auckland and captain of Great Britain's Olympic Games Soccer Team in 1948, was once again deprived of the one honour that had eluded him throughout his distinguished playing career, an Amateur Cup Winner's medal. Yet, as he gallantly declared afterwards, in the finest British sporting spirit to mock all cynicism about bad winners and good losers: 'Somehow, it's different this time. Pegasus deserved to win and it means so much to football.' His colleagues agreed.

Hence, that lobbed pass by Dutchman from which Potts drove in the first goal with his fair head was a variation of the Tottenham Hotspur free-kick precision move which had gained for the League Champions so many goals and points throughout the season. The second goal by Tanner, after Pawson and Dutchman had worked the opening and the centre forward had swerved round the centre-half, was taken in a manner and crowned a display of which G.O. himself could well have been proud. Indeed, in the light of our knowledge of Tanner's school and University it was only fitting that one of the chroniclers of this match, Alan Hoby, should have aligned the Pegasus centre-forward with the greatest of them all when recording the game in the *Sunday Express:*

'Hero of the match was that modern G.O. Smith, former Oxford captain and English amateur international, John Tanner.

'Tanner was always moving the ball around and dribbling with the superb speed and skill of one of those old-time masters we hear so much about.

'I can pay him no higher compliment than to say that I doubt if the great G.O. Smith himself could have played much better than Tanner did against Auckland's centre-half, R.W. Davison. Tanner "lost" Davison for speed.

'It was a top-class performance by a man who was once told after a particularly trying thigh injury that he would be well advised not to play football again.'

Yet the whole Pegasus team were heroes: from Saunders the captain who was now amply consoled for having missed his year of captaincy of Oxford's soccer side through a serious illness; from Dutchman, who was nearly left in the dressing-room at half-time with a badly gashed leg and had prepared for the replayed Semi-Final on stimulants after collapsing at the end of the first; down, to Brown in goal who had scared his cheek against a goalpost in effecting a save and had survived the second Hendon game despite an injured thumb. The Tottenham Hotspur touch throughout the whole team (unanimously acknowledged by the whole sporting Press) from Brown in goal with his Ditchburn-like throwing, Platt with his Nicholson-style of tackling at right-half, down to Potts on the wing with the effervescence of Medley, could clearly be recognised. The wheel had now indeed turned full circle with the amateur students, whose ancestors had preceded the professionals, triumphing as twentieth-century pioneers upon professional teachings.

Here indeed, was the best of both worlds, the Corinthian spirit with the Spurs skill wedded to a display of football that gave for the game a future hope which the throes of the thirties had at one time threatened to destroy. On this performance those white shirts of Pegasus could easily have been mistaken for those worn by the other two great clubs, Corinth and Tottenham Hotspur: they might also have been associated with a third great white-shirted side who, on this very day, became champions of the Second Division of the Football League in attempting to regain the lost glory of other days - 'Proud' Preston. For Pegasus were surely, and rightly, entitled to become proud.

TUTORS AND PUPILS

TOTTENHAM HOTSPUR – LEAGUE CHAMPIONS – 1951

Group – (Back, l. to r.): Withers, Ramsey, Nicholson, Ditchburn, Burgess, Clarke, Arthur Rowe (Manager), C. Poynton (Trainer), Bennett. *(Front):* Walters, Murphy, Duquemin, Bailey, Medley, Willis.

PEGASUS – F.A. AMATEUR CUP WINNERS – 1951

Group – (Back, l. to r.): J. Platt, K.A. Shearwood, J.A. Dutchman, R. Cowan, D.F. Saunders (with Cup), J.D.P. Tanner, B.R. Brown, H.A. Pawson, D.B. Carr. *(Front):* J. Maughan, H.J. Potts (back to camera), Dr H.W. Thompson (Hon. Secretary).

The teams were as follows:

PEGASUS
Goal
B.R. BROWN
(Mexborough G.S. & Oriel College, Oxford)

2. Right-back	3. Left-back
J. MAUGHAN	R.COWAN
(Stanley G.S. & Keble College, Oxford)	*(Chorlton H.S. & Queens' College, Cambridge)*

4. Right-half	5. Centre-half	6. left-half
J. PLATT	K.A. SHEARWOOD	D.F. SAUNDERS
(Hulme G.S. & St.John's College, Cambridge)	*(Shrewsbury & Brasenose College, Oxford)*	*(Capt.)(Scarborough*
H.S. & Exeter College, Oxford)		

8. Inside-right	10. Inside-left
J.A. DUTCHMAN	D.B. CARR
(Cockburn H.S. & King's College, Cambridge)	*(Repton & Worcester College, Oxford)*

7. Outside-right	9. Centre-forward	11. Outside-left
H.A. PAWSON	J.D.P. TANNER	H.J. P0TTS
(Winchester & Christ Church College, Oxford)	*(Charterhouse & Brasenose College, Oxford)*	*(Stand G.S. & Keble College, Oxford)*

●

11. Outside-left	9. Centre-forward	7. Outside-right
B. EDWARDS	H.J. McILVENNY	J.W.R. TAYLOR
	(Capt.)	

10. Inside-left	8. Inside-right
K. WILLIAMSON	W. ANDERSON

6. Left-half	5. Centre-half	4. Right-half
J. NIMMINS	R.W. DAVISON	J.R.E. HARDISTY

3. Left-back	2. Right-back
L.T. FARRER	D. MARSHALL

Goal
W.H. WHITE
BISHOP AUCKLAND

Although the teams on this occasion gave the Final a South v. North aspect, Pawson alone of all the players from the winning eleven came from the Southern Counties. Yet perhaps this was significant, for the word Pegasus, apart from suggesting a winged horse, also connotes astronomically a constellation of northern stars around the planet Jupiter. Already before the Final, Brown, Cowan, Potts and Tanner had received their amateur international caps as Shuttleworth had done the previous year. Now Pawson and Saunders were selected to play against Finland for the next England Amateur XI chosen after the Final. By the end of 1954 their number had been increased by another half a dozen, so that within their six short years of existence Pegasus could field a full team English international players plus reserves, though in the amateur sphere alone. Indeed, the selectors might well have followed the precedent of their predecessors who had selected the Corinthians as a team to represent England v. Wales in 1894 and 1895 and have changed the

Pegasus crest on ten white shirts and the goalkeeper's jersey for that of England. Certainly the recognition from the Football Association's headquarters at Lancaster Gate was sufficient proof, if proof were ever needed, of the Club's material contribution to the game, and the F.A.'s justifiable confidence in it from the beginning.

The following season saw an anti-climax similar to that after the Bromley story. Buckingham departed for deserved recognition of his cultured touch, firstly with Bradford (Park Avenue), and subsequently with West Bromwich Albion Dutchman had left to join the Casuals, while Donald Carr' was away as vice-captain of M.C.C.'s side touring in India. Yet in the First Round Pegasus seemed to carry on where they had left off. Thanks to Peter May at inside-forward and John Tanner, a scratch team had no trouble in romping home by four clear goals in Surrey against the reasonably strong Kingstonian side, themselves past winners of the trophy. The New Year tour in Switzerland now followed to enable Reg Flewin of Portsmouth, that season's coach, to knit the side together, and when they went north once more to Durham for the Second Round tie with Crook Town, tradition was followed by the loss of a goal within five minutes. Yet on a mudheap which completely clogged their style, Pegasus managed to equalise and also to miss a penalty. A week later at the replay, the soccer ground at Iffley Road and not a few ideals were sacrificed for the better equipped University Rugby pitch next door with its uneven surface which checked the flow of Pegasus passes. So Nemesis overtook this flirtation with fate and Rugby.

Crook Town snatched an early goal, and although the last quarter of an hour saw the now traditional Pegasus flourish and rally, the gods and goals were this time not on their side. Perhaps it had been forgotten, or never known, that when the Corinthians ventured on to a Rugby ground they stuck to the game for which it was prepared - and won!

A year later, George Ainsley, the former England professional, was appointed coach. At the outset it was understood that with a greater concentration on defence he would try and adapt the push-and-run style of Tottenham Hotspur to the individual talents of the Pegasus players in the manner proved so successful in 1951. The First Round of the Amateur Cup, however, played a week after the Varsity match in December would have taken place for the first time at Wembley Stadium but for fog, hardly gave time to effect this. Against Hayes in Middlesex the University players turned up with hopes of finding time to develop an understanding. While they were doing so, the familiar story began and half-time found them 0-2 down. Immediately after the interval, however, Lunn set the tempo for his own success that season by reducing the lead; but despite the rising tide of Pegasus attacks the score remained 1-2 until three minutes were left. Then Sutcliffe was tripped in the penalty area and Carr made it 2-2. Lesser mortals would now have been content; but Hayes were to follow Hendon. As *The Times* Association football correspondent wrote, 'the finish defies description ... In the final judgment Hayes were found wanting. They collapsed like a pack of cards.' Seconds later Sutcliffe ran in from the left to Pawson's centre from the right-wing, saw an opening and took advantage of it. In the next and last minute Laybourne made the score 4-2 and the forward march was on.

Cockfield came to Oxford from Durham only to leave with five goals in their net and none to show for their own courageous and sporting efforts. Clearly the Pegasus New Year tour of Yorkshire and the North-East, sandwiched between the two rounds, had merged the players into a force that amateur soccer could only fear and admire. Yet, did they but know it, their greatest crisis was now at hand.

Two days after the Cockfield rout, the draw for the Third Round was announced. It brought Pegasus, away once more, to their step-brothers-in-arms, Corinthian-Casuals, at the historic Kennington Oval. This was the draw all had feared and dreamed might happen, but not before the Final. Insole, the Casuals' captain, who had played for Pegasus in that first game against the Arsenal, summarised the feelings of many when he said after the pairing was known that it was 'like crossing swords with a fellow idealist. All the present Pegasus side have played for us: seven of our boys have turned out for them.' Dr Thompson, too, echoed many feelings when he declared: 'It is the worst thing that could have happened to *amateur* football. It should have been reserved for Wembley. The winners must play in the Final.' So they did; but not the winners many had secretly or openly hoped.

Apart from the tension that had arisen between the clubs over the relaxation of the Pegasus qualifying rule and the Club's subsequent success, the belief had arisen that the Oxford men generally decided to throw in their lot with Pegasus and the Cambridge players, a year after they went down, with the Casuals. This was far from being the true position.

Beneath the friendly rivalry on the surface, therefore, something deeper was at stake. The sporting press did not assist the atmosphere, and Leslie Nichol, in the *Daily Express,* typified this by suggesting: 'One question this match will supply; who are the present mid-century Corinthian,: Pegasus or Corinthian Casuals?' That position, of course, had been settled at Wembley in 1951, and, indeed, acknowledged by Leslie Nichol himself throughout the whole of that year. The tragedy of it all is clearly the true Corinthians could have risen again and that recaptured all the old glory in the Amateur Cup, continuing their missionary work while leaving the Casuals to continue their associations with the Isthmian League and Pegasus, if necessary, as a nursery in the Universities. Indeed, there are reasons to think that Pegasus had tried to achieve such a position by constructive proposals in 1951 - but these had been turned down. As it is, Pegasus alone have assumed the role fulfilled by the Corinthians of redressing the balance of the professional influence; and having once done so, they have a duty to fulfil their mission and destiny.

It should not be forgotten, as has been shown, that the Corinthians did not limit their membership to Oxford and Cambridge players exclusively. So the Corinthian Casuals against Pegasus at the Oval contained eight Cambridge Blues, two London University Purples, and a goalkeeper from a London bank. Pegasus that day contained four Cambridge Blues and six from Oxford, as they did at Wembley in 1951, and an international goalkeeper, Brown, who graduated from Oxford to research work at Cambridge without gaining his Blue from either. So the tie underlined the paradox of two clubs professing *presumably* the same object with one major source of membership. At the time of the draw the *Oxford Mail* commented: 'It is not generally known that a proposal to amalgamate Pegasus and Corinthian-Casuals was the subject of lengthy discussions not long ago at St John's College, but came to nothing'; and Geoffrey Green mysteriously ended his report of the game, in *The Times,* with the closing words that 'by then the pale sun had gone down on the Casuals, and all those who would wish to serve two masters.'

Before the game began, the atmosphere had been intensified by an interview given by Insole, the Casuals' captain, to the London *Evening Standard.* For there he was recorded as having said, quite unjustifiably as is now known, Pegasus v. Corinthian Casuals match is mostly Oxford v. Cambridge. The Cambridge men stick to the former idea that the new Pegasus Club exists only for undergraduates and those down for less than a year, then they move over to the Casuals. At Oxford they go riding the flying horse even into their thirties.'

Unfortunately for Insole and his fellow Casuals, the oldest of those riders in the thirties, Pawson, flew the ball and horse into the Casuals' net twelve minutes after the start to win a disappointingly scrappy game that never lived up to the heights of expectation. Three of the losers had played for Pegasus at Wembley in 1951; and with Casuals now deflated, Pegasus had completely vindicated their claim to be the sole and rightful heirs to the true Corinthian tradition. Providence and their destiny once more now pointed in one direction Wembley.

Pegasus supporters in the 12,000 crowd,
at the 1953 Oval Cup-tie.

The draw for the next round, Slough Town, away, underlined that pointer. Slough Town had been victims of Pegasus in the Second Round *en route* to Wembley in 1951. Some regarded it as a chance now for revenge; others as an omen. Spurred on by Saunders' unobtrusive yet effective captaincy at left-half, Sutcliffe and Tanner settled any doubt with a goal each in the second half. So once more it was the Semi-Final and Highbury.

Southall this time were the problem; and like Hendon before them, they gave Pegasus a fright. For once, Pegasus scored first and then forgot their attacking traditions to allow the Athenian League team to equalise. Yet, as in the Hendon game, Highbury once more produced a 1-1 draw and a mixture of artistry and rhythm, chiefly supplied by Pegasus with the thrills and heart-pangs that Cup-Ties alone can bring. For the replay at Craven Cottage, Fulham, as against the Casuals, Pegasus took no chances. They had the wisdom to listen to

the guidance of their coach: kept Southall's defence at full stretch with their mixture of long and short passing, and utilising the speed of their wings, gained a two-goal lead, which they held until reduced to the odd goal near the end. J.P.W. Mallalieu generously wrote of this game in the *Spectator,* after mentioning his local town club, Huddersfield, that he had been present at 'about the best football match I have ever seen since the war'; and on the same afternoon, ten seconds and a fatal pass back against Blackpool in the F.A. Cup Semi-Final at Villa Park prevented Tottenham Hotspur from once more joining hands to celebrate with their pupils. For the second time the University club that is not a club had reached the final stage.

At the start of the season the Pegasus players were very amused to hear one of their most ardent supporters, coming like many of their regular followers from Morris Motors rather than from the Universities, tell an uninitiated enquirer, who had asked where Pegasus usually played, 'Well, sometimes we play at Oxford and sometimes we play at Cambridge, but you might say our home ground is - Wembley.' Nor was the answer as funny as it may seem. For in the previous three years they had been drawn at home only once in Cup games and played at Wembley twice. On this second occasion they appeared as experienced and redoubtable Cup-fighters, no longer the fortunate babes who were supposed to have fluked their way to the right of meeting and beating the leading Amateur Cup club in the country.

Harwich and Parkeston from the shattered East Coast flood areas supplied the opposition on this occasion. Not since 1899 had they reached the final stage, when they lost 0-1 to Stockton. Now they came full of confidence with victories over such amateur giants as Leytonstone and Walton and Hersham. For ten minutes their confidence was justified. Then Pegasus scored against the run of play. The flood-gates were opened, and the tide from the teachings of the professionals mounted wave upon wave of lashing controlled attacks to break through the helpless Harwich defence on five more occasions.

The losers may not have been as great a side as Bishop Auckland; but they resisted as bravely as had their neighbours in more desperate circumstances under the assault of the cruel sea. Unhappily for them, they found a somewhat more balanced Pegasus, certainly more balanced in defence, than in 1951 had shocked all the football world except themselves and their closest admirers. With Cowan having departed for the Casuals, another Cantab, Alexander, not unlike Ramsey in build and style, formed with McKinna from Oxford as solid and constructive a pair of backs as had the famous Hotspur with his professional colleagues for Tottenham and England, or Oakley and Lodge from Oxford and Cambridge respectively, for Corinth in the Golden Age; and like that famous University pair they once more brought the Universities to England for international duty. Vowels, then Cambridge captain, replaced Platt at right-half to blend with Saunders' delicacy and retain a Light Blue in the half-back line; and further Cambridge additions appeared as Sutcliffe, hero of some of the 1951

games, came in for Potts at outside-left and Laybourne for Tanner at centre-forward. Lunn from Oxford completed the replacements, at inside-left in place of Carr, who had taken the position of Dutchman at inside-right; and with the old guard of Brown in goal, Shearwood and Saunders in the half-back line and Pawson and Carr in the attack there was no doubt now that 1951 had been no chance accident.

With the sunshine girdling the flawless turf as if to form a halo around these Bachelors and Masters of Arts, they demonstrated to a perfection unattained in 1951 all the art and science of the world's most beautiful game. Only Matthews could be said to have bettered it among the twenty-two professionals three weeks later in the more thrilling but aesthetically less satisfying Final between Blackpool and Bolton Wanderers. Alan Hoby in the *Sunday Express,* though before the pluperfect displays by F.I.F.A. and Hungary six months later, recorded: 'At its best the football played by these students and graduates of Oxford and Cambridge is the purest I have seen at Wembley since the war.' The six goals came with clockwork regularity, spaced at ten to fifteen minute intervals, as though controlled by some preconceived plan which no defence could hold: and the audience showed its appreciation by staying to the end.

During the seasons between Portsmouth's 1934 and 1939 Cup-Finals, I had seen the tutors of Pegasus, Tottenham Hotspur, then in the Second Division of the Football League, play the more favoured Hampshire side from the First Division at Fratton Park in a Third Round F.A. Cup-Tie. After twelve minutes the Londoners had opened the scoring; by half-time they had anticipated Pegasus and led 3-0. A few minutes after the interval they scored their fourth goal; yet long before their fifth goal without reply sent the home team to the bottom of its famous Harbour and out of the Cup for that year, I shall always recall the gleaming regalia of the Lord Mayor and the Admiral of the Fleet departing from the Directors' Box. The winners had played their traditionally fast and clean sporting game. But no one could leave Wembley Stadium on Saturday, 11th April, 1953, before the final whistle. For the onlookers were treated to a feast of the arts of football surpassed only by F.I.F.A. and the Hungarians at the famous Stadium six months later.

It is of some significance, too, that the continental countries, unhampered by the sophistication of overloaded professional League and Cup competitions, place their faith in the basic skills demonstrated by the Corinthians and their contemporaries of the Golden Age. The high standard of these very same skills attained by the Spurs and Pegasus has been the reason for both their successes.

Before the first Hendon Semi-Final at Highbury in 1951 one telegram among the countless received by Pegasus contained a special message: 'Make it simple, make it quick.' It was sent by the manager of Tottenham Hotspur, Arthur Rowe. Two years later the theme had not been forgotten when George Ainsley was making his own polished contribution to perfection. So Frank Coles, in the *Daily Telegraph,* recorded: 'This latest edition of Pegasus moved with the precision of well coached professionals; indeed, their ground passing, use of the telling short ball and speedy running into position would have done credit to the Spurs at their best.' In place of the glory that was Corinth a fresh force had arisen; the power that is Pegasus had spread its wings. The teams were:

PEGASUS

Goal
B.R. BROWN
(Mexborough G.S. & Oriel)

2. Right-back
F.C.M. ALEXANDER
(Wolmer's Jamaica & Caius)

3. Left-back
G.H. McKINNA
(Manchester G.S. & Brasenose)

4. Right-half
R.C. VOWELS
(Brentwood & Emmanuel)

5. Centre-Half
K.A. SHEARWOOD
(Shrewsbury & Brasenose)

6. Left-half
D.F. SAUNDERS
(Capt.) (Scarborough H.S. & Exeter)

8. Inside-right
D.B. CARR
(Repton & Worcester)

10. Inside-left
R.G. LUNN
(Holme Valley G.S. & St. Edmund Hall)

7. Outside-right
H.A. PAWSON
(Winchester & Christ Church)

9. Centre-forward
J.S. LAYBOURNE
(Hookergate G.S. & Emmanuel)

11. Outside-left
R. SUTCLIFFE
(Chadderton G.S. & St John's, Cambridge)

●

11. Outside-left
V. JENNINGS

9. Centre-forward
D. DAVIES

7. Outside-right
H. STREMP

10. Inside-Left
R. COOPER

8. Inside-right
S. PEARSON

6. Left-half
R. HAUGH

5. Centre-half
K. BLOSS

4. Right-half
P. CHRISTIE

3. Left-back
E.TYRELL

2. Right-back
B. NIGHTINGALE

Goal
B. KING

HARWICH AND PARKESTON

PEGASUS SPREADS ITS WINGS

PEGASUS – 1953 – F.A. AMATEUR CUP WINNERS

Bottom Group – (Back, l. to r.): Dr H.W. Thompson (Hon. Secretary), A.H. Chadder (President), G.E. Ainsley (Coach), R. Sutcliffe, G.H. McKinna, B.R. Brown, R.G. Lunn, J.S. Laybourne, W.V. Cavill (Hon. Treasurer), L. Laitt (Trainer), J.L. Weinstein (Ass. Hon. Secretary). *(Front):* K.A. Shearwood, J.D.P. Tanner*, H.A. Pawson, D.F. Saunders (Capt.), F.C.M. Alexander, R.C. Vowels, D.B. Carr.

⋆ Did not play in the Final.

Success, of course, begets success. Of the victorious Pegasus side against Harwich and Parkeston four were capped in the next amateur international against France, and Brown the goalkeeper was chosen as reserve. Invitations came pouring in from Europe, from Australia, from America. Floodlit matches were requested by professional clubs of all standards; and within a few weeks of the beginning of the following season the new 'Corinthians' were receiving the spontaneous and sincere plaudits from the supporters of Portsmouth in the First Division and Watford in the Third. The only problem was how to maintain the standard.

The success of coaching for Pegasus was obvious. As Vic Buckingham had said after the Bishop Auckland game: 'These fellows, being university men, think fast. You can train them from the head downwards, and not from the feet upwards. Likewise as George Ainsley said after the Harwich and Parkeston game: 'These boys are grand to coach. They begin movements in their head, then tell their feet what to do.' Looking back now I find that about the time that the foundation of Pegasus was being considered, in 1948, I wrote in the *Amateur Football Yearbook 1948-49*: 'Without practice and some attempt at training the Universities can never hope to raise their standards from the rut into which they have fallen, let alone approach the favour that Rugby deservedly holds ... If the Varsity soccer standards and prestige are raised, as a consequence the more ambitious grammar schools (and most of them are so) will have an incentive, lacking to-day, to train their boys for a coveted Blue, equal in status to that awarded for Rugby. The progress of the one is complementary to the other.'

Did I but know it at the time, Pegasus, already born, was then gaining strength to spread its wings and gospel into the four corners of the land; and on the Monday after the defeat of Harwich and Parkeston the *Daily Mail* contained the following suggestions by its experienced Rugby correspondent, Roy McKelvie, alongside Geoffrey Simpson's enthusiastic account of the match:

'The challenge to Rugby football presented by the success of Pegasus in the Amateur Cup should not he taken lightly. In recent years the Rugby Union have made great efforts to convert, among others, grammar schools from one code to the other. They have had their successes. To-day the majority of players representing England, Oxford and Cambridge are gramrnar-school boys.

But Pegasus and the Soccer clubs of these two leading universities draw most of their players from the grammar schools, and it is therefore on that field that Rugby and Soccer do battle. The inspiration of Pegasus will give headmasters and governors of grammar schools doubts about converting to Rugby. Moreover, Rugby, for all its camaraderie, social life, and manliness, has this season done itself little good by the way it has been played - excessive numbers of penalties, lines-out, the use of obstructing tactics, and dull negative play.

These have not only tried the spectators whose support maintains the big clubs and representative games, but they also appear to have inspired a good deal of hot-headedness and bad temper. Despite England's popular success in the international championship this season, there has been much unworthy play in representative Rugby.'

The same comment was hardly applicable to representative soccer during that or any recent season at either the professional or amateur level. Once the true position is realised by head masters and governors whose prejudices, like most prejudices, stem from crass ignorance alone, then the boys who endure the tyranny of playing a game they detest may be given that freedom of choice which at present exists only between Association football or Rugby and hockey. There are few schools to-day, whether in urban or rural areas, that do not possess the facilities or the numbers allowing Association football and Rugby to live side by side or alternate through the Michaelmas and Hilary terms. Both are fine games in their own way, making their own individual contributions to the community. For one to arrogate a superiority over the other that is contrary to the true facts, reflects neither credit on the claimant nor, one would imagine, an admirable attitude to life.

Meanwhile, the progressive accumulation of defects in the modern Rugby game mentioned by Roy McKelvie culminated after that second Pegasus triumph in what the All-Blacks' captain, Bob Scott, described as, even for New Zealanders, the game of the year - Oxford v. Cambridge. This match, more so than either the Cup-Final or England v. Scotland in the soccer calendar is regarded as the apotheosis of the Rugby season; and if the Universities cannot control themselves before Queen Elizabeth, the Queen Mother, and Princess Margaret, as the Twickenham crowd shamefully observed in 1953, what is one to expect of the rest? For after 9 of the 12 points in a 6-6 draw had come from penalties, *The Times* Rugby correspondent was constrained to write, 'Most of it was the merest rough and tumble, punctuated by thud and blunder.'

Yet although in April, 1953, the joint University side drew 100,000 to Wembley for the second time while the Varsity Rugby match at Twickenham in the previous December had attracted a mere 45,000, the postponed Varsity soccer match played for the first time at Wembley in March, 1953, with five of the Pegasus team on view, a month before the Pegasus-Harwich Cup-Final, could gather within the famous Empire Stadium only 5,000. A week later when those five joined their Pegasus colleagues for the first Southall Semi-Final, just under 30,000 turned up at Highbury, and for the re-play a week later at Fulham there were 22,000. Here, then, is the greatest mystery in amateur soccer. Were it not for Pegasus and the existence of a similar position in G.O.'s day, the reason could well be regarded as a hangover from the thirties.

Perhaps the truth lies in realising that whereas the two University elevens and a few seniors combined as Pegasus can produce the finest exhibition of pure football given by Englishmen at Wembley for years, Oxford and Cambridge in opposition before 1953's brilliant game on the seventieth anniversary of the match were rarely able to attain such heights of perfection. Consequently their appeal must always suffer by comparison with that of professionals and Pegasus: whereas the Varsity match at Twickenham in the past was expected to produce some of the highest quality domestic and Dominion Rugby - whatever that is worth. Meanwhile, the Association game must await the realisation among those who arrange such things that until the Universities in opposition at soccer can produce the appeal of their combination as Pegasus, the Varsity match must not be played at Wembley Stadium. Even the fog stepped in during December, 1952 - when the pathetic sale of tickets in advance warned the authorities of the certainty of the fiasco which occurred three months later. The handful dotted round the huge bowl immediately recalled the haunting memory of the Corinthians farewell to London at the White City in 1937; and had it not been for the Pegasus performance a month afterwards there is no knowing what harm could have been done to the cause for which so many have worked with so much success. It is a pity that those responsible for the decision to take the game to Wembley had not let the wisdom of those who opposed the move prevail. if the conflict between Corinthian-Casuals and Pegasus cannot permit a return of the Varsity match to the Oval where this inter-University contest began in 1874, then no better resting place can be found than at White Hart Lane where it was welcomed and supported by its largest post-War crowd. In view of the influence of the Spurs on Pegasus, Tottenham is perhaps a more natural home in 'the football world' of to-day than the Oval with its ghosts of the old Corinthians from an age now faded and never to return. At Tottenham, too, would the influence of the Varsity match on the game in general be greatest. Moreover, with the continued success of Pegasus, the Varsity soccer match might well replace the Varsity rugger match as the social event of the football year.

It was in North London, at half-time during that memorable 5-4 Oxford victory in 1948, that G.O.'s successor at Ludgrove, A.T. Barber, suggested to me that he would always take his boys to Tottenham for the Varsity match. His silence as to what other matches he would take them to was more significant than any words. Yet this famous Corinthian of the thirties, in his study at Ludgrove, amidst the Berkshire meadows, had recalled nostalgically for me his own appearance for the Corinthians at the Arsenal Stadium in the same Sheriff of London Shield Competition which had produced G.O.'s most memorable game - against Aston Villa. Perhaps he would have thought differently had he seen the Tottenham Hotspur players throughout that and the coming seasons practising what they were to preach to their Pegasus pupils.

The style has, I think, always been unique and never entirely absent, even in the club's worst years. The chief thing about it is the "straight ahead" theory. The forwards play a good open game, without any crowding, taking the ball on the run and making quick for goal without dallying. The passing is crisp, quick and along the ground; the shooting is done from all angles. There is plenty of hard charging, but never a suspicion of foul play. There is any amount of life and go, and no one ever slacks. In fact, the impression one gleans from watching is that they play to win the game and to enjoy themselves while doing so.' Of Tottenham Hotspur was this written? It could have been, as we shall immediately see; but that was how Stanley Harris described the Corinthians in 1906.

Forty-five years later Clifford Webb used almost identical phrases in the modern idiom of his *Daily Herald Football Handbook for 1950-51* to summarise the season which saw Tottenham Hotspur race to the top of the Second Division of the Football League prior to their Championship of the First Division:

'The comparatively young Hotspur players swept through their League and Cup matches with a bubbling infectious enthusiasm which was a rare and timely tonic for English football. Wonderful five-in-a-line attacks smashed through the dourest defences. No wonder Spurs not only gained promotion to the First Division but had capacity attendances for almost all their home games. The entertainment value of the football at White Hart Lane came to be almost legendary last season. Similarly, when Spurs travelled they invariably pulled in bigger-than-usual gates on the grounds of their opponents. The North London Club did a great deal for football in England last season. The hope is not only will they continue to sparkle in the First Division but that they will persuade other Clubs to throw aside in dull defence and endeavour to emulate their methods.'

This they did with Pegasus. A generation before them at the height of Arsenal's third-back success, that club's great inside-forward, David Jack, wrote in his book, *Soccer:* 'The successful Tottenham Hotspur team of 1933-34 appears to be doing its utmost to prove that the five-in-line attack and a roaming centre-half-back [Arthur Rowe] can still more than hold their own under modern conditions, but they are the exception rather than the rule.' While even before the great team of the early 1920s under Grimsdell's captaincy we find *Gibson and Pickford* writing at the time of Stanley Harris's assessment of the Corinthians: 'Than the famous Spurs there is probably no more popular club in England. The reasons are not far to seek. Did the Spurs not recover the Association Cup for the South? Do they not play pretty and effective football? Are they not scrupulously fair? Are they not perfectly managed?'

Whatever their modern supporters may occasionally think of to-day's management, it has come about that the professionals at Tottenham played pure Corinthian football after the Corinthians had disappeared, and then handed on the quality to the natural inheritors of the Corinthian tradition. Corinthans - Spurs - Pegasus, here is the perfect football trinity, dissolving the prejudice and barriers that have been erected ever since the 'split' in 1907 and the advancement of professionalism with its occasionally objectionable publicity. Now that University football has once more returned to its standards and, of even greater importance, to its status of the nineties, the attention paid by the public to the professionals which hitherto has almost eclipsed the University player, has returned after half a century to the start of it all. As Dr Thompson wrote in the Wembley programme for the seventieth Varsity soccer match after the F.I.F.A. and Hungarian fiascos: 'Amid all the torrent of self-criticism from recent events there is the realisation that pure orthodox football remains supreme, the sort of game in fact which the Universities and the Corinthians themselves long ago made so appealing.'

The Varsity match itself of that year, 1954, bore that out; and thanks to Pegasus, no longer need the gulf between the professional and amateur branches of the game in the land where it was born create false impressions in the minds of the public. At cricket, the difficulties of Association football have never been considered because the Universities and Public Schools have never lost control of the M.C.C. at Lord's. At soccer, from the time of 'Pa' Jackson and his objection to professionalism, the Public Schools and Universities have slowly surrendered the reins to the administrators from the professional clubs, who were eventually to lose their sense of proportion in safeguarding the interests of the game. Yet whatever may have occurred in the committee rooms or council chambers by way of changes from the past, they have never been visible on the field of play at football apart from the distinctions of stamina between the fully trained professional and the amateur.

Further, the golden strand of duality running throughout the history of English football and cricket has reappeared through Pegasus to emphasise, although emphasis is in no way needed, their full inheritance of the traditions and position in English sport of the Corinthians. For not a few Pegasus players have reflected perfectly that versatility which the four generations of Corinthians before them so nobly displayed. I was able to draw attention to this by pointing out in *The Cricketer* during 1951 that three Oxford cricket Blues were in the Pegasus forward-line at Wembley. There might also have been another, J.D. P. Tanner, as *Wisden* for 1950 suggests, if the Oxford wicket-keeper in 1949 had been chosen on

form and not from a schoolboy's statistical reputation. As it was, the Old Carthusian amateur international was selected as twelfth man while D.B. Carr, his inside-left at Wembley, played at Lord's and the following year, 1950, played there again as captain. H.J. Potts, who had headed that first Pegasus goal at Wembley, also played at Lord's in 1950. Later he went on to assist the Lancashire 2nd XI after the selectors from Lancaster Gate in the previous winter had awarded him his first amateur international soccer cap. His fellow winger, H.A. Pawson, gained his first recognition from the F.A. over three years after scoring his century and then captaining Oxford at Lord's in 1947 and 1948 respectively; and K.A. Shearwood from centre-half was selected for an F.A. tour of the Channel Islands after a deserved appearance as wicket-keeper and batsman for Derbyshire against Goddard's fizzers on a Bristol sand-pit in Gloucestershire.

From Cambridge, D.J. Insole, later captain of Essex, might well have been playing at Wembley, too, if he had not appeared earlier in the competition for the Corinthian-Casuals at inside-right, the position from which he captained the Light Blues soccer side of 1948 which included two other cricket Blues, G. M. Shuttleworth and G.H.G. Doggart, both in their turn soccer captains. They have all appeared for Pegasus in its short life along with P.B.H. May, of the Surrey and England cricket sides, who also captained the Cambridge soccer side in 1951; and just as G.O. turned up at Lord's three months after playing for England against Scotland, so Alexander and McKinna, the pegasus full-backs who played against Harwich and Parkeston at Wembley in April 1953, appeared for their respective Universities at Lord's three months later; when they caused the score-card to register the following entry in the Cambridge second innings: F.C.M. Alexander, b. G.H. McKinna . . 16.

Yet is it so surprising that these young men should have two strings to their sporting bows? When 'Pa' Jackson founded the Corinthians we have seen how he swiftly drew from the Public School and University recruiting-grounds footballers who had gained equal if not greater renown at cricket.

With the decline, before 1914, of the standards set by George Brann and C.B. Fry, R.E. Foster and G.O. himself, the hopes after 1918 for a revival of Corinthian fortunes were not high. Yet we saw a new generation of cricketing Corinthians, including the brothers Ashton, A.G. Doggart, R.W.V. Robins and A.T. Barber arise to leave fresh memories of that Club's fighting spirit against the rapidly advancing soccer professionals. Then came the slump in the thirties, amalgamation with the Casuals and another war. And what has happened now? Another line of cricket and football Blues in the true Corinthian tradition, now no longer able to compete for reasons of training and stamina against professionals, but, in a lower key, in their own amateur spheres, have done what we have thrilled to see them do, as well as raise fresh hopes for the future of British sport.

It was hardly surprising, therefore, that when Peter May and Colin Cowdrey (who had assisted Brasenose with two goals to win the Oxford University Association football College Cup Final in 1953) thrust home the bowling benefits of Statham and Tyson to win the Sydney Test Match for England against Australia on Christmas Eve, 1954, Neville Cardus wrote home for the *Manchester Guardian:* 'Not for many years has English cricket had cause for so much rejoicing and expressions of relief as now, in the moment of revival of the young amateur batsman in English cricket. As I watched May and Cowdrey at Sydney I had a vision of young Maclaren and young R.E. Foster on the same ground, a vision from the Golden Age. The wheel is circling.'

With Pegasus the wheel has turned full circle. By linking with Tottenham Hotspur to share their talents and ideas the University players have set an example to others in re-establishing the old relations between Gentlemen and Players in foot. ball. They have also created an atmosphere within which football in its native land, despite continental challenges, has as great a future to look forward to as has been its heritage in the past.

For the benefits each section of the community can confer upon the other are beyond the realm of imagination.

Following upon the Pegasus success in 1951, the *Tatler and Bystander* generously offered a silver model ship to be known as the Argonaut Trophy, to be competed for annually by the Oxford University Centaurs, the first winners, Cambridge University Falcons, finalists in the next two years, and other amateur clubs from the services, military and civil, and business houses, who would not normally take part in competitive football. Moreover, as experienced a chronicler of the professional game as Charles Buchan, the former Sunderland and Arsenal international forward, echoed many feelings when he observed in *A Lifetime in Football:* 'What I should like to see is some amateur club like Pegasus take over the mantle of the old Corinthians and join the League. I am sure they would be welcomed by all clubs, just as Queen's Park are favourites in the Scottish League.'

The realities of the time have left little enough scope for an effective interpretation of such a thought. Yet its significance will always remain. For when Pegasus spread its wings not only did it symbolise the spirit of an age in which the conquest of the air has created new aristocracies but it also conjured up a past to which it had already given a new dynamic: a past which is all too easily forgotten, or, in the world of football at least, is generally not known.

After the Amateur Cup triumph of 1951 *The Christian Science Monitor* from Boston, U.S.A., recorded: 'There is no doubt at all that the bold experiment of the few Varsity soccer stalwarts has been well worth making. In making it they have made no small contribution to sporting history. They have also, perhaps unknown to themselves, made no small addition to their own glorious inheritance.

CHAPTER X

TOWARDS A NEW SPORTING ERA

Back to the future is a modern cliche which not only links the past to present and future times. It also turns history's wheel full circle in the context of these pages.

They began with my Second World War schoolboy's quest for the autograph of a retired headmaster whose signature had been targeted for his fame as the greatest centre-forward in the history of Association Football. They now re-appear four decades later in this unaltered re-issue while the game he graced grapples with the long-term effects of the European Court of Justice judgment, gained by the Belgian footballer Jean Marc Bosman against the Belgian and UEFA (Union of European) Football Associations on 15 December 1995. This outlawed within the European Union the controversial transfer system with its inflated payments and UEFA's artificially limited number of foreign players in a team. It applies to all professional sportsperson nationals of the 15 Member State countries in the European Union, and it also covers the member countries of the European Free Trade Association (EFTA). Its impact and repercussion will still be debated when and long after these pages are published during the autumn of 1996; but the unrestricted freedom for players to negotiate as free agents their new contracts of employment upon termination of an existing one will have one inevitable consequence.

The Coat of Arms granted to the Corinthian-Casuals in 1959, by the College of Arms in recognition of the Club's services to football. A unique honour.

This will be the crucial need for anyone concerned with the long-term replacement recruitment sources for public performance to fix their minds and eyes upon the game's only natural origins: the schools and local clubs and those who teach and coach in them. For while the multi-million television business deals negotiated globally and domestically within England by Premier League Clubs guarantee a regular flow for English clubs of overseas developed and mature talents, their inevitability could divert attention from developing the grass roots from which natural team selections can be nurtured.

Furthermore, it is to be hoped that the English football sources will not experience what has been recorded in the definitive treatise on *"The Bosman Case"* by Professor Roger Blanpain and Rita Inston [1996].

"It took dozens of legal actions, which were brought by parents driven by anxiety and which the Belgian Football Association lost humiliatingly time and time again, before any action was taken within the association to call a halt to the buying and selling of child players in Belgian football. If then".

In this context, Bernard Darwin wrote during and at the end of the Second World War in his *British Sport and Games* essay in a *British Life and Thought* series, as already cited in the original text, with words which have stood the test of time:

"... Great as is the interest in the big matches, in particular those of the professionals at Association, it would be a complete mistake to think of football as purely a gladiatorial exhibition. If it is the game which the mass of the people watch and read about, it is also the game which they play and know because they have played it. There is scarcely an open piece of ground where you may not see a band of small boys playing football with no better goal-posts than those made by piles of thrown-off coats, and you may see it almost as often out of the official season, in midsummer as in winter.

Association football is *the* game of the people in Britain and it has so remained throughout the war though naturally under new conditions."

This perceptive assessment from the 1940s by Charles Darwin's kinsman, an Old Carthusian and *The Times* Golf Correspondent, transcended the then greatly misunderstood belief that the game was the opiate of the cloth-capped masses, while ignoring the sustained activity of the Arthur Dunn Cup Competition schools. Nevertheless, the misconception was sufficiently entrenched in the public consciousness at that time, by way of contrast to the current cult status of the game today, for the creator of Pegasus, Dr (later Sir Harold) Thompson to write on the eve of their first Wembley FA Amateur Cup Final in 1951 as cited in the original text:

"Three years ago Pegasus FC was little more than a thought in the minds of a few Soccer enthusiasts at Oxford. While admiring the rising skill of the professional game, they saw with some dismay the effects of prejudice by others against it, for this prejudice was providing a channel for the flow to Rugby football in many schools all over the country. Within a generation this might prove disastrous and damage our national prestige even in the world of International Soccer which this country has done so much to create, for without a veritable host of amateurs behind them, the professional ranks must surely dwindle ... So, in order to strike one modest blow in Soccer's cause, the founders of Pegasus at Oxford and Cambridge determined to experiment with a new club, strictly amateur, formed from members of the two Universities."

How that experiment succeeded appears throughout the preceding chapter (IX) *Pegasus Spreads Its Wings*. Advancing years and an enveloping professionalism and shamateurism within the game led to its decline and, indeed, in 1974, abolition of the FA Amateur Cup Competition. Nevertheless, the principle of amateur recruitment for the professional game from schools and clubs to sustain an effective national representative team remains now even more essential at school than it did then at University levels in the wake of the potentially unforseen overseas fall-out to English professional clubs from the unfolding Bosman legal process which began as a spin-off in the Aldershot County Court for Ralph Banks while preparing the original text of this book. It is consistent with what C.B. Fry and his genius perceived as long ago as the opening paragraph of his Foreword in 1955 to be......

"a great formative era of what is now a great national and international entertainment. Some would say an industrial entertainment".

In one crucial active area sport differs from every other aspect of that exploding industry. For what is ignored by many within sport itself, as well as by even more outside it, is that the skills and techniques refined by C.B. Fry's

"great national and international entertainment"

are regulated by the particular laws applicable to each individual recreational and sporting discipline in addition to the national laws of every land where sport is played. Furthermore, the basic playing laws do not differ in their application between public, professional and private amateur performances, except for differentials in sizes for playing areas and equipment for differing age groups and degrees of fitness, such as disabled or other disadvantaged participants.

Thus a well publicised Arsenal supporter in a House of Lords debate [5 July 1996] explained

"We take it for granted that you cannot play a game of football without rules. Rules do not get in the way of the game; they make the game possible."

Dr George Carey, the Lord Archbishop of Canterbury, was speaking when he initiated a House of Lords debate on *'Society's Moral and Spiritual Well-being'*. He was followed ultimately by Lord [Denis] Howell, Britain's longest serving Minister with responsibility for Sport who observed,

"As a referee, I am grateful that someone pointed out today that we must observe the rules";

and it was England's World Cup referee, Philip Don, who told Michael Parkinson in the *Daily*

Telegraph during the opening days of the 1994-5 season after the red and yellow card proliferation during that 1994 competition,

"The laws weren't changed. All that FIFA did was to remind referees of what their responsibilities are".

That was why Patrick Barclay wrote in the *Sunday Telegraph* after the Croatia -v- Turkey game, as cited in the new Preface to this edition,

"No matter how many treats Euro '96 has in store, the Croatian substitute Goran Vlaovic's late winner against Turkey will go down among the goals of the tournament. It ought also to be hailed as a vindication of strict refereeing. The liberal use of yellow and red cards may be hurting, but this was a spectacular piece of evidence that it's working .... Cynics argued afterwards that Alpay/Ozalen of Turkey should have sacrificed himself [by committing a foul with a consequential suspension] ... The game's rulers should be congratulated on their campaign against such debilitating negativity, even if it seems to be taking an age for some observers to recognise the link between the hard line established in the 1994 World Cup and a perceptible tilting of the balance towards entertainment,

The complaining classes tend to forget how morally brutalised top level football had become before FIFA, alarmed by the dull, fear-filled World Cup of 1990 and the distressing submission of a great player,

Marco Van Basten, to a violent tackle from behind, at last resolved to act".

It was too late, by thirty years at least, to save the artistry of the great Pele, from being criminally and civilly assaulted out of the 1966 World Cup, as he explained in detail at pages 258 of the text *My Life and the Beautiful Game* [1977]

"... I had been the target of merciless attacks from Zechev of Bulgaria throughout the entire game ... Morais, of Portugal, had a field day fouling me, eventually putting me out of the game. He tripped me, and when I was stumbling to the ground he leaped at me, feet first, and cut me down completely. It wasn't until I actually saw the films of the game that I realised what a terribly vicious double-foul it was".

Objectively and more recently, Brian Glanville, football's leading international chronicler, has explained in *The Sport of the World Cup* (1993) on the eve of the 1994 World Cup,

"... there was no excuse, not even that of cynical necessity, for Morais to chop down Pele. Later Pele would say that it was only when he saw the incident on film that he realised how bad it was. He would swear, then, never to play in the World Cup again. The indulgent, flaccid English referee, George McCabe allowed Morais to say on the field, so that now Portugal were virtually against ten men".

During the Euro '96 recollections of that 1966 World Cup tournament, no reference, not even in Patrick Barclay's brilliant analysis cited above, referred to this outrageous breach of the Law XII

of the game against violent foul play and the common law of criminal and civil assault, known as trespass to the person. Pele, and his national team, Brazil were denied continued lawful participation in that international competition; and against that background can be seen the manner in which the encroachment of the law of the land to protect injured victims of unlawful misconduct has unsheathed its weaponry which had rusted in the case precedent books since their creation from even before the days of G.O. Smith and his Corinthians of a century ago.

The prosecution during 1995 by Scotland's Procurator Fiscal of the international striker Duncan Ferguson when playing in Scotland for Rangers for head-butting and thereby assaulting John McStay, during a Scottish Premier League game, is consistent with a precedent which has existed since 1878 *(R -v- Bradshaw)*. The legislation and litigation which followed from the Bradford City fire and Hillsborough stadium disasters were consistent with a legal liability which first surfaced in the courts four years after a collapsed grandstand at the traditional Cheltenham Race Festival 130 years ago in 1866 *(Frances -v-Cockerell* [1870]). The legal principle of a duty to take care to prevent injury, first traced there as its earliest application to a sporting situation, has been threaded down the years in different sporting circumstances most recently to the successful claim (subject to appeal) against the rugby union referee in 1996 for allowing the scrum to collapse in an under-19 Colts match *(Smolden v Whitworth v Nolan)*.

On that occasion the trial judge decided unequivocally that the referee had failed to understand and apply the relevant law within the rugby union game. It also merits recalling within the context of this decision and Dr. Carey's recognition,

"Rules ... make the game possible",

how the original text demonstrated that the Football Association was created in 1863 from a need to harmonise the different school and club rules under which the games had been played until

144

rules under which the games had been played until then; and the Rugby Football Union in 1871 developed from a disagreement with the Blackheath Football Club and its wish to retain the concept of hacking an opponent's shins against the majority decision of the founders of the newly-formed Association. The detailed explanation of how all that happened from the sports loving barrister Montague Shearman's (later Mr. Justice Shearman) scholarly analysis appeared in the Badminton Library: *Athletics and Football*, 1st Edition in 1887, almost symbolically in the year when Daimler produced the first 4-wheeled motor car. For nine years later, in the year of G.O. Smith's match winning Varsity match century three months after leading England's professionals against Scotland at Ibrox, Glasgow, 1896, the Highways Act of that year abolished the 4 mph outside town, and 2 mph inside it speed limits for driving horseless carriages.

The significance of those dates is directly relevant to the state of play and public attitudes today towards the law's involvement with sport, and particularly inside the touchline, boundaries and boardrooms.

For the progression of Road Traffic legislation and litigation via speed limits, radar traps and alcohol tests to regulate the dangerous and reckless driving with the daily lethal and severely injurious consequences to victims of all ages and status, motorists, passengers, pedestrians is no different in principle and logic from the need to protect victims of criminal and negligent misconduct by players, promoters and administrators from the frequent lethal and severely injurious consequences to victims of all ages and status.

The necessity to state such self-evident parallel circumstances is required because of the culture gap which surfaces on each occasion when a victim of sport misconduct is brought to court. It happened after the Duncan Ferguson conviction, and the rugby referee's liability for negligence. Yet Mr. Justice Drake who denied Paul Elliot's claim for damages compensation against Dean Saunders and Liverpool during 1994 explained

unequivocally,

> "If the injury was caused by another player acting in a wholly unacceptable manner, for example, by intending to cause injury, or being reckless, not caring whether or not injury was caused, then surely it is right that the injured person should be able to claim compensation ...
>
> ... There is no doubt at all, and the parties to the action agree, that the law does provide an injured sportsman with the right to claim compensation. The right is a very old one".

Of equal antiquity is the right which ended in the European Court of Justice with Jean Marc Bosman's claim against various European parties. If the Old Etonian goalkeeper from England XI -v- Ireland and FA Cup Final fixtures in 1882 thirty years later, in 1912, had not failed to spot the restraint of trade open goal in the claim by Aston Villa's Harry Kingaby against the then Football League, he would have been supported by earlier precedents of 200 years antiquity available for citation. When I raised its flag on behalf of Ralph Banks in the Aldershot County Court after he had been transferred to the town's club from Bolton Wanderers, following his appearance in the memorable Matthews 1953 Coronation Cup Final, almost simultaneously with publication of these pages in 1955, one of the leading and most thoughtful writers of the period who was often heard on the BBC *Sports Report* programme, J.L. (Jim) Manning, wrote in the Sunday Despatch,

> "Barrister Edward Grayson, whose book "Corinthians and Cricketers" has just been published and who has written articles in the FA's official bulletin, argued the case for Banks. I am wondering how much of Corinthian

Precious little. For let me remind those who think the phrase "soccer slave" is just a joke, that the case of Ralph Banks proves that it has cruel substance".

Soccer Slave was the title James Guthrie gave to his own biography as the theme behind his campaign as the Union chairman that footballers were "the last bonded men in Britain". In due course there he explained how it led on to George Eastham's case against Newcastle United and the game's governing bodies during 1963, when Guthrie published his own story in 1976. Two years further forward in 1978 the Packer revolution in cricket completed the picture after 31 days in court and a five hour judgment, which added to Douglas Insole's cricket and football playing honours his immortal citations in the formal law reports listings as a representative defendant in its legal source as *Greig -v- Insole*. The Belgian footballer Jean Marc Bosman's arrival at a comparable decision to the Banks and Eastham English judgments, in the European Court of Justice during the end of 1995, almost forty years to the day and month after *Corinthians and Cricketers* was published initially in 1955, squared the circle which had begun during its preparation as explained here.

During the intervening period since then all the current developments which now dominate the sporting scene which C.B. FRY in that Foreword forty years ago to the initial publication correctly described as "an industrial entertainment", have unfolded from a vacuum to their present recognisable forms which also require a regulatory legal framework to keep abreast of kaleidoscope changing developments.

The creation of secretary-captains for county cricket clubs led to the abolition formally in 1962 of the feudal distinctions between Gentlemen and Players at Cricket (they had disappeared at football before the First World War). Denis Compton's fan mail resulted in his invoking the services of Bagenal Harvey as the first full-time agent to administer his off the field activities. This led to the famous sponsored advertisement for Brylcream hair dressing (and almost symbolically Harvey's barrister brother authored the standard employment law text book under the title *Harvey on Industrial Relations and Employment Law*). Today FIFA and the Premier League require agents to be licensed.

A year after Gentlemen and Players fixtures disappeared from cricket's calendars they were replaced in 1963 with the first sponsored knock-out cricket competition on the lines of the FA Cup, the Gillette Cup, now the Nat-West Trophy. Yet sponsorship in cricket had almost a century old precedence when the first ever cricket tour to Australia in 1861 was sponsored by two expatriate Englishmen Felix Spiers and Christopher Pond who had established catering contracts for their supply of refreshments to the Melbourne and Ballarate Railway. When they returned to England their famous catering company containing their joint names was absorbed ultimately by the famous Express Dairy Group.

Around that period two other enterprising cricket sponsors John Wisden and James Lillywhite conceived the idea of advertising and marketing their sports goods lawfully through annual publications and shops which survive until today. In a different sphere but in line with customers, participants and spectators' initiatives the laws of contract, defamation, restraint of trade, taxation and charity began to stir with court cases concerning sport. That collapsed grandstand at the traditional Cheltenham Races Festival in 1866 ended with judicial decisions in 1870 consistent with the principles which have been applied alongside parliamentary legislation to more modern and more disastrous experiences after the Ibrox, Glasgow (1971), Bradford City fire (1985), Heysel and Hillsborough (1989) tragedies. Criminal precedent prosecutions since the first in 1878 and 1898 for football field fatalities, coincidentally each at Leicester Assizes, have been activated regularly. Injuries to participating players have come before the courts frequently since the first ever traceable claim from an illegal soccer tackle and the first ever damages award, for a broken leg evidenced at a Lewes Assizes trial in 1969 to an amateur player who had played for fun, and lost his job because of the injury.

Parliament has been required to legislate almost annually for crowd control, public order and violent hooligan offenders. Judicial Reports from Lord Wheatley after Ibrox (1971); Mr. Justice Popplewell after Bradford (1985); Lord Justice Taylor after Hillsborough (1989-1990), were all in line with comparable enquiries after the first fatal free Wembley Cup Final in 1923 and; the Bolton Wanderers fatalities in 1946. They all resulted in substantive public safety legislation. Women's team sports have now followed their individual ladies' triumphs in athletics track and field, golf, swimming, tennis and every other individual activity, with authentic recognition by the governing bodies for the established team games of cricket, rugby and soccer football; and television brings every sporting activity for which sponsorship can be obtained into an ever increasing audience.

Yet as prizes and pressures predominate, the need to regulate temptations to bend and break the laws of play intensify with every raising of the ratchets of rewards for results. The Gilbertian concept "to make the punishment fit the crime" rarely appears to be understood by the voluntary administrators and their inadequate instructed paid executives; but as sport and the national team games continue in a revolutionary changed social climate from that which dominated the C.B. Fry - G.O. Smith-Corinthian era, the need for preservation of Corinthian ideals emerges with greater urgency almost every passing day.

Football no longer is the misconceived opiate of the masses alongside its sustained survival within the Arthur Dunn Competition and the Public Schools and the village greens where it began. It has become a cult concept, over-indulged and self-consciously analysed in academic and pseudo-self-styled-intellectual circles, epitomised by the theme behind the Euro '96 competitions: "Football comes home". Very few, if at all anyone, acknowledged publicly that what came home was not within its own native shores the game which Britain exported to the world. What came home from Europe was the style of football which the Corinthians developed for Brazil to create the Sport Club Corinthians Paulista, or the London University expatriates took to Moscow in 1914, explained in the original text by Sir Godfrey Ince's citation.

No longer will as distinguished a headmaster as G.O.'s successor at Ludgrove, Alan Barber, be able to cause me to write as I did in the original text,

> "that he would always take his boys to Tottenham for the Varsity match. His silence as to what other matches he would take them to was more significant than any other words";

and it is difficult to believe that any biographer of *"The Lyttletons: A Family Chronicle of the Nineteenth Century"* as Betty Askwith wrote in 1975, would today studiously ignore or demonstrate a complete unawareness that in the latter part of that nineteenth century, the Honourable Alfred Lyttleton, father of Viscount Chandos in Churchill's war-time government, and uncle of today's leading jazz trumpeter, Humphrey Lyttleton, was England's first ever double International, FA Cup winning Finalist, and wicketkeeper in the famous Ashes Test Match at the Oval in 1882.

Yes, football has come home; not as the cliche riddled mantra for its inherent talent, when nearly all the television commentators discuss about the ball going to "his **good** foot", or "his **bad** foot" recognising the basic technique inadequacies of modern United Kingdom performers. It has come home, in Napolean's nation of shopkeepers, and Bernard Shaw's nation of snobs, to the whole nation, transcending classes in John Major's thoughtless concept of a "classless society": and above all else, it has come home for recognition as a mirror for social conduct, and a yardstick for differentiating between right and wrong.

Finally, a touchstone of the unawareness among those who purport to provide a form of leadership in society of the impact of sport within the community, was witnessed by the paucity of response to the Archbishop of Canterbury's recognition of the rules of play with his initiative for opening the House of Lords debate on *Society's Moral and Spiritual Well-being* (5 July 1996). Only Lord Borrie who had created the Institute of Judicial Administration at Birmingham University as Professor Gordon Borrie and Lord Howell as Denis Howell, who had been Britain's longest serving Minister with special responsibility for Sport, took up this theme.

Lord Borrie began by saying,

> "... society's moral well-being is, or should be, an important objective for people of all religions and, indeed, for those who have none. The most reverend Primate the Archbishop of Canterbury has, no doubt very rightly, put an emphasis on the responsibility of schools".

He continued,

> "However, this afternoon I should like to stress not just the responsibility of schools and other educational institutions, and, of course, parents, in all such matters, vital though that is, but also the responsibility of influential leaders in our society. Most obviously, I refer to our politicians and other business and commercial leaders. I suppose that there is also a responsibility, though it may be less easy to persuade them, on all the people whose utterances and behaviour have an impact on citizens of all ages, especially the young.
>
> I include among those people

editors, sporting heroes and pop stars. They can be role models. They may not choose to be influential but, whether or not they choose to be so, their impact through the publicity given to their activities and behaviour both on and off the sports field and on and off the stage involves, to my mind, a responsibility to behave in a moral and ethical way."

Not surprisingly Lord Howell followed through from his experiences during Euro '96 with the following ending to his contribution to the debate.

> "When the most reverend Primate was at Wembley I do not suppose that he realised - I certainly did not, in my ignorance at that moment - that UEFA, which organised that wonderful competition had produced a code of ethics dealing with football. I have a copy of that code if anyone wishes to see it. It is an outline of good ethics for players, coaches, referees and team officials. It is first class.
>
> As a referee, I am grateful that someone pointed out today that we must observe the rules and, I might add, to acknowledge that the referee is always right even when he is wrong. That is a good precept. The code of ethic states:
>
> *'Through such a code of ethics, sport is recognised as a social and cultural institution which, when played in a spirit of Fair Play, enriches society and promotes friendship between individuals, groups of*

individuals, nations, etc. Sport offers the opportunity for self-knowledge, fosters self-expression, and encourages skill, social interaction, enjoyment and health.

Ethics mean not only adherence to written rules, but also involve a correctness of attitude among players, coaches, referees and team delegates, who should be encouraged to behave in a fitting spirit'.

None of us could have written that better. It was written by a football organisation. Nobody knows about it because it was not mentioned by the press. I have discovered that UEFA held a conference about it in the middle of the competition. I hope that the Football Association will send a copy of this document to every football team in the country.

My only complaint about that competition was that penalties were used to decide matches. That is an extraordinary decision because matches are then decided on the basis of a failure. Failure is elevated so that it becomes vitally important.

I am also a patron of an organisation called Christians in Sport, which does a great deal of work within sport. That organisation has drawn my attention to what Mr Berhard Langer, that famous golfer, said when he missed that vital putt, which we can all remember, in the Ryder Cup. He said that it was not the most important thing in the world to miss that putt on which the whole of European gold depended and that his relationship with God and with Jesus Christ put all that into perspective.

I hope that when Gareth Southgate, who plays for Aston Villa contemplates the over-exposure of his missed penalty, he will think the same.

I end by urging all teachers to realise that the practicalities of life can be drawn upon by using sporting illustrations. That can be vital to them in

their work in schools. There are two regrettable incidents in cricket when the England captain put grit in his pocket to rub on the ball and somebody else tried to pick the seam of the ball to achieve an unfair advantage. Those incidents should have been taken up and discussed in the schools. I agree that ethics cannot be taught but they can be discussed in order to achieve an understanding of them. I believe that sport, probably more than anything else in the lives of youngsters, should enable us to achieve that objective".

Happily, England won the Fair Play Trophy, and Lord Howell would not have been aware that while these pages were being prepared, the headmaster of C.B. Fry's old school, Repton, G.E.Jones, wrote to me explaining that he wished to preach a sermon to his boys and girls after the Easter Holidays of 1996, and having seen a letter I had written to *The Times* on the Corinthian spirit and also having been lent the first edition, could I help on the origin of the club's name? Regretfully, I could do no more than refer him to Hubert Doggart with his family associations, and to the only other chronicler so far as I am aware who had correspondence with a Corinthian. Hubert offered the First Appendix to the 2nd Butterworths edition of *Sport and the Law*. I suggested that other source of *Letters to Corinthians* with which I have ended each of the first two editions of Butterworths *Sport and the Law*. I shall always continue so to do with all future editions.

In conclusion, today's gap between the £15m. price tag on England's centre-forward of 1996, Alan Shearer, and his Oxford University cricketing and Old Carthusian predecessor of 1896, can never be exaggerated sufficiently. Nevertheless at differing periods of time they will always reflect different values. Each will always be a hero to his own generation. History alone will judge whether both will become immortal.

———————————

1988. After over 100 nomadic years,
the Corinthians at last move into a permanent home

APPENDIX - STATISTICS

G.O. SMITH
INTERNATIONAL MATCHES FOR ENGLAND

1. v. IRELAND, Perry Bar, Birrningham, 25th Feb., 1893: 6-1.
C. Charsley (Small Heath); A.H. Harrison (Old Westminsters), F.R. Pelly (Old Foresters); A.Smith (Nottingham Forest), W.N. Winckworth (Old Westminsters), N.C. Cooper (Cambridge Univ.); R. Topham (Wolverhampton Wanderers), G.O. Smith (Oxford Univ.)(i), G.H. Cotterill (Old Brightonians), W.E. Gilliat (Old Carthusians), R.R. Sandilands (Old Westminsters).

2. V. WALES, The Racecourse Ground, Wrexham, 12th March, 1894: 5-1.
L.H. Gay (Old Brightonians); L.V. Lodge (Cambridge Univ.), F.R. Pelly (Old Foresters); A.H. Hossack (Old Chigwellians), C. Wreford Brown (Old Carthusians), A.G. Topham (Casuals); R. Topham (Casuals), R.C. Gosling (Old Etonians), G.O. Smith (Old Carthusians), J.G. Veitch (Old Westminsters), R.R. Sandilands (Old Westminsters). *(All Corinthians.)*

3. v. SCOTLAND, Parkhead (Celtic Park), Glasgow, 7th April, 1894: 2-2.
L.H. Gay; Clare (Stoke), F.R. Pelly; Reynolds (Aston Villa), Holt (Everton), Needham (Sheffield Utd.); Bassett (West Bromwich Albion), Goodall (Derby County), G.O. Smith (Old Carthusians), Chadwick (E) (Everton), Spiksley (Sheffield Wednesday).

4. v. WALES, Queen's Club, West Kensington, 18th March, 1895: I-I.
G.B. Raikes (Oxford Univ.); L.V. Lodge (Cambridge Univ.), W.J. Oaklcy (Oxford Univ.); R.R. Barker (Casuals), C. Wreford Brown (Old Carthmians), A.G.Henfrey (Old Wellingburians); R.R. Sandilands (Old Westminsters), R.C. Gosling (Old Etonians), G.O. Smith (Old Carthusians) (1), G.P. Dewhurst (Liverpool Ramblers), M.H. Stanbrough (Old Carthusians). *(All Carthusians)*

5. v. IRELAND, Cliftonville Grounds, Belfast, 7th March, 1896: 2-0.
G.B. Raikes (Oxford Univ.); L.V. Lodge (Cambridge Univ.), W.J. Oakley (Oxford Univ.); Crabtree (Aston Villa), Crawshaw (Sheffield Wed.), Kinsey (Derby County); Bassett, Bloomer (Derby County), G.O. Smith (Oxford Univ.) (1), Chadwick (E), Spiksley.

6. v. WALES, Cardiff Arim Park, 14th March, 1896: 9-1.
G.B. Raikes (Corinthians); W.J. Oakley (Corinthians), Crabtree; A.G. Henfrey (Corinthians), Crawshaw, Kinsey; Bassett, Bloomer, G.O. Smith (Corinthians) (2), Goodall, R.R. Sandilands (Corinthians).

7. v. SCOTLAND, Parkhead (Celtic Park), Glasgow, 4th April, 1896: 1-2.
G.B. Raikes; L.V. Lodge, W.J. Oakley (Corinthians); Crabtree, Crawshaw, A.G. Henfrey (Corinthians); Bassett, Goodall, G.O. Smith (Corinthians), Wood (Wolverhampton Wanderers), C.J. Burnup (Cambridge Univ. and Corinthians).

8. v. IRELAND, Trent Bridge, Nottingham, 20th Feb., 1897: 6-0.
Robinson (Derby County); W.J. Oakley (Corinthians), Williams (West Bromwich Albion); B. Middleditch (Corinthians), Crawshaw, Needham; Athersmith (Aston Villa), Bloomer, G.O. Smith (Corinthians) (Capt.), Wheldon (Aston Villa), Bradshaw (Liverpool).

9. v. WALES, Bramall Lane, Sheffield, 29th March, 1897: 4-0.
Foulke (Sheffield Utd.); W.J. Oakley (Corinthians), Spencer (Aston Villa); Reynolds, Crawshaw, Needham; Athersmith, Bloomer, G.O. Smith (Corinthians) (Capt.), Becton (Liverpool), Milward (Everton).

10. v. SCOTLAND, Crystal Palace, 3rd April, 1897: 1-2.
Robinson (Derby County); W.J. Oakley (Corinthians), Spencer; Reynolds, Crawshaw, Needham; Athersmith, Bloomer, G.O. Smith (Corinthians) (Capt.), Chadwick (E), Milward.

11. v. IRELAND, Cliftonville Grounds, Belfast, 5th March, 1898: 3-2.
Robinson (New Brighton Tower); W.J. Oakley (Corinthians), Williams; Forman (Frank) (Nottingham Forest), Morren (Sheffield Utd.), Turner (Derby County); Athersmith, Richards (Nottingham Forest), G.O. Smith (Corinthians) (Capt.), Garfield (West Bromwich Albion), Wheldon.

12. V. WALES, The Racecourse Ground, Wrcxham, 28th March, 1898: 3-0.
Robinson; W.J. Oakley (Corinthians), Williams; Perry (T) (West Bromwich Albion), Booth (Blackburn Rovers), Needham; Athersmith, Goodall, G.O. Smith (Corinthians) (Capt.), Wheldon, Spiksley.

13. V. SCOTLAND, Parkhead (Celtic Park), Glasgow, 2nd April, 1898: 3-1.
Robinson; W.J. Oakley (Corinthians), Williams; Forman (Frank), C. Wreford Brown (Corinthians) (Capt.), Needham; Athersmith, Bloomer, G.O. Smith (Corinthians), Wheldon, Spiksley.

14. v. IRELAND, Roker Park, Sunderland, 18th Feb., 1899: 13-2.
Hillman (Bumley); Bach (Sunderland), Williams; Forman (Frank), Needham, Crabtree; Athersmith, Bloomer, G.O. Smith (Corinthians) (2) (Capt.), Settle (Bury), Forman (Fred) (Nottingham Forest).

15. v. WALES, Bedminster, Bristol, 20th March, 1899: 4-0.
Robinson (Southampton); Thickett (Sheffield Utd.), Williams; Needham, Crabtree, Forman (Frank); Athersmith, Bloomer, G.O. Smith (Corinthians) (4) (Capt.), Settle, Forman (Fred).

16. v. SCOTLAND,Villa Park, Birmingham, 8th April, 1899: 2-1.
Robinson; Thickett, Crabtree; Howell (Liverpool), Forman (Frank), Needham; Athersmith, Bloomer, G.O. Smith (Corinthians) (1) (Capt.), Settle, Forman (Fred).

17. v. IRELAND, Lansdowne Road, Dublin, 17th March, 1900: 2-0.
Robinson; W.J. Oakley (Corinthians), Crabtree; Johnson (Sheffield Utd.), Holt (Reading), Needham; Turner (Southampton), Cunliffe (Portsmouth), G.O. Smith (Corinthians) (Capt.), Sagar (Bury), Priest (Sheffield Utd.).

18. v. WALES, Cardiff Arms Park, 26th March, 1900: 1-1.
Robinson; Spencer, W.J. Oakley (Corinthians); Johnson, Chadwick (A) (Southampton), Crabtree; Athersmith, R.E. Foster (Old Malvernians and Oxford Univ.), G.O. Sniith (Corinthians) (Capt.), G.P. Wilson (Corinthians), Spouncer (Nottingham Forest).

19. v. SCOTLAND, Parkhead (Celtic Park), Glasgow, 7th April, 1900: 1-4.
Robinson; Crabtree, W.J. Oakley (Corinthians); Johnson, Chadwick (A), Needham; Athersmith, Bloomer, G.O. Smith (Corinthians) (Capt.), G.P. Wilson (Corinthians), Plant (Bury).

20. v. SCOTLAND, Crystal Palace, 30th March, 1901: 2-2.
Sutcliffe (Bolton Wanderers); Iremonger (Nottingham Forest), W.J. Oakley (Corinthians); Wilkes (Aston Villa), Forman (Frank), Needham; Bennett (Sheffield Utd.), Bloomer, G.O. Smith (Corinthians) (Capt.), R.E. Foster (Corinthians), Blackbum (Blackbum Rovers).

21. v. GERMANY, White Hart Lane, Tottenham, 21st Sept., 1901: 12-0.
W.H. Waller (Richmond Association); A.W. Parsons (Clapton), W. Blackburn (Oxford Univ.)*;
T. Marshall (Bishop Auckland), H. Thwaites (Corinthians), H. Vickers (Casuals)*; L. Hales (Crewe Alexandra), C.F. Ryder (Old Carthusians)*, G.O. Smith (Corinthians) (Capt.) (2), R.E. Foster (Old Malvernians) *, A.S. Farnfield (Casuals). (* Corinthians)

ENGLISH DOUBLE INTERNATIONALS

Name	Soccer	Cricket
Hon. A. Lyttelton (Cambridge University, Old Etonians and Middlesex)	1877 v. S.	1880, 82, 84 (2) *v.* A.
William Gunn (Notts County and Nottinghamshire)	1884 v. W., S.	1886/87 (2), 88 (2), 90 (2), 3 (3), 96 , 99, v. A.
L.H. Gay (Cambridge University, Corinthians and Somerset)	1891 v. C; 1893 v. S.; 1894 v. W., S.	1894/95 v. A.
R.E. Foster (Oxford University, Corinthians and Worcestershire)	1900 v. W.; 1901 v. I., W., S., G.; 1902 v. W.	1903 v A, (5); 1907 v. S.A. (3)
C.B. Fry (Oxford University, Corinthians and Sussex)	1891 v. C.; 1901 v. I.	1895/96 (2), 1907 (3), 1912(3) v. S.A.; 1899 (5), 1902 (3), 1905 (4), 1909 (3), 1912 (3) v. A.
Jack Sharp (Everton and Lancashire)	1903 v. I., 1905 v. S.	1909 (3) v. A.
Harry Makepeace (Everton and Lancashire)	1906 v. S.; 1910 v. S.; 1912 v.W., S.	1920/21 (4) v. A.
H.T. Wally Hardinge (Sheffield United and Kent)	1910 v. S.	1921 v. A.
Andy M. Ducat (Woolwich Arsenal, Aston Villa and Surrey)	1910 v. I., W., S.; 1920 v. W., S.; 1921 v. I.	1921 v. A.
John Arnold (Fulham and Hampshire)	1933 v. S.	1931 *v.* N.Z.
Willie Watson (Sunderland and Yorkshire)	1950 v. I., It.; 1951 v. W., Y.	1951 (5) v. S.A.; 1952 v. In.; 1953 (3) *v.* A.; 1953/54 (5) v. W. I.

NOTES:
E. ('Patsy') Hendren (Brentford and Middlesex) appeared 51 times in Test Matches and played v. Wales in 1920 in a 'Victory' International. Denis Compton (Arsenal and Middlesex), with over 60 Test Match appearances, also played in a 'Victory' International, in 1946, v. Scotland, as well as in 11 war-time Internationals.
PUBLISHER'S NOTE: Since the first edition of '*Corinthians and Cricketers*', there is one player to add to the above list: **Arthur Milton** (Arsenal, Bristol City and Gloucestershire) - Soccer 1951 v. Austria, plus six Cricket appearances for England (1958 and 1959)
Abbreviations:　　A.= Australia, C. = Canada, G. = Germany, I. = Ireland, In. = India, It. = Italy,
　　　　　　　　N.Z. = New Zealand, S. = Scotland, S.A. = South Africa, W. = Wales, Y. = Yugoslavia.

DOUBLE INTERNATIONALS – SOCCER AND CRICKET

ANDY DUCAT
Woolwich Arsenal, Aston Villa
and Surrey.

L.H. GAY
Corinthians and Somerset.

C.B. FRY
Corinthians and Sussex.

HARRY MAKEPEACE
Everton and Lancashire.

Hon. A. LYTTELTON
Old Etonians and Middlesex.

WILLIE WATSON
Sunderland and Yorkshire.

R.E. FOSTER
Corinthians and Worcestershire.

WALLY HARDINGE
Sheffield United and Kent.

JACK SHARP
Everton and Lancashire.

WILLIAM GUNN
Notts County and Nottinghamshire.

JOHN ARNOLD
Fulham and Hampshire.

FIRST-CLASS CRICKETERS WHO GAINED
F. A. CUP WINNERS' MEDALS

Name

Lubbock, E.	Wanderers, Old Etonians	1872 & 1879	Kent
Kenyon Slaney, W.S.	Wanderers	1873	M.C.C.
Ottoway, C.J.	Oxford University	1874	Kent and Middlesex
Nepean, C.E.B.	Oxford University	1874	Middlesex
Birley, F.H. .	Oxford University	1874	Lancashire and Surrey
Renny-Tailyour, W.H.	Royal Engineers	1875	Kent
Whitfield, H.	Old Etonians	1879	Sussex
Wynyard, E.G.	Old Carthusians	1881	Hampshire
Paravicini, P.J. de .	Old Etonians	1882	Middlesex
Daft, H.B.	Notts County	1894	Nottinghamshire
Devey, (J.)	Aston Villa	1895 &1897	Warwickshire
Needham (E.)	Sheffield United	1899 & 1902	Derbyshire
George (W.)	Aston Villa	1905	Warwickshire
Sharp, (J.)	Everton	1906	Lancashire
*Makepeace (H.)	Everton	1906	Lancashire
Ducat, (A.M.)	Aston Villa	1920	Surrey
Hulme, (J.H.A.)	Arsenal	1930 & 1936	Middlesex
Carter, (H.S.)	Sunderland and Derby County	1937 & 1946	Derbyshire
Compton, (D.C.S.).	Arsenal	1950	Middlesex
Compton, (L.H.) .	Arsenal	1950	Middlesex

* Harry Makepeace holds a unique record at soccer and cricket: (a) F.A. Cup Winner's Medal with Everton, 1906; (b) Football League Championship Medal with Everton, 1915; (c) County Cricket Championship Honours with Lancashire, 1926-27-28-30; (d) Soccer Internationals for England, 1906 v. S.; 1910 v. S.; 1912 v. W., S.; (e) Test Matches for England, 1920/21 (4) v. Australia.

[N.B. Above list is as appeared in the original, 1955, edition of *Corinthians & Cricketers*]

INDEX (To chapters 1 - 10 only)

EPILOGUE 1955 and 1996

From the preceding pages it should now be evident that the Football and cricket triumphs of to-day, or any day, which are created from merit as distinct from mere chance, can be fashioned with dignity and satisfaction only by applying the principles of play which the Corinthians and their contemporaries fashioned for the world on British football and cricket grounds in the era of G.O. Smith - the Golden Age. Trevor Wignall, the doyen of modern sporting writers, neatly summed it all up after the end of the Second World War when he wrote in his reminiscences, *Almost -Yesterday:* 'Those who assert that the playing of games is not very different from what it was one hundred years ago are not far wrong ... The kicking of a goal by Tom Lawton, or the heading of it, is much the same as it was when G.O. Smith was banging them in, and the scoring of a century by Walter Hammond calls for the same strokes that were employed by W.G. Grace. Sport has undoubtedly been developed out of recognition, but not so much in its expositions as in the finer workmanship that has been acquired, and in the enormous crowds it hails and holds.'

When these elementary conclusions are acknowledged as fundamental to the understanding of modern sport, recognition will be granted to the fact that inferior performances by British football and cricket teams against overseas opponents are not only a sign of progress elsewhere: they also reflect a departure from Britain's own high standards and traditions in the past. A return to those levels, harnessed to 'the finer workmanship that has been acquired,' can alone raise the nation's prestige in the world of football and cricket to the position it belongs as of right. Whenever and wherever that will be, the shades of G.O. Smith and his fellow Corinthians and Cricketers will always be guiding the destinies of soccer and cricket in England. For the influence of these pioneers will and should never be forgotten as the years fly by and add new peaks of achievement to our national games which others have made so international.